SO-BTC-595

Also by
VIRGIL THOMSON

The Musical Scene

THIS IS A *Borzoi Book*
PUBLISHED BY *Alfred A. Knopf* IN NEW YORK

The Art of Judging Music

THE ART OF JUDGING MUSIC

VIRGIL THOMSON

1948

ALFRED A KNOPF : *NEW YORK*

Copyright 1941, 1943, 1944, 1945, 1946, 1947, 1948 by Virgil Thomson

All rights reserved. No part of this book may be reproduced in any form without permission in writing from the publisher, except by a reviewer who may quote brief passages in a review to be printed in a magazine or newspaper.

Manufactured in the United States of America.
Published simultaneously in Canada by The Ryerson Press.

FIRST EDITION

29738

EXPLANATORY NOTE

The essay from which this book takes its title was delivered as an address in Sanders Theater, Cambridge, Massachusetts, on May 2, 1947, at the Harvard Symposium on Music Criticism. It was later published in the Atlantic Monthly. *The other pieces appeared originally in the* New York Herald Tribune, *most of them between September 1944 and August 1947.*

V. T.

New York, 1947

Contents

Contents

Contents

The Art of Judging Music

THE ART OF JUDGING MUSIC

THE LAYMAN is under no obligation to exercise judgment with regard to musical works, to describe to himself their characteristics, or to estimate their value for history. He can take them to his heart or let them alone. He does not have to be just or fair, or to reflect about them in any way. He can accept, reject, tolerate, using only caprice as his guide. The professional has no such liberty. Neither has any musical patron or amateur who has chosen to follow in his role of music consumer the standards that govern the music producer.

These standards are not immutable, but they do exist. They exist because being a professional involves, by definition, the assumption of a responsible attitude both toward the material with which the profession deals and toward society in general, which the profession unquestionably serves. Service, indeed, is the price of any profession's toleration by society. And the acceptance of money for professional services rendered is the criterion by which professionalism is determined. This transaction is no guarantee of quality delivered, but it *is* a symbol of responsibility accepted. And once that responsibility is accepted, the workman must be at least morally worthy of his hire, however limited his skill or mental powers may be. He must be willing, in other words, to rise or fall professionally by his sincere opinions, as expressed in his professional actions.

Every musician, therefore, is a music critic. He is obliged to make musical judgments and to act on them. This necessity obtains primarily, of course, with regard to the work of other musicians, living and dead, in so far as his work is at all a comment on theirs or an interpretation of it, which nine tenths, at least, of anybody's musical work is. Even the composer, no less than the scholar, the pedagogue, the executant, and the reviewer, is constantly under the necessity of making a fair estimate, and a decently responsible one, of other people's musical output.

The making of such an estimate, hasty or slow, involves three possible operations. The first operation has nothing to do with deliberate fairness. It consists of listening to a piece, or of reading it, rather in the way that a cook tastes food. This act of cognition, this beginning of acquaintance, is probably a more powerful determinant in our final judgments, the ones on which we act, than the subsequent cerebrations are by which we endeavor to correct them. And one cannot prepare for it by purifying the spirit. One does not need to, as a matter of fact, because curiosity is stronger than prejudice. Any musician, faced with a new piece, will listen. He may not listen long, but he will submit himself to it, if only for a moment. He will listen, in fact, as long as he can, as long as it holds his attention.

The second stage of the first operation, after the initial tasting, is going on listening, the experience of having one's attention held. Not all pieces hold one's attention. One is regretful when they don't, but one must never undervalue the fact of their doing or not doing so. Fatigue here is of no more importance than prejudice. In reasonable health, and awake, any musician will listen to music, to sound of any kind, rather than merely ruminate, just as a painter will observe or a dancer will move around. That is why he is a musician to start with, because listening is his line of least resistance. When a musician can't keep his mind on a piece of music, that fact must be considered when he comes to form his judgment.

The final stage of the first operation is the aftertaste, the image that the whole piece leaves in the mind for the first few moments after it ceases to be heard (I say *heard* because reading a piece is hearing it in the mind, in however attenuated a fashion). This is as significant a part of its gustation as the first taste of it and the following of it through. It is a recalling of the whole while memory is fresh and before correction and reflection have begun to distort it. Never must one forget, never does one forget, hearing for the first time a work that has absorbed one from beginning to end and from which one has returned to ordinary life, as it were, shaken or beatified, as from a trip to the moon or to the Grecian Isles.

All new music does not produce this effect. But the degree to which it does is as valuable a datum for judgment as any that can be found on subsequent analysis. A great deal of subsequent analysis, as a matter of fact, is a search for the reasons why the piece did or did not hold one's attention on first hearing. And the initial taste or distaste for its qualities will constantly return to plague one's researches or to illumine them, to discourage or to inspire one in the process of making fuller acquaintance.

If tasting or savoring a piece is the first operation, the prelude to judgment, making its fuller acquaintance is the second. The latter depends, of course, on the success of the first. If first acquaintance has proved agreeable or interesting, one undertakes the second. The undertaking is a result of first judgment, though not necessarily of reflection. The whole first operation, let me insist, is spontaneous; and so is the initiation of the second. At this point, however, spontaneity ceases to be the main highway to experience, the guide to knowledge. We must now amplify and correct our first impression. If our first impression of a piece was gained from auditory means, from hearing only, we must now see the score. If it was gained from a score, we must hear it in execution. Many pieces look better than they sound, and even more of them sound better on first hearing than their design justifies. Because ordered sound is usually pleasant in itself, whether or not high intrinsic interest of an expressive or of a textural nature is present. In the case of executant musicians there is a constant shifting, during the study of a work, between score reading and execution, each approach to the piece correcting the other till the artist's interpretation is fully formed as a concept and completely clothed in sound. Thorough acquaintance with any piece of music, its mastery for responsible professional purposes, is not possible without this double possession, visual and auditory. At such a point of mastery one has material for a reflected judgment, and one *formulates* that judgment if there is any necessity for doing so. Otherwise one continues to study and to correct until interest lags.

The third operation of judgment, which is revisiting, can be undertaken only after a period of rest, of vacation from the subject. One has to forget the study period and its results, to approach the work all over again from a distance. Here the acquisition of experience and those shifts in the center of emotional interest that come from growing older are capable of lighting up the work in a new way. Sometimes they make it appear nobler; sometimes they show up shoddy material or poor workmanship; sometimes one can't see why one ever bothered with the piece at all. As in reading old love letters, however, or reviving an old quarrel, one's former emotion is still a fact to be dealt with. It involves one in loyalty or ruthlessness, in any case in lots of remembering. The music is no longer new and shining; nor has it been kept bright by continual use. It has acquired a patina that must be rubbed away before one can see the object as anything like its old self. Restudy and more rehearsing are therefore necessary if a new judgment has to be made. And one does have to be made if one is going to use the work again for any purpose whatsoever.

No judgment, of course, is ever final or permanent. At any stage of musical acquaintance action may become necessary; one may have undertaken to perform the work or to explain it to students or to describe it in public. For any of these purposes one must formulate such judgment as one has arrived at to date, if not about its value, at least about its nature. This formulation can take place at any point of experience. Reviewers often describe new music from one hearing, as pedagogues criticize student compositions from one reading. In nine cases out of ten this is sufficient for the purpose, and no injustice is done. Works of standard repertory are more often described after both hearing and study, that is to say, after the second phase of acquaintance, such acquaintance being easily available nowadays to all, though the press is not invariably as well prepared in standard repertory (by score study) as it might be, and many members of the teaching profession have not always as broad a prepared repertory as might be desired for the answering of student questions and for exposing to the young all the kinds of music that there are. The press in general tends to express judgments of new work from hearing only, just as historians, especially those dealing with remote periods, are obliged to describe from score a great deal of music that they have never heard at all.

In order to make a fair judgment from only the first stage of acquaintance, either from hearing or from reading, one is obliged to have recourse to the aid of clues or clinical signs. The clinical signs of quality are three: 1) the ability of a work to hold one's attention, 2) one's ability to remember it vividly, and 3) a certain strangeness in the musical texture, that is to say, the presence of technical invention, such as novelty of rhythm, of contrapuntal, harmonic, melodic, or instrumental device. The pattern that a score makes on a page can be enticing, too, even before one starts to read it. In the matter of attention, it is not germane that one should be either delighted or annoyed. What counts is whether one is impelled to go on listening.

"Can you listen to it?" and "Can you remember it?" are, I think, answerable in the affirmative only when real invention is present. Everybody likes novelty. People's responses to novelty are diversified, however, since the amount of it that anyone can take in is a personal quotient. Some like a little; some like a lot. This is why strong feelings of pleasure or displeasure are likely to accompany its encounter. These feelings, like those of love and hatred, reverse themselves with the greatest of ease. Their value as a clinical indication that one is probably in the presence of strong music lies in their strength, not in their direction.

It is necessary to keep wary, too, and to examine one's mind constantly for possible failure to make the cardinal distinctions. The cardinal distinctions in music are also three: 1) design *vs.* execution, or the piece itself as distinct from its presentation; 2) the expressive power of a work as distinguishable from its formal musical interest; and 3) a convincing emotional effect *vs.* a meretricious one.

One must ask oneself always, therefore: 1) "Have I heard a pretty piece or just some pretty playing?" 2) "Is this just a piece of clockwork, or does it also tell time?" and 3) "In the process of receiving its message, have I been moved or merely impressed?"

Study and reflection will provide answers to all these questions; but when one has to act quickly, one must assume that one's first impression, so far as it goes, is a true view. And it is, in fact, as true a view as any, since most of what is revealed on further acquaintance is of a descriptive nature, a more detailed picture, filling in outlines already sensed. This is not always so; but far more often than not it is so. In the case of successive contradictory impressions, it is the first, I think, that tends to survive.

And so to recapitulate.

First, one votes about a piece, spontaneously, sincerely, and more often than not, permanently; one adopts it or rejects it. Liking is not necessary for adoption, but interest is. If interest is present, one can study the work further with profit. If not, one tends to forget it. After study one can forget it too, but not completely. In this case one can revisit it after a time. But at any time when the formulation of a judgment or opinion is found to be desirable, that formulation must be based on a description of the work. The techniques of musical description are:

1) *Stylistic* identification, recognizing its period or school from internal evidence, from the technical procedures of composition employed. Identifying these procedures will answer the question, "What is it like?"

2) *Expressive* identification is the second technique of musical description. One must decide whether a piece depicts the cadences of speech, bodily movements, or feelings (that whole series of anxiety-and-relief patterns that constitutes our emotional life). This decodifying is a more difficult operation but also a more important one, since one can, if necessary, and the passage of time aiding, neglect stylistic differences or even abstract them from the problem, whereas one cannot perform, communicate, or in any other way *use* a piece of music until one has found an answer, correct or incorrect, to the question, "What is it about?"

3) The third technique of description consists in summoning up the classical aids to memory. These are the known methods of melodic, harmonic, orchestral, and formal analysis. They are of little value without stylistic and expressive identification; but they help one to remember detail, provided one has first understood stylistically and emotionally the whole. By *understand* I mean *accept*, be satisfied with something. George Bernard Shaw once showed the futility of a formal analysis of art without reference to its content in a parody of program notes such as might have been written about the most famous of the five Hamlet soliloquies. He begins (I quote from memory): "The theme is first stated in the infinitive mood, followed immediately by its inversion." Analysis is an indispensable procedure, but the analy-

sis of a given piece is valueless to anyone who does not have some previous knowledge of the piece. That is why one must first, in describing a work verbally, answer the questions, "What is it like?" and "What is it about?" before attempting to answer, "How does it go?"

4) The fourth procedure of musical description is verbal formulation. This is, of course, a literary rather than a musical problem; but no one escapes it, not the teachers, the conductors, nor the string-quartet players, any more than the historians and the journalists. In some of the musical branches it is easier than in others. Vocalism is particularly hard to teach otherwise than by example, or to describe in any circumstance, because there is no standard vocabulary for the purpose. Instrumental terminology is richer, though most of this is borrowed from the language of painting. Composition is chiefly described in metaphor, though the stylistic and expressive identifications do have a scholastic terminology. That for styles follows the history of the visual arts except for the years between 1775, say, and 1825, where the visual artists discern a classic-revival period and the musicians a Classical one (with a capital C). The classification of musical phraseology as strophic, choric, or spastic is valuable; but the last division, which includes so much of our grander repertory, is incapable of further precision than that available through poetic allusion. The same is true of musical landscape painting. Here one must use similes; there is no other way.

You will note that I have said nothing about communicating one's passion with regard to a work. I have not mentioned it because it presents no problem; it takes place automatically and inevitably. Insistence on it, moreover, is immodest. What is most interesting about any musical judgment is the descriptive analysis on which it is based, or, if you like, since one's judgment is likely to precede the analysis, by which it is defended. This is revelatory and stimulating. The fact that one man likes or does not like the finale of Beethoven's Fifth Symphony will influence nobody. The fact that I for one consider that piece to be, shall we say, more like a newspaper editorial about something than a direct transcript of personal sentiments is, however right or wrong, convincing or foolish, possibly worth following up, if only for refutation.

The public does not have to be right. Musicians do not have

to be right. Nobody has to be right. Any opinion is legitimate to act on, provided one accepts in advance the responsibilities of that action. Any opinion is legitimate to express that can be stated in clear language. And any opinion at all is legitimate to hold. As I said before, it is not the yes or no of a judgment that is valuable to other people, though one's original yes or no about a certain kind of music may have determined a whole lifetime's activity. What other people get profit from following is that activity itself, the spectacle of a mind at work. That is why, just as an emotional reaction is more significant for its force than for its direction, a musical judgment is of value to others less for the conclusions reached than for the methods by which these have been, not even arrived at, but elaborated, defended, and expressed.

ORCHESTRAS, CONDUCTORS, RECITALISTS

The Philharmonic Crisis

ARTUR RODZINSKI has gone and done it. For years the knowledge has been a secret scandal in music circles. Now he has said it out loud. That the trouble with the Philharmonic is nothing more than an unbalance of power. Management has usurped, according to him, certain functions of the musical direction without which no musical director can produce a first-class and durable artistic result. He has implied that no conductor, under present conditions, can keep the orchestra a musical instrument comparable to those of Boston and Philadelphia. He points to Arthur Judson, a powerful business executive who manages the orchestra as a side line, as the person chiefly interested in weakening the musical director's authority. He is right; he is perfectly right; he could not be more right. An orchestra can use one star performer and one only. And such a star's place is the podium, not the executive offices.

The American symphony orchestra, like the American government, is an operation of three powers. Its trustees are the power responsible to the community. They provide (or collect) money and determine how it is to be spent; they hire a manager to handle the business details of concert giving; and they entrust to a conductor the production of music for these. The manager in his office and the conductor before his orchestra both have full authority to run their departments, the trustees preserving a veto power over policies only. The trustees, a self-perpetuating body, are thus the initiators of the orchestra as a project and the court of final appeal about everything regarding it.

The musical director's job is the most responsible post of its kind in the world. He has all the authority of a ship's captain. Hiring and firing of musicians, their training and discipline, the composition of all programs and their public execution are his privilege. Any visiting conductor or soloist is a guest in his house. The manager's job is purely organizational, a routine matter that anyone can handle who has a knowledge of standard business methods and some diplomacy. The latter is essential for him, serving constantly, as he does, as go-between in whatever brush-ups occur between the conductor and the trustees. Since the symphony orchestra is a nonprofit-making institution serving the community in a cultural capacity, its trustees must be men and women of culture and of unquestioned civic responsibility, its conductor a musician with courage and judgment as well as technical skill, its manager a model of integrity and of tact.

The Philharmonic case is simple. Arthur Judson is unsuited by the nature and magnitude of his business interests to manage with the necessary self-effacement a major intellectual institution doing business with his other interests. He is also a man of far too great personal force to serve effectively as a mediator between a proud musician and the equally proud trustees. That is probably why no conductor ever stays long enough with the Philharmonic to accomplish the job that everybody knows should be done, namely, to put the orchestra permanently on an artistic equality with the other American orchestras of comparable financial resources.

Artur Rodzinski has done more for the orchestra in that respect than any other conductor in our century has done. Mahler and Toscanini were greater interpreters, were not such great builders. If Stokowski and Muench, also great interpreters, have been able this winter, as guests, to play upon the orchestra in full freedom and to produce from it sonorous and expressive beauties of the highest quality, that achievement has been made possible by Rodzinski's personnel replacements and his careful training. Such an achievement on the part of guest conductors has not heretofore been possible. Today the Philharmonic, for the first time in this writer's memory, is the equal of the Boston and Philadelphia orchestras and possibly their superior.

Stabilization of these gains is the next step indicated. With that in mind the trustees in December voted Mr. Rodzinski a long-term contract "without strings attached." One gathers that the contract he actually received contained not strings but chains, that his right to decide who besides himself shall conduct his orchestra, to confer with his guests about their programs, even to determine in full freedom his own was seriously jeopardized. It seems doubtful that any conductor would leave so important a post unless the working conditions were about to become intolerable. So far, they have not been that for him, and the orchestra's improvement under his leadership has proved that they were not.

What awaits his successor is anybody's guess. Dramas and heartbreaks probably, unless the trustees decide to hire another such orchestra builder and give him full power to go ahead and build. In that case, it is scarcely worth while to have provoked the present conductor into resigning. (The contention that he resigned merely because a better job was offered him is not credible, because there is no better job.) In any other case, the Philharmonic will decline as an orchestra as inevitably as winter will return. There is only one way to have a first-class orchestra and that is to let the conductor run it. If he fails, he can be replaced. But while he lasts he has to be given full musical authority as that is understood in the major symphonic establishments.

Rodzinski's career will not be gravely interrupted, we hope, by his courageous gesture. New York will miss him and regret his musical benefits bestowed. The last and greatest of these will have been the most valuable of all, if his exposure of what has long been known in music circles as a scandal and a shame shall encourage the trustees to correct it. There is no reason why the Philharmonic should not remain what it is now, the tip-top executant musical organization of the world. All it needs is a competent and energetic musical director and a disinterested management.

February 9, 1947

The "New Friends"

A PROSPECTUS announcing next year's plans for the New Friends of Music concerts arrived recently at this desk accompanied by a letter from Ira Hirschmann, president of the society. "Am I right," he asks, "in saying that very few enterprises of any kind, especially those that deal with the living spirit of music, can show a record of the consistency we were privileged to practice; and do you think it is of sufficient interest to you to justify the republication of these aims?

"I hope," he continues, "that you are not disappointed with our next year's plans."

One cannot deny that the aims stated in the original prospectus of 1936 are excellent and that the New Friends have pursued them assiduously. They are:

1. To offer the best in the literature of chamber music and lieder.

2. To embrace complete cycles of composers' works rather than "little pieces," wherever possible.

3. To conceive the music in the season's programs as a unit divided into sixteen concerts, with a view to offering the subscribers as complete a representation of the literature of individual composers as feasible.

4. To perform neglected music in unusual instrumental and voice combinations along with better known chamber music works.

5. To build the programs first and choose the artists on the basis of the programs.

6. To make this music available at very low prices on a subscription basis; most cases under $1 and student tickets at 25 cents.

7. To eliminate all elements foreign to the music itself, such as exploitation of artists' personality, display pieces, encores, flowers, interruptions between movements, intermissions, etc.

8. To offer no free passes, with a hope of helping to curb this practice, so unfair to artists and managers.

9. To attempt to demonstrate that there is a large public for

the best in music and that even at low prices, under careful management, the best music can be self-supporting without patrons or patronesses.

As to whether I am disappointed with next year's plans, yes, Mr. Hirschmann, since you ask, I am. Devoting the season to Bach, Schubert, and Brahms seems to me a retracing of your footsteps. For eight years the society gave nothing but Central European music. In its ninth it began to branch out and spent half its time on French music, ancient and modern, the other half being given over to Mozart. Evidently the Germanically schooled element among the subscribers did not like this admission that chamber music exists beyond the West Wall, since a more timorous retreat could scarcely be imagined than your announced return to the triple fortresses of Bach and Schubert and Brahms.

"To offer the best in the literature of chamber music and lieder" could not have been accomplished without the admission of French repertory. To do the job completely would still require that Italian (at least the madrigal literature) and English and Russian chamber music be included. There are vast repertories of chamber music written outside Central Europe, in fact, that a comprehensive program should have dealt with before going into such minor masters, as the New Friends did a few seasons back, as Mendelssohn and Dvořák. To turn tail on the non-Germanic world after one brief expedition into France I find a little cowardly.

The announced return to Central Europe is no doubt the result of subscriber pressure. Certainly the Germanic-minded are the most faithful element in the New Friends' audience. Dealing with their conservatism and their prejudices is your problem, Mr. Hirschmann, not mine. But since you have asked me for my sentiments about next year's program announcement, I am obliged to express the disappointment that your question foresaw. And I should like to take this occasion to bring out another complaint that has been burning my pocket for a long time. I find not only that the programs are weighted unjustly on the Central European side but that the choice of interpreters is, too. If we must be limited in our repertory by the Rhine, the Danube, and the Curzon line, couldn't we maybe have some of it played more often by French quartets? Turning over French music this year to too many German-school executants was a mistake, I think. But the opposite procedure has long been known to produce excellent results. French and Italian interpreters often do a better job, in fact, on the German classics than the Germans themselves do.

Lest any one imagine that I am trying to drag our present war with the Central Powers over into the field of art, I hasten to add that I have no unfriendly feeling at all toward German music and German musicians, ancient or modern. I merely insist that the German tradition is not the whole story of chamber music. Any attempt to pretend that it is is just ostrich tactics. And I deplore obscurantism in all its forms, especially on the part of a society that furnishes to New York most of the classical chamber music we hear. The New Friends are no longer just a private society, entitled to play what they please. They have assumed a responsible role in our cultural life. And the carrying out of their obligation requires that they continue to give us not only "the best in the literature of chamber music and lieder" but *all* that best, however unfamiliar some of it may be to music lovers of strictly Teutonic upbringing.

March 25, 1945

Pierre Monteux

PIERRE MONTEUX's two-week visit as guest conductor of the Philharmonic-Symphony Orchestra, which ends today, has led music lovers of all schools (the critical press included) to two conclusions: namely, that this conductor has drawn from our orchestra more beautiful sounds and more beautiful mixtures of sound than any other conductor has done in many years, and that his readings of Brahms are highly refreshing.

It has been a long time, a very long time, since our Philharmonic sounded like an orchestra. It has always been an assemblage of good players; and the changes of personnel operated last year by Mr. Rodzinski, on his accession to the conductorship, have improved further its musical potentialities. Sometimes of late the playing has been most agreeable. Sometimes, too, no matter who was conducting, the performances have sounded more like a reading rehearsal than like a prepared execution. This lack of dependability in the ensemble — so noticeable in contrast to the solid teamwork, no matter who conducts them, in the orchestras of Philadelphia, Boston, and Chicago — has long been a trouble. As far back as 1936 Sir Thomas Beecham, who served a half-season that year as guest, annoyed the directors considerably by replying, when asked to diagnose the musical ills of the organization, that though it contained many excellent players it was not an orchestra.

Many conductors, Mr. Rodzinski included, have produced a pretty good balance of timbres and made music, usually unfamiliar music, sound pretty well. Arturo Toscanini has occasionally, without any beauty of sheer sound being involved, made familiar music sound unusually eloquent. It has remained for Pierre Monteux to achieve what many of us thought was hopeless. He has made the Philharmonic play with real beauty of tone, many kinds of it, and with perfect balance and blending — to sound, in short, like an orchestra, a real, first-class orchestra requiring no apology. And he has also played music as familiar as that of Brahms and Beethoven (not to speak of Debussy) with not only a wonderful beauty of sound but a far from usual eloquence as well. This is the way a real orchestra *should* sound, the way the first-class orchestras of the world all *do* sound. And this is the way many musicians have long wished the music of Johannes Brahms could be made to sound.

It is a strange anomaly that although Brahms's symphonic music is extremely popular (in some years it tops even that of Beethoven for frequency of performance), almost nobody's reading of it is thoroughly satisfactory. How to discern the rhythm that underlies its slow and its energetic passages, to make these sound in any given piece as if they are all parts of the same piece, is one of the unsolved problems in music. Certainly the meditative ones require to be read as inward rather than as extrovert sentiment. And certainly the animated ones and the passages of broad eloquence, such as the codas and finales, tempt any conductor to make oratory out of them. But alternations of introversion with extroversion do not make a unity in the reading of anything, and there is no reason to suppose that so experienced and so consecrated a musician as Brahms was basically incoherent in thought. It is far more likely that his exact poetic temper, being profoundly personal, escapes us.

In my time only the late Frederick Stock of Chicago has been able to envelop the Brahms symphonies with a dreamy lilt that allowed the soft passages to float along and the loud ones to sing out as elements of a single continuity. A rhythmic propulsion that was steady without being rigid was the basis of these readings. Orchestral tone that was light in texture and wholly transparent was its superstructure. Mr. Monteux is less expert than Dr. Stock was at preserving a poetical and rhythmic unity throughout, but he is more expert than anybody at lifting the velvet pall that is accustomed in our concerts to lie over the Brahms instrumentation and allowing everything, middle voices too, to shine forth with translucency. His strings never obscure the woodwinds. His trumpets and trombones never blast away the strings. His horns, when force is indicated, play very loud; but their loudness is bright, not heavy; it is a flash of light rather than a ton of bricks.

Both these conductors have been celebrated for their renderings of French music, especially of Debussy, which requires a similar rhythmic continuity and identical refinements of balance. Sheer weight, like sheer brilliance, must always, in this kind of music, be avoided, because it destroys the translucency that is the music's main means of evoking an atmosphere. And the rhythm must be alive but steady, the cantilena floating on the delicate wavelike motion of this without effort or any insistence. Mr. Monteux, when playing both these composers, sometimes allows the slower passages to go dead. At these moments the rhythm stops supporting the flow of sound, all animation disappears, and the sounds themselves lose their ability to blend. But these moments are never long. As soon as the rhythm reasserts itself, the tonal fabric comes to life again and breathes like a sentient being.

Listening lately to Pierre Monteux conduct Brahms and Debussy on the same program brought to mind how much the music of these two authors is alike, or at least demands like treatment. The secret of their rhythm is very much the same secret And nonviolation of their rhythm is essential and preliminary to producing among their orchestral sounds luminosity. That and the use of transparent, or nonweighty, orchestral tone.

By what occult methods Mr. Monteux produces in our Philharmonic-Symphony Orchestra a real community of rhythmic articulation, not to mention the delights of delicate balance and
blending that proceed from this, I cannot even guess. The guest
conductors who have failed where he has succeeded would like
to know, too, I imagine.

November 12, 1944

The Sanguine Temperament

ROCHESTER PHILHARMONIC ORCHESTRA, *Sir Thomas Beecham,* conductor, concert in Carnegie Hall Saturday night.

SYMPHONY NO. 93	HAYDN
SUITE FROM BALLET THE GREAT ELOPEMENT	HANDEL-BEECHAM
(First New York Performance)	
SYMPHONY NO. 7, IN A MAJOR. OP. 92.	BEETHOVEN
MARCHE TROYENNE	BERLIOZ

THE CONCERT that Sir Thomas Beecham conducted with the Rochester Philharmonic Orchestra in Carnegie Hall on Saturday night
was a personal triumph for the English leader. The massive applause that greeted, in a far from full house, his incomparable
readings of Haydn, of Beethoven, of Berlioz, and of his own
ballet music (out of Handel) could only have been gratitude
for the grandeur and buoyancy of those readings as such, since
the orchestral execution of the Rochester society is certainly no
marvel for fine finish. When, at the close of the concert, the audience demanded extra numbers (the Andante from Elgar's String
Serenade and the March from Sibelius's *Karelia* suite were what
they got), it seemed reasonable to suppose that what they wanted
was not so much further acquaintance with the pleasant but
roughish playing of the Rochester band as more of Sir Thomas's
deeply joyous music making.

This reviewer confesses to a similar predilection for the
Beecham readings. His Haydn has gusto and sentiment along
with its grace. It breathes with ease and steps a real measure. It
is no line drawing of antiquity but a full evocation in the round
of music that everybody knows to have passion as well as de-

corum, but that no other conductor seems able to bring to life with quite that ruddy glow.

The new Handel-Beecham suite, which received its first New York hearing on this occasion, is out of a ballet entitled *The Great Elopement,* undertaken, I believe, for the Ballet Theater, but not yet produced on any stage. Here is no sullen expatriate Handel, yearning after the unhappy Germany he grew up in (and never liked) or after the perverse and monumental Italy of his youth. It is the British Handel, as square-toed as a country squire, as witty as a London playwright, as dainty as a beau of Bath, as expansive as the empire itself. One looks forward to a stage performance of the work. Frederick Ashton would probably be its ideal choreographer.

Beethoven's Seventh Symphony received the roughest execution of the evening but the most enlightened reading it has had in my lifetime. Nothing in its whole progress was either long or wrong. And when one remembered the innumerable booby traps for conductors with which that work is sown, it was with amazement and respect that one observed Sir Thomas sidestepping them all and going straight to the heart of the matter. This heart is the funeral-march Allegretto, the saddest, mostly deeply tragic piece Beethoven ever wrote, surrounded and framed by three of the most exuberant affirmations that exist in musical literature. We have had choleric Beethoven of late and melancholy Beethoven and even some lymphatic. Myself I like it sanguine, because I think that is the kind of man Beethoven was. And Sir Thomas's Seventh Symphony, for all its studied proportions, was abundantly that.

March 10, 1945

The Ormandy Case

PHILADELPHIA ORCHESTRA, *Eugene Ormandy,* conductor, opening concert of the season in Carnegie Hall last night:

SYMPHONY NO. 4, E MINOR	BRAHMS
CONCERTO FOR ORCHESTRA	KODÁLY
TWO NOCTURNES: NUAGES; FÊTES	DEBUSSY
DAPHNIS ET CHLOË, SECOND SUITE	RAVEL

THE PHILADELPHIA ORCHESTRA, which opened our indoor orchestral season last night at Carnegie Hall, has a sound that is pungent and mellow like the smell of fall fruits. No other instrumental assembly has quite the quality of impersonal, almost botanical, beauty that this one possesses; and none of the other conductors who appear regularly before us has quite Eugene Ormandy's way of offering really excellent workmanship without personal insistence.

Persons who cherish star quality in public performers often feel let down by Mr. Ormandy, though it is surprising how satisfactory the work he does with his orchestra turns out to be on accustomed acquaintance. There is, indeed, no final flame of eloquence in it and no categorical authority. But there is always beauty and order and an approach to all kinds of music that, if it does not manifest the ultimate of sensitivity, is nevertheless marked by an understanding of all the musical languages, that is at once sensuous and delicate.

With no preparation, for instance, by early training or by residence, for the playing of French music, and with, to this day, an incurably Viennese irregularity of rhythmic scansion, he manages to expose French music with less distortion of its original sense than almost any of the other interpreters do, saving only those of extended Parisian experience. He does this by cultivating in his orchestra the whole gamut of sounds and colorations of sound — not just the pushing or the throbbing ones — that are the full French orchestral palette. And he keeps these cleanly separate from one another, equilibrating and contrasting, as is the custom of the French conductors, rather than mixing them.

He just misses full identification with the French style in his rhythm. He has neither the instinct nor the training for exact quantities that are characteristic of French musicians and that are necessary above all for the lucid exposition of Debussy. And he does not quite seize the strophic nature of French musical discourse. What is meant for a simple breath, a hesitation, becomes too often a hiatus. His whole rhythmic outline is too flexible for full metrical clarity.

All the same, French works, as he plays them, come out less distorted than is usual here and with far more vibrancy of timbre than is common anywhere. The trumpet passages that start the march section in Debussy's *Fêtes*, for instance, were articulated last night so brightly, and yet so softly, that one might easily have taken them for an off-stage effect. I have never before heard trumpets to be played so quietly and still to sound like trumpets.

The novelty of the evening was a Concerto for Orchestra (it might as well have been called an overture) by Zoltán Kodály, written for the fiftieth anniversary season of Chicago's Symphony Orchestra and performed there in 1941. This is a lively piece, gay and clean and fresh and soundly sonorous. Mr. Ormandy read it straightforwardly and with full appreciation of the special Hungarian savor that characterizes the work of this composer, who was, in fact, Mr. Ormandy's teacher.

October 4, 1944

Wrestling and Shadow Boxing

NEW YORK CITY SYMPHONY, *Leonard Bernstein,* conductor, concert last night at the New York City Center.

BRANDENBURG CONCERTO NO. 3, IN G MAJOR	BACH
THE CREATION OF THE WORLD	MILHAUD
SYMPHONY NO. 2, IN C MAJOR	SCHUMANN

THE NEW YORK CITY SYMPHONY gave a concert last night at the City Center of Music and Drama that was in every way vigorous and refreshing. The new conductor, Leonard Bernstein, is on the whole rather too vigorous for the complete enjoyment of this sedate observer. But the freshness of his attack on musical problems both technical and interpretative is a delight to bear witness to. And if his work more resembles to the eye shadowboxing than standard orchestral conducting, there is auditory proof aplenty that this gifted young musician is also wrestling with angels.

He came off best last night, it seemed to me, in his bout with the spirit of Robert Schumann. One so rarely nowadays hears this composer's Second Symphony at all that there was double pleasure in hearing it read with such romantic brio. I have not heard such a warm and spirited rendering of any orchestral piece by Schumann in a long time.

The same warmth was Mr. Bernstein's downfall in the Third Brandenburg Concerto of Sebastian Bach. Like many of his elders, in dealing with this music, he mistakes dynamic exaggeration for fullness of utterance. Fullness in the Baroque style comes from rhythmic exactitude, not from runaway tempos, from the line nobly curved in repose, not from gasping phraseology. Solidity of pace becomes it, and all brilliance of tone, rather than breathless passion and huskiness.

Darius Milhaud's masterpiece, *The Creation of the World*, had brought out a lively audience; and there seemed to be no public disappointment with the work. Myself I was a little disappointed in Mr. Bernstein's reading of it, though hearing at all a piece so famous and so seldom presented was perhaps enough to have asked. All the same I regretted, as I had in the Bach, that overweening dynamism in the beat ended by obscuring somewhat the static and primeval character of this jazz poem.

The music itself alternates so sharply between tranquillity and syncopation that any reading of it based on whipping it up and then letting it down tends to let the whole piece down. Its continuity requires a steady rhythm and the avoidance of all excitement on the conductor's part. He must traverse it as if it were a massive and sluggish river with whirpools in it. Having fun in the whirlpools is tempting, I know; but keeping the boat in equilibrium gives the passengers a better view of the stream.

November 20, 1945

You Can Listen to Him

BOSTON SYMPHONY ORCHESTRA, *Leonard Bernstein*, conductor. Heard last night at Carnegie Hall.

SYMPHONY NO. 7, IN C MAJOR   SCHUBERT
LE SACRE DU PRINTEMPS   STRAVINSKY

STRAVINSKY'S *Rite of Spring*, which closed last night's concert of the Boston Symphony Orchestra in Carnegie Hall, is probably the most influential work of music composed in our century and the most impressive in performance. Not having heard its execution in November by the Philharmonic under Artur Rodzinski, the present writer has no basis for a comparison of that reading, which was much admired, with last night's by Leonard Bernstein. He has heard many another, however; and none has seemed to him more straightforward or more moving.

The work does not stand much interpretative tinkering, as a matter of fact. The more rigid its beat the greater its expressive power. What it needs is clean rhythm, clean tonal balances, and understanding. Its subject, human sacrifice, is too grand and terrible to permit personal posturing. And Mr. Bernstein, often a sinner in that regard, gave it none. If he did not extract from the score one tenth of the detailed refinement that older hands at it do — conductors like Monteux and Ansermet and Désormière — he nevertheless got the rhythm right and made the meaning more clear than usual. One felt that he loved the music, understood it, and submitted his will in all modesty to its relentless discipline.

The work is not a clear masterpiece, like the same composer's *Petrouchka;* but it is more original. It cuts farther below the surface of musical convention, goes straight to the heart of the whole stylistic problem of Romanticism, comes out both deeply expressive and completely impersonal. Its complex rhythmic interest, its high harmonic tension, and its rigid orchestral textures are justly famous. Its patent of nobility, however, lies in the extreme beauty of its melodic material. Partly Russian folklore and partly inventions in the same manner, its themes are short, diatonic, and narrow. They rarely cover a larger range than the perfect fifth. They are as plain as granite and as resistant to time. If the work did not lose intensity in the early part of its second half, it would be the solidest single monument of musical art our century has erected. Just possibly it is that in spite of everything.

Mr. Bernstein's reading of the Schubert C-major Symphony, which preceded the Stravinsky work, was open-hearted, animated, youthful, and full of life. Texturally it was a little rough, and at no point was it particularly Viennese in lilt. But it was passionate and sweet. Anybody can question another artist's interpretation. What seems to be beyond question in Mr. Bernstein's case is that he is a real interpreter. His orchestral hand is still young and a little heavy, and sometimes his personal projection is overweening. But his is a real temperament for making music. What he conducts rarely sounds beautiful to a sensuous spirit. And his musical culture is far from mature. But you can listen to him. That is the first and the last test of any interpreter.

February 13, 1947

Among the Best

PHILHARMONIC-SYMPHONY ORCHESTRA, *Charles Muench*, guest conductor (New York debut), concert last night at Carnegie Hall.

WATER MUSIC SUITE	HANDEL
SYMPHONY No. 3 ("Liturgique")	HONEGGER
(First Performance in the United States)	
IBÉRIA	DEBUSSY
DAPHNIS ET CHLOË, SUITE No. 2	RAVEL

CHARLES MUENCH, who conducted last night's Philharmonic concert in Carnegie Hall, has been for some fifteen years, till recently, conductor of France's oldest and best-known orchestra, that of the Société des Concerts du Conservatoire. Alsatian by birth and a French citizen by adoption (in 1918), Mr. Muench, who was at one time first violinist of the Cologne Orchestra and long a pupil and protégé of Furtwängler, would seem admirably prepared to bridge, as an interpreter, that ever-widening gap between the German and the French musical styles which is one of the most troublesome musical phenomena of our century.

All the same, and with a vast experience behind him on both sides of the Rhine, he remains Alsatian. You never know quite where his musical sympathies lie. He plays German music, particularly Beethoven, better than most of the French conductors now working in France. And he certainly plays French music better than any of the German conductors now working in Germany, though many a German not now working in Germany, Furtwängler included, has had a sounder understanding of the French Impressionist style.

Last night he played Handel's *Water Music* (arranged by Sir

Hamilton Harty), a new symphony by the Franco-Swiss Honegger, and familiar works by Debussy and Ravel. The first was charming and animated, the second, if one could judge in an unfamiliar work, a masterful rendition. The last two readings, though impressive enough as a display of both technics and temperament, missed the musical point of both pieces about as completely as could be imagined.

In the Debussy *Ibéria* Mr. Muench sacrificed color to dynamics, and metrics to accent. He took romantic liberties with the sentiment and with the time and leaned on all the melodic lines. As a result, the piece sounded like an unsuccessful attempt on Debussy's part to write real Spanish music instead of a successful attempt to evoke poetically, as in a dream, the whole sensuous panorama of a Spain he had never seen.

Ravel's second *Daphnis and Chloë* suite was similarly weakened by the imposition on it of a personal romanticism that it was never made to support. By taking its tempos consistently rubato and by exaggerating the climaxes, Mr. Muench managed to make it sound like an inferior *Tristan and Isolde,* which it is not, instead of like the superior *Scheherazade* that it is. This was all very disappointing from a conductor who has been both a first-class musician and a Frenchman long enough to know better.

Arthur Honegger's Third (or "Liturgical") Symphony consists of three symphonic odes that express the emotional content of the Dies Irae hymn, of the De Profundis psalm, and of the final phase, "Dona nobis pacem," from the Agnus Dei of the Mass. They do this most effectively indeed in a turbulent and dissonant style that is not difficult to follow and that is rhythmically far from platitudinous. If the harmonic and orchestral seeming complexity is a little bit, with regard to the thematic, the melodic content, like sauce cooking that conceals the poverty of the basic food materials, the result is tasty all the same. The work is both meritorious and masterful, and it is interesting to listen to. It is also a shade theatrical in the sense of obvious.

The public received both Mr. Muench and the Honegger symphony warmly. All present seemed to recognize, in spite of a certain expressive poverty, the high qualities of skill and temperament that characterize the work of both and place it among the best of our time.

January 21, 1947

Birthday Salute

ARTURO TOSCANINI will be eighty years old on Tuesday, March 25. The occasion is notable not merely for the fact that age has not withered nor custom staled his infinitely satisfactory musicianship, but also for the reminder that he is today, exactly as he has been for twenty years, the first conductor of the world. His primacy in the field of opera has been clear for nearer forty years, since his appearance at the Metropolitan Opera House in 1908, in fact. Since 1926, when he first conducted the New York Philharmonic Orchestra, his mastery of the concert style has been equally unquestionable. From that day till now it has not been possible for any musician or musical observer to list the great living conductors of an age that has been glorious for great conducting without putting Arturo Toscanini's name squarely at the top.

His most remarkable quality as a public performer has always been his dependability. He never lets his audience down nor lets music down. When announced to appear, he appears. When he conducts any work, however familiar, unfamiliar, difficult of execution, facile of sentiment, no matter what kind of work or by whom, he knows the score and gives it as careful, as polished a reading as if his whole musical life depended on that single work. It is this unusual dependability, indeed, that has given rise to the legend of his musical infallibility. Actually he misses the point of a piece, misunderstands a composer's thought as often as any other musician. Where he does not fail is in the ability to call forth on any platform the full resources of his own musical interest and attention. Music, any music, all music stimulates in him as automatically as in the proverbial circus horse the full functioning of his professional capacities.

Those capacities derive not only from a nervous stability superior to that of any of the other great living conductors, but also from a musical instinct as simple and as healthy as that of a gifted child. Toscanini, and let us make no mistake about it, is a natural musician. His culture may be elementary but his ear is true. He makes music out of anything. And the music that he makes is the plainest, the most straightforward music now available in public performance. There is little of historical evocation in it and even less of deliberate emotional appeal. It is purely auditory, just ordered sound and very little else. There is not even much Toscanini in it. For in spite of his high temperament, this musician is strangely lacking in personality.

That is why, I think, he has based his interpretative routine on a literal as possible an adherence to musical texts. A respect for the written note and the adherence to any composer's clearly indicated intent have always been the procedure of first-class conductors of ensemble music. But the composer's expressive intent is more often than not far from clear; and musical notation, particularly as regards phraseology and rhythmic inflection, is extremely imprecise. Imagination and a deep historical culture are the classical approaches to the problem of invigorating the music of the past. Toscanini has no such culture to channelize his imaginative faculties. He is not in any sense an intellectual. He is not ignorant; he has heard, read, and played vast quantities of music; and his mind is as sound as his body. But he has not the humane letters of a Beecham, a Reiner, a Monteux, the refined sensuality of a Stokowski, an Ormandy, the moral fervor and sense of obligation toward contemporary creation of Koussevitzky. He simply sticks as closely to the text as he can and makes music.

Actually, of course, he takes as many liberties with a text as any other executant. He neglects Beethoven's metronome marks, as everybody else does. He corrects a balance for clarity's sake. He speeds up a finale for general excitement. He has gravely falsified, moreover, the musical tradition of our time by speeding up the Mozart minuet movements to a point where all memory of the court dance has disappeared from them. What he does not do is to personalize his interpretations. He adds a great deal of excitement to any piece, but that excitement is of a purely auditory and cerebral, rather than of an expressive character. His appeal is thus deeply contemporary to an epoch which has accepted abstractions in art, in science, and in politics as the source of its most passionate loyalties.

Nobody else in our time has been so simple or so pure toward music as Toscanini. He will not loom large, I imagine, in the history books of the future, because he has mostly remained on the side lines of the creative struggle. And music's history is always the history of its composition. Toscanini has radically simplified the technique of orchestral conducting, and he has given a straightforwardness to all interpretation in our time that cannot fail to facilitate the execution problem for living composers. But his involvement with the formation of our century's musical style, with the encouragement of contemporary expression in music, with the living composers, in short, whose work will one day constitute the story of music in our time, has been less than that of any of today's other orchestral great. He has honor and glory now, but by posterity his work will probably pass unremunerated.

That is why we must enjoy him and be thankful for him and cherish him. For when he leaves there will be little left save a memory and a few gramophone records; and these give hardly any idea of his electric powers as a public performer. By a miracle we have him with us still and, by a greater miracle, in full possession of his powers. That those powers are without peer in our time cannot be denied by anybody. That they may long be preserved to him and to us is the prayer of every living musician and lover of music.

March 23, 1947

The Koussevitzky Case

SERGE (or Sergei) Koussevitzky, conductor of the Boston Symphony Orchestra since 1924, is an aristocrat among American conductors and in Boston music circles something of an autocrat. Born seventy-two years ago in Russia and reared there in poverty (his family, though Orthodox Jews, never lived in a ghetto), he has attained wealth, world-wide fame and the highest distinction in his profession. As a virtuoso on the double-bass viol and as a conductor his ranking, by any standards, has been for many years among that of the very greatest in our time. As a composer he has contributed to the reputable literature of his instrument. As a publisher and a patron of contemporary music he has probably made a more lasting contribution to the art than any other single person living, excepting five or six composers. His place in its history is already assured and glorious.

Just to make assurance doubly sure, the Boston immortality machine has started issuing this winter what looks like a series of books bearing the papal imprimatur of the good doctor (LL.D., *honoris causa,* Harvard, 1929, and elsewhere). M. A. DeWolfe Howe, official biographer to the Bostonian great, has furnished *The Tale of Tanglewood, Scene of the Berkshire Music Festivals* (Vanguard Press, New York, 1946, $2), prefaced by Mr. Koussevitzky himself. And Hugo Leichtentritt, a musicologist of repute and a former Lecturer of Harvard University, has fathered *Serge Koussevitzky, the Boston Symphony Orchestra and the New American Music* (Harvard University Press, Cambridge, Mass., 1946, $3).

Both volumes are slender, and their tone is unctuous. The first sketches ever so lightly the history of the celebrated summer festivals that have now grown into a training school for composers, conductors, and orchestral musicians. The second enumerates the American compositions played by Serge Koussevitzky and the Boston Symphony Orchestra (sometimes under other leaders) since 1924. The list is large and impressive. If Mr. Leichtentritt's critical paragraphs are weakened by the fact that he has neither heard many of the works nor had access to their scores, the tabulation of Mr. Koussevitzky's public encouragements to American composers alone is of value as proving once and for all (if Walter Damrosch, Frederick Stock, Pierre Monteux, and Leopold Stokowski had not proved it before) that a sustained program policy supporting contemporary composition does not keep subscribers away from symphony concerts.

And now to supplement these two books, which are clearly official and more than a little superficial, arrives a full-length biography of the maestro which is neither. It is entitled simply *Koussevitzky,* by Moses Smith (Allen, Towne, and Heath, New York, 1947, $4). Announced for sale on February 15, its distribution has been held up for the time being by an injunction that prohibits its publication, sale, and distribution till Justice Shientag of the New York Supreme Court shall have determined whether the book's circulation will do its subject "irreparable harm." If the present writer, who has read an advance copy received before the injunction was issued, is in any way typical of the American reading public, it certainly, in his opinion, will not. The only possible harm he can envisage to so impregnable a reputation as that of Serge Koussevitzky is that already done by his own efforts to suppress the book.

Moses Smith, a trained newspaper man, for many years music critic of the *Boston Evening Transcript* as well as a friend of Mr. Koussevitzky, has produced a far more thorough study, a better work of scholarship than either Mr. Howe or Mr. Leichtentritt, scholars both by trade. There seems little in the book of factual statement that is subject to question. Whether Mr. Koussevitzky, in view of his great devotion to the memory of his second wife, is made unhappy by mention of his first marriage, hitherto not publicized in America, is scarcely germane. Neither is his possible sensitivity to reports of his quarrels with musicians and with blood relatives. These are, as a matter of fact, common knowledge; and they legitimately form part of the whole story of his musical life, just as his first marriage does of any complete biography.

Judgments and opinions, expressed over any writer's signature, are, of course, personal. The conductor's legal complaint objected to Mr. Smith's statement that Koussevitzky had succeeded as a conductor in spite of imperfect early training in musical theory and score reading. This also, if I may make so bold, has long been common knowledge among musicians. Nor is the estimable doctor unique among the conducting great for being in a certain sense self-taught. Leopold Stokowski, Sir Thomas Beecham, and Charles Muench, great interpreters all of them, did not come to conducting through early mastery of the conservatory routines. They bought, muscled, or impressed their way in and then settled down to learn their job. They succeeded gloriously, as Koussevitzky has done. All honor to them. They have all, Koussevitzky included, contributed more of value to the technique of their art than most of the first-prize-in-harmony boys ever have.

But great pedagogues, and the good doctor is one, do hate hearing that their own education has not been conventional, though it rarely was. And all great artists loathe criticism. They do; they really do. What they want, what they need, what they live on, as Gertrude Stein so rightly said, is praise. They can never get enough of it. And sometimes, when they have come to be really powerful in the world, they take the attitude that anything else is libel and should be suppressed. Dr. Koussevitzky's complaint, as I remember, did not use the word "libel." It spoke of possibly "irreparable injury." Well, criticism is often injurious; there is no question about that. Many a recitalist, receiving unfavorable reviews, finds it more difficult to secure further engagements than if the reports had been less critical. Minor careers have been ruined overnight that way. Major careers are rarely harmed by criticism, because major artists can take it. They don't like to; but they have to; so they do. All the same, it is the big boys, the great big boys that nothing could harm, that squawk the loudest. I know, because I have been in the business for several years now.

Mr. Smith's book makes Koussevitzky out to be a very great man indeed, but it also makes him human. Gone is the legend of his infallibility. Renewed is one's faith in his deep sincerity, his consecration, his relentless will to make the world permanently better than he found it. Nobody, I am sure, can read the book through without admiring him more. And the faith of the pious need not be shaken by reading that he has not always been toward his fellow man just and slow to anger. Civilization would be just a racket if we had to learn all we know about the lives of great men from their paid agents.

Mr. Koussevitzky is not the only first-class conductor in the world, though he is one of the best. Nor is he the only first-class conductor the Boston Symphony Orchestra has enjoyed. Nor does he any longer play the double bass in public, though when he did he was, by common consent, world champion. His unique position in a world full of excellent conductors, many of them devoted to contemporary music, is that he has played more of it, launched more of it, published more of it, and paid for more of it than anybody else living. That is the clear message of Mr. Smith's biography. Everything else, a petulant gesture here and there, a musical or family quarrel, a pretentious remark, a vainglorious interview, the present court action—all these things serve the picture; they bring him more vividly to life. How can anyone mind knowing them? Only he himself, apparently, hasting fearfully toward Parnassus, though his throne there has long been reserved for him, and involved, no doubt, in a publicity apotheosis that has already begun, would see any value in posing before an already worshiping universe without the customary habiliment of one human weakness. His lawsuit, of course, adds to the tableau that he has essayed so carefully to compose just that.

February 23, 1947

The Horowitz Mood

VLADIMIR HOROWITZ, pianist, second New York recital of the season last night at Carnegie Hall.

SONATA IN E FLAT MAJOR, OP. 78	HAYDN
FANTASY IN C MAJOR, OP. 17	SCHUMANN
TOCCATA, OP. 11	PROKOFIEV
BRUYÈRES; GENERAL LAVINE; ETUDES: Pour les arpèges; Pour les cinq doigts, D'après Monsieur Czerny	DEBUSSY
BALLADE IN G MINOR, OP. 23, No. 1; MAZURKA IN F MINOR, OP. 63, No. 2	CHOPIN
MENDELSSOHN'S WEDDING MARCH AND VARIATIONS (after Liszt)	HOROWITZ

VLADIMIR HOROWITZ, who played last night in Carnegie Hall his second piano recital of the season, is justly famous as a marksman of the keyboard. To play the piano quite that loud and quite that fast with accuracy is given to few in any generation. To project at the same time so strongly a sentiment of controlled and relentless violence is given to none other in ours. It is, no doubt, the very intensity of this characteristic Horowitz mood, or expression, that makes his quieter passages sound mostly, by comparison, tame. By themselves they are pretty good music making, though not invariably of the best. Heard beside his bravura work, it becomes clear that they are not what one has come to hear, what anybody present would come a second time to hear.

Just as there is a characteristic Horowitz mood of expression, there is also, equally characteristic, the Horowitz piano tone. This is plangent, brassy, and dark in color. It evokes the trombone rather than the trumpet. And it is most richly in evidence in loud passages. At any dynamic level lower than mezzo forte it fails to vibrate. From mezzo forte to fortissimo and beyond it is commanding and, because of this artist's unusual finger and arm-weight control, varied and interesting. This is why, I think, Mr. Horowitz's public is likely to be a bit restless in the early part of a program or during the meditative and poetic parts of any long piece. One is waiting for the moment when both the characteristic sound and the characteristic fury will be turned loose, when Horowitz will stop being respectful of the classics and start being his unafraid self.

The Horowitz tone is not varied in color. Debussy shows up that weakness in it. But it is so highly varied in weight and articulation (in staccato playing he uses at least four different shortnesses) that its coloristic monotony is compensated for by its wide gamut of dynamic differentiation. Abstention from excessive use of the sustaining pedal brings out all this variety of percussive attack with a dryness and a clarity unequaled in the work of any other pianist now appearing before the public.

Nevertheless, for all the technical mastery displayed and all the real musical excitement provoked, Horowitz's playing is monotonous and, more often than not, musically false. He never states a simple melody frankly. He teases it by accenting unimportant notes and diminishing his tonal volume on all the climactic ones. The only contrast to brio that he knows is the affettuoso style. Only when handling the objectively picturesque, as in Debussy, does he seem at home in soft music. There, though he lacks the lighter, brighter colorations, he tampers little with the plain expressivity and gives, in consequence, a reading musically acceptable. But even here he is more convincing in the technically elaborate Études than in the poetically more delicate Préludes.

Last night's big show of the evening was a fancied-up version, by himself, of Liszt's Variations on the Mendelssohn Wedding March. Last year it was Sousa's *Stars and Stripes Forever,* complete with piccolo part. Another time it was Saint-Saëns's *Danse Macabre.* There is always something of the kind. Nobody else plays that kind so devastatingly well. Your reviewer always regrets there isn't more of it on any program. When a man can play hard music like that so satisfyingly, one regrets that he should spend so much of the evening worrying standard repertory.

April 9, 1946

Money's Worth

ALEXANDER BRAILOWSKY, pianist, recital last night at Carnegie Hall.

Toccata and Fugue in D minor	Bach-Busoni
Rondo Favori	Hummel
Sonata in B minor	Liszt
Intermezzo in B flat minor	Brahms
Scherzo from Midsummer Night's Dream	
	Mendelssohn-Rachmaninoff
Reflets dans l'eau	Debussy
Toccata	Ravel
Fantasy in F minor; Ecossaises in D major and D flat major; Waltzes in A minor and A flat major; Andante Spianato and Grande Polonaise	Chopin

Alexander Brailowsky's recital of piano music last night in Carnegie Hall was a model of the "good show" produced by legitimate means. He dramatized the music that he played, and he dramatized the excellence of his excellent execution. He dramatized these as a harmony, too, not as a conflict of opposing elements. Everything he played was consequently a human, as well as a musical, pleasure. Not a very deep pleasure, perhaps, but a real one.

Mr. Brailowsky has a natural gift for making music, untainted by intellectuality, and a masterful hand. His instincts are as gracious as his technique is sound. He exploits sentiment without getting hot around the collar, brilliance and brio with a visible delight. He paces a piece, any piece, as if it were an act of a play, builds it up, tapers it off, without hurry and without lingering. And he plays the right notes.

No audience can fail to respond to such charm, such competence, such courtesy. This member of last night's audience responded most vigorously to the Liszt Sonata, which offered the further delight of an apt stylization. This consisted of executing all its rolling and rumbling figurations with the driest, cleanest, and most exact modern finger mechanics. To the mere power of its climactic moments, which was already considerable, there was added thus an incisiveness that this work rarely enjoys; and its Romantic fury took on, in consequence, a diabolic quality at once terrifying and completely appropriate.

Mr. Brailowsky's Chopin benefited from the same clarity of articulation; and so did his Hummel Rondo, his Mendelssohn, Debussy, and Ravel. A Brahms Intermezzo, though cleanly read, lacked intimacy. And the Bach organ Toccata and Fugue in D minor (in the Busoni transcription) rather missed out all around. This is a clocklike piece, not a storm in the mountains. Its themes and its figurations are all mechanistic. Its expressive power in performance comes from playing up this mechanical quality rather than from trying to conceal it. Any organ transcription, moreover, must derive on the pianoforte any overpowering effect that is desired from a relentless rhythm rather than from mere pounding.

With these two exceptions, the evening was full of good musical value. No revelations, mind you. Mr. Brailowsky projects little original poetry and almost no novel meanings. But he makes music harmoniously, brilliantly, and quite soundly enough for anybody's price of admission. He is an honest virtuoso.

December 6, 1945

The Noble Style

ALEXANDER BOROVSKY, pianist, recital last night at Carnegie Hall.

ORGAN PRELUDE AND FUGUE IN A MINOR	BACH-LISZT
TWO PRELUDES AND FUGUES from THE WELL-TEMPERED CLAVI-CHORD, BOOK II	BACH
THIRTY-TWO VARIATIONS	BEETHOVEN
SONATA IN B FLAT MINOR, OP. 35	CHOPIN
PRÉLUDES: Cloches d'angoisse et larmes d'adieu and Le nombre léger	MESSIAEN
(First Performance)	
DANZA, OP. 32	PROKOFIEV
(First Performance)	
SARCASM, OP. 14, No. 5	PROKOFIEV
PRELUDES IN E FLAT MAJOR AND C MINOR, OP. 23	RACHMANINOFF
SONNETTO DEL PETRARCA, No. 104; ÉTUDE TRANSCENDANTE in F minor	LISZT

ALEXANDER BOROVSKY, who played a piano recital last night in Carnegie Hall, is a technician of the first water and a musician of impeccable taste. He is businesslike, forthright, masterful. Nowhere in his work is there any vulgarity, any obscurity, or any inadequacy. Few pianists give such deep satisfaction and oppress the spirit so little, and only a very few great have his rhythmic solidity. His work is serious, solid, sound, and sober.

It is sober, not from any lack of fire in the temperament, but rather from the nature of Borovsky's piano tone, which is all of one color. This is not at all an ugly tone, but neither is it exactly pretty. It is merely a little lacking in variety. It is hugely varied in weight, or loudness, and most exact about durations. But it lacks on its palette the lighter colorations. Its noble unity at all the levels of loudness has been achieved, apparently, at the sacrifice of brightness, brilliance, and liquidity.

This artist, a very great one and a man of broad musical understanding, is at his best, consequently, in music that calls for little coloristic expression. His Bach and his Beethoven last night were admirable in every way, though the present reviewer could have wished for a less consistent legato in the former, a more pointed evocation of harpsichord sonorities. His Prokofiev and Rachmaninoff were impressively sonorous too, dark-sounding, clear, and harmonious.

All the music of the Parisian school—Chopin, Messiaen, and Liszt—though thoroughly eloquent and lucid—left one longing for a sweeter caress, a gratuitous beauty of sound, a more imaginative orchestration. Color is part of such music's planned expressivity. A black-and-white photograph of it shows the formal composition but does not make a complete communication. In all these works Mr. Borovsky achieved effects of no mean grandeur, but the poetry of them all was pale from a lack in their performance of full tonal luminosity. Mr. Borovsky is at his best in the noble, or massive, style.

March 18, 1947

Grace and Power

GEORGE CHAVCHAVADZE, pianist, recital last night at Carnegie Hall.

SONATA IN C MAJOR, OP. 53 ("Waldstein")	BEETHOVEN
SUITE ON THEMES from EL AMOR BRUJO	de FALLA-CHAVCHAVADZE
SUITE FOR THE PIANO	DEBUSSY
MAZURKA, OP. 17, No. 4; BALLADE, OP. 23, No. 1; BERCEUSE,	
OP. 57; POLONAISE IN A FLAT, OP. 53	CHOPIN

GEORGE CHAVCHAVADZE, who gave a piano recital last night in Carnegie Hall, his first appearance here in several years, is one of the most delightful pianists of them all. There is variety in his work and spirit and imagination. His are a high color-range and a broad dynamic gamut. There are force and tenderness in him, relentlessness of rhythm and flexibility, wide sweep in any piece's progress, and an incredible luxury of detail. And always he plays with freshness, so that even works as familiar as the Chopin G-minor Ballade or Beethoven's "Waldstein" Sonata become absorbing to listen to, as if one had not heard them in twenty years.

The sources of that freshness are several. One is a natural feeling for Romanticism, a gift for moving about with grace among the passions. Another is the kind of alertness that keeps his full musical faculties employed in what he is doing. He never gets bored and begins to pound. Still another is his quite phenomenal finger agility, which enables him to sweep clearly through complexity and right up to a climax without any hesitation. He dramatizes the music, not his technical accomplishments. These last are many, but he does not throw them at you. He is an artist fecund of thought, rich in sentiment, and vastly abundant as to means.

His whole program was a delight for the genuine originality of his readings, an originality all the more welcome for being at no point arbitrary. He played the first movement of the "Waldstein" Sonata somewhat faster than we are used to hearing it, gave it by that means a fury that becomes it well. His Debussy suite *Pour le piano* had a breadth all unusual to it, but one that the work sustains without giving at the seams. His Chopin was a dream of supple grace, sweet, full, passionate, and grand. And if, in the great A-flat Polonaise, his finger strength was less impressive in the mounting scales than that, say, of Horowitz, the beauty of his tone at all the levels of loudness, from a whisper to full military evocation, was more consistent, more varied in all imaginable kinds of loveliness than almost anybody else's ever is.

Mr. Chavchavadze's own Suite on themes from Falla's *El Amor Brujo* is a masterpiece of piano transcription. It evokes the very sound of de Falla's orchestra. Whether the work, as played last night, is perhaps a little long for concert usage remains to be ascertained from further performances. Few theater works are tight enough in structure to support concert exposition at the length of more than fifteen minutes. The present version is nowhere lacking in interest for piano detail, but the original work was not built for concert conditions. It is quite possible that the omission of certain passages that seem musically static in the concert hall would lighten the suite up and give it the full force of its great musical beauty without the loss of pianistic brilliance.

March 24, 1947

In the First Category

MARYLA JONAS, pianist, recital yesterday afternoon at Carnegie Hall.

PASSACAGLIA	HANDEL
ANDANTINO	ROSSI
VARIATIONS	HAYDN
CAPRICCIO	W. F. BACH
RONDO IN D	MOZART
SONATA NO. 3	SCHUBERT
IMPROMPTU NO. 3 IN G MAJOR	SCHUBERT
POLONAISE, OP. 71, No. 2; TWO MAZURKAS; NOCTURNE; WALTZ;	
GRANDE POLONAISE, OP. 44	CHOPIN

MARYLA JONAS, who played the piano yesterday afternoon to a packed Carnegie Hall, is everything the reviewers said of her last spring. One can like or not this-that-or-the-other about her performance, but she is a solo pianist of the first category in any meaning of that term.

Her technique is clean and dry, her tone agreeable and varied in color, her musical understanding sound, her communication straightforward. Straightforwardness, indeed, is the quality of her work that lifts it above mere competence and puts it among that of the great. There is nothing kittenish about it or affected or flamboyant or timid or tentative or ostentatious. Miss Jonas makes her every musical point in the most direct manner imaginable. All is under control: her thought, her feeling, her fiery Polish temperament; and her technical powers respond without hesitancy to every expressive demand.

The basis of this alacrity, the organizing force behind all her skill and knowledge, is a rhythmic instinct unspoiled by bad training or mental cross-purposes, refined, on the contrary, by a far from superficial musical culture. In the classic style, playing Handel and Haydn and Mozart and Beethoven, the metrical march of her readings is as relentless as Landowska's. And when she plays the high Romantics, like Schubert and Chopin, her rubato, at the height of its freedom and fancy, never lets one forget for one instant that rhythmic freedom is a comment on measure, not a violation of it. Only first-class musicians ever work in this way.

Another region in which this artist's work is more sophisticated than that of ordinary good pianists is that of dynamic relief. When she plays plain chord passages she plays them with all voices equal. But when the musical texture is more complex, which is most of the time, she organizes her melody, her accompanying figures, her bass, her countermelody, and her interjected melodic comments at different levels of loudness, using also different kinds of tone, orchestrating the piece, so to speak, for clarity. The variety in dynamic relief that she employs is very great indeed, and the boldness with which she brings forward or almost whispers that which merits such treatment is invariably justified by the lucidity that results. She oversimplifies nothing; she merely amplifies emphasis by composing her dynamics rather elaborately.

Nor does she shy away from sentiment. When she makes a crescendo on a rising melodic curve, she lets it continue to the top of the curve. When passage work is fast and furious she keeps it fast and furious, no matter what technical difficulties it may present. She deals with every kind of emotion frankly and with every executional problem courageously. This frankness and courage are the marks of her individuality as a performer. As for mere mannerisms, technical or expressive, she has fewer, probably, than any other artist of her class now working before the public.

That she is a curious and wonderful Romantic survival, as many thought on hearing her last season, I do not believe. Schooled quality like hers and working methods of that efficiency are not atavistic throwbacks. They imply a musical understanding that can meet more emergencies than those of any particular repertory. That Miss Jonas is at home in all the centuries was proved yesterday by her impeccable renderings of both the early eighteenth century and (in the encores) of our own. She is a modern musician so thoroughly equipped that she can even play the Romantics convincingly. Being Polish, of course, helps.

December 8, 1946

Incomparable Chopin

GUIOMAR NOVAES, pianist, recital yesterday afternoon at Town Hall.

TOCCATA AND FUGUE IN D MAJOR	BACH
SONATAS IN E MAJOR AND D MAJOR	SCARLATTI
SONATA IN D MINOR, OP. 31, No. 2	BEETHOVEN
IMPROMPTU IN F SHARP, OP. 36, SONATA IN B FLAT MINOR, OP. 35	CHOPIN
EVOCATION	ALBÉNIZ
TOCCATA	GUARNIERI
FEUX-FOLLETS	ISIDOR PHILIPP

GUIOMAR NOVAES gave yesterday afternoon in the Town Hall the most absorbing, as well as the most convincing, rendition of Chopin's B-flat minor Sonata that this reviewer has ever heard. Her whole recital, indeed, was lovely and sensible. Bach, Scarlatti, Beethoven, and divers light modern pieces were interpreted with full competence both mental and fingerwise. But the poetry and the grandeur of the Chopin sonata were beyond all comparison with any reading of the work that this student has previously encountered. Cheers seemed to indicate that the audience was impressed, too.

Against all precedent, Miss Novaes dramatized the piece itself instead of the difficulties of its execution. These she accepted as incidental, as something never to be allowed to get in the way of the musical discourse. She took up no time reaching for notes or hesitating before heavy chords. She played her climaxes as musicians think them, on the upward sweep of feeling. As a result, the piece came off with a spontaneity and a conviction that left one no less swept away by her eloquence than admiring of her markmanship.

The climactic section of the work, in Miss Novaes's reading, was the Funeral March. The passionate earlier movements led up to the tragic calm of this; and the finale was like a coda to it, light as the wind, brief, desolate, all passion spent. The March itself was majestic in rhythm, impersonal in pathos. It was the evocation of a burial scene, not any artist's display of grief. And the softly soaring middle section was little but a melody and a bass, its inner notes as light as a harp or a clarinet heard outdoors with the wind blowing the other way.

It seemed rather a pity that so great a pianist as Miss Novaes (who is no newcomer to New York, either; she has appeared here pretty regularly since 1915) should have accepted to play on such an inferior instrument as the Steinway she used yesterday. Its tone was brassy throughout and lacking in depth. Its one virtue was the uniformity of its sound. It was not, like so many of the pianos heard nowadays in concert halls, all bass and high treble with no proper resonance at all in the center of the scale. In a season full of ugly-sounding pianos, however, it was the least agreeable your announcer has encountered.

October 27, 1946

Warm Welcome

DAME MYRA HESS, pianist, first New York recital in seven years yesterday afternoon in Town Hall.

FRENCH SUITE NO. 5, IN G MAJOR	BACH
SIX VARIATIONS, OP. 34	BEETHOVEN
SONATA IN A FLAT, OP. 110	BEETHOVEN
SONATA IN F MINOR, OP. 5	BRAHMS

DAME MYRA HESS, who played a pianoforte recital yesterday afternoon in the Town Hall, has, as a musician, instinct and intelligence. She has the quality which in France is called *musicalité*, the gift for making music sound like music. Also, she is a workman of taste and refinement. She takes convincing tempos, phrases soundly, analyzes a work correctly, executes it with ease and distinction. What she lacks is temperament, the power always to respond in public to her music's own sound and to add, inevitably, communication. She plays intelligently and she has a natural nobility. But she doesn't easily "give," as the young people would say.

Her playing yesterday of a Bach French Suite was pleasant, of two Beethoven works (the Six Variations, Opus 34, and the A-flat Sonata, Opus 110) pretty but distant. It was as if, having known them all her life, she were reminding other musicians of how they went. She did not so much play them as strum them. She exposed them clearly, sounded them out agreeably, but abstained from any personal involvement with their expressive content. The result was hard for a disinterested listener to keep his mind on. And her constant imposition of slight crescendos and descrescendos on every phrase removed from musical design its expressive urgency, reduced all to a restful lullaby.

Halfway through the Brahms F-minor Sonata (Opus 5) a change took place. She got into the scherzo through its rhythm, stopped strumming and really played the piece. From there to the end of the work she made music squarely, forthrightly, convincingly, instead of just dreaming about it in a flowing robe. One realized then that her celebrity is not due merely to her admirable wartime activities. Here her work had a plainness of speech, an impersonal grandeur that was served rather than diminished by refinements of touch and phraseology.

Dame Myra is no devotee of the big tone, though she can play loud enough when she needs to. It is the breadth of her musical thought that gives dignity to her execution. For all the gentleness of her sentiments, the grace of her musical ornaments, the wit of her dry little scale passages, she is not a finicky musician. She is sensible, straightforward, and noble, when she gets warmed up.

Yesterday she was rather slow warming up, though the massive audience had warmed to her from the beginning, had stood up, indeed, to welcome her. Perhaps the gracious speech she made at the end of the first half of the program, in which she thanked America so prettily and with such sweet sincerity for its moral and financial help in continuing throughout the war daily free concerts at the National Gallery in London, had broken down by verbal means her previous emotional reserve. In any case, she was first-class when she finally got going.

October 13, 1946

Violence and Charm

RUDOLF FIRKUSNY, pianist, Carnegie Hall, 8:30.

FANTASY IN C MINOR	MOZART
SONATA IN C MINOR	HAYDN
FOUR ÉTUDES	CHOPIN
SONATA IN C MAJOR, OP. 53 ("Waldstein")	BEETHOVEN
FANTASY AND RONDO	MARTINŮ
TWO CZECH DANCES	SMETANA

RUDOLF FIRKUSNY, who played a recital of piano music in Carnegie Hall last night, is a dynamic temperament with lots of punch in his fingers. He plays very loud and very fast most of the time. He plays most of the written notes, too, and often adds extra ones by accident. I once heard him play a concerto with orchestra most prettily. But concerto playing doesn't show up faults of musicianship as a recital does. Last night's concert revealed a pianist with far from negligible (though not complete, by any means) keyboard mastery and a musical temperament of such banal violence as it has not often been my lot to encounter among reputable performers.

Excepting for two of the Chopin Études, which were sensibly and agreeably read, everything — literally everything — was so deformed by speed and pounding that it was difficult to tell one piece from another. Under such circumstances it was not possible for one to have any clear impression of Martinů's Fantasy and Rondo beyond recognition of the fact that it is a work of serious intentions and some length. What a listener not familiar with Beethoven's "Waldstein" sonata might have made of the piece is difficult to imagine. It was recognizable to your reviewer only by the notes of it, its expressive content, as rendered, being chiefly reminiscent of the movie pianism of his youth.

The first movement might have been entitled "A Day at the Races," with steeplechase hazards being got over at full speed and ponies constantly coming lickety-split down the homestretch. The rondo was like the accompaniment to a class-B Western. A young miss of pastoral upbringing had apparently been seized by a band of outlaws on horseback, taken to a lonely spot, and left there. She was very sad about this, and then the outlaws took her to an even lonelier place and tied her hands behind her. A gallant young cowboy, however, came to her rescue and galloped her away. On the ride home the two had a tender moment in which she thanked him for his trouble. And when they got back to town there was general dancing.

If you think I am making fun of either Beethoven or Mr. Firkusny, just try playing the "Waldstein" Sonata at 120 half-notes to the minute. You will see that the effect is somewhat as I have described it, especially if you play all the passages marked f as if they were marked $ffff$. The result is both piquant and trite. If you play a whole program through in this way you will discover that only so tough a work as this particular sonata is capable, under the speed-up and the pounding process, of sounding as if it had a subject at all. Music fast and furious is not always fun. If Mr. Firkusny were less charming as a platform personality, it is doubtful whether his kind of music making would be as appealing to music lovers as it clearly was, I must admit, to last night's audience.

December 14, 1944

Too Fast for Brilliance

SIMON BARERE, pianist, recital last night at Carnegie Hall.

CHROMATIC FANTASIA AND FUGUE	BACH
SONATA IN A FLAT, OP. 110	BEETHOVEN
FANTASIE IN F MINOR; ANDANTE SPIANATO AND GRANDE POLONAISE	CHOPIN
ISLAMEY	BALAKIREV
PRELUDE IN G SHARP MINOR	RACHMANINOFF
ÉTUDE IN C MAJOR	GLAZUNOV
GNOMENREIGEN	LISZT
WALTZ FROM FAUST	GOUNOD-LISZT

SIMON BARERE, who played a piano recital last night in Carnegie Hall, is justly famous for his technical skill. For finger agility and velocity execution he has few equals. But he is also a better musician than one would expect a pianist to be who is celebrated chiefly for technical prowess.

Curiously enough he plays easy pieces more effectively than he does hard ones. In the technical repose of the former his honest and graceful readings are most agreeable. In difficult pieces he almost invariably plays too fast. Not too fast for accuracy; at any speed he plays the right notes, all of them. But too fast to make a really brilliant effect.

Brilliance is the dramatization of speed. It is the throwing of it into relief by the use of great variety in rhythmic articulation and in loudness. Mr. Barere has a steady rhythm but not, in loud fast passages, much variety of accentuation. Here is where his high speeds become ineffective. A harmonious acoustical blur is produced that lacks the final clarity of dramatized emphasis. He proves that almost any piece can be played faster than is customary, but he does not prove that any brilliance or other expressive value is added to it by this fact. On the contrary, he demonstrates rather that pieces have a "critical" speed, as the physicists might say, beyond which added velocity of execution produces diminishing expressive returns.

From an expressive point of view his most powerful execution last night was that of Bach's Chromatic Fantasia and Fugue.

Here the rapid swoops of the ornamentation, played without weight, were highly dramatic in contrast to the chordal phrases of the Fantasia and to the clear articulation of the successive thematic entries in the Fugue.

Liszt's *Gnomenreigen,* also played softly, was interesting as a velocity stunt only. In the Chopin works Mr. Barere played the slow soft passages charmingly, missed the grand accent of the loud fast ones. The *Faust* Waltz, in Liszt's transcription, was welcome for its rarity on contemporary programs. It was played too fast for real brilliance; but it has pretty tunes and its acrobatics are no end fun.

November 19, 1946

Sound without Fury

ALEXANDER UNINSKY, pianist, recital in Carnegie Hall last night.

THREE SONATAS: F MINOR, F MAJOR, C MAJOR	SCARLATTI
PRELUDE AND FUGUE IN D MAJOR	BACH-BUSONI
"CARNAVAL."	SCHUMANN
BALLADE IN F MINOR, OP. 52; TWO MAZURKAS: B FLAT MINOR, OP. 24; C SHARP MINOR, OP. 63; THREE ÉTUDES: C MAJOR, OP. 10, No. 1; F MINOR, OP. 10, No. 9; G SHARP MINOR, OP. 25, No. 6	CHOPIN
VOILES; CE QU'A VU LE VENT D'OUEST	DEBUSSY
DANSE RUSSE, from PETROUCHKA	STRAVINSKY

ALEXANDER UNINSKY, who played a piano recital last night in Carnegie Hall, is a sound artist both technically and intellectually. He plays correctly, and he understands the rhetoric of music. He knows about styles, too; and he respects the texts of the historic masters. He is a completely accomplished musician. And that is about the list of his qualities.

It is not quite the list, because there are certain special beauties in his execution that are beyond this stipulation. These consist chiefly in the advantages of a wide dynamic range. He can play softer and louder without sounding ugly than almost anybody else. And from his tiniest pianissimo to his majestic forte the control is perfect, the crescendo constant. One is grateful for such care. And so satisfying an amplitude of sound is not often at the disposition of any soloist.

One is grateful, too, for musicianly readings; and one wishes these were sufficient satisfaction for concertgoing. But they are not. We like personal poetry and passionate clarity and something of the unforeseen. Lightness of hand is not full compensation for the heaviness of a methodical spirit. And a magnificent loudness, though pleasant enough in itself, adds little to the meaning of the music of Robert Schumann. We forgive more easily, I think, an inspired misconception than we do a stodgily reasonable rendering of familiar pieces.

The stodginess in Mr. Uninsky's work is due largely to a not very interesting rhythmic articulation. His beats and quantities are all in place, but they are read rather than felt. His rhythm lacks tension and breath. As a result his piano playing always sounds like piano playing, never like singing or trumpets or harps or wind or quiet rain. It evokes no orchestra, no landscape, no dancing, no meditation, and no fury. The notes are there, and the sound of them is good. But they carry one nowhere save right back to the printed page they came from. Perhaps also a bit to Russia, where Mr. Uninsky originally came from. Because there is a kind of Muscovite crudeness beneath all his studied imitation of flexibility. He has facility, schooling, and knowledge, but no real ease.

In view of the reverberant acoustics of Carnegie Hall, it might be a good idea if pianists playing there would use a minimum of pedal instead of the more customary maximum. A dry articulation, especially in the left hand, is always of advantage in rooms where the cessation of sound is not instantaneous. That particular room gives its best result to pianists when all middle and low-lying passages are kept brittle.

January 18, 1945

Young Man, Why So Serious?

WEBSTER AITKEN, pianist, recital in Town Hall yesterday afternoon.

TOCCATA, C MINOR	BACH
RONDO, A MINOR (K. 511)	MOZART
"DIABELLI" VARIATIONS	BEETHOVEN

WEBSTER AITKEN, who gave the first of a series of three piano
concerts yesterday afternoon in Town Hall, is a master pianist
and a master musician. He can play anything and play it right.
His tone is beautiful; his execution is dry and clean; his rhythm is
impeccable; and everything sings. Really, one doesn't hear piano
playing like that every year. Technicians of that order do not
commonly toe so strict a line between sweetness and virtuosity,
all the while keeping everything intense.

What bothered this writer about yesterday's concert was what
seemed to him an excessive seriousness about the whole thing,
both program and playing. It is proper enough to begin with a
Bach toccata and a Mozart rondo, and certainly both were executed yesterday with admirable clarity and with an amazingly
straightforward loveliness. Perhaps it was frivolous to wish for
something lighter to follow up these substantial matters. In any
case, Beethoven's "Diabelli" Variations seemed to him a heavy
dish, handsomely presented though they were.

And they must have had something of the same effect on the
pianist himself, because after the fifty-one minutes that they required of continuous and thorough music making, he responded
to the warm applause of the house with seven or eight returns
to bow, but refused firmly to play any encores. Not a tidbit or
sweetmeat did we get, though we all wanted something of the
kind and needed it to activate digestion.

There was nothing wrong about the "Diabelli" Variations except the work itself, which is laborious, cumbersome, and long.
As read by Mr. Aitken, it was far from boresome, which it can
so easily be. But it was tiring, nevertheless. It brought out all
the rather heavy seriousness of this pianist's temperament, offered

no play at all to his gift for simple song or to his genius for American-style, twentieth-century rhythmic scansion. He plays the Variations too beautifully for one to mind greatly his putting them on the program. But this reviewer kept wishing, all the same, that Mr. Aitken had had the wit to be less ponderous. It was a throwing away, as if deliberately, of his genuine charm and youth for an old-master effect that seemed all the more inappropriate for being so complete.

January 21, 1945

Intensity and Brains

ROSALYN TURECK, pianist, recital last night at Town Hall.

PRELUDES AND FUGUES from THE WELL-TEMPERED CLAVICHORD:
  IN C SHARP MAJOR, BOOK I; A MINOR, BOOK II   BACH
SONATA IN C MAJOR (K. 330)   MOZART
SONATA IN F MINOR, OP. 57 ("Appassionata")   BEETHOVEN
SONATA   AARON COPLAND
VARIATIONS AND FUGUE ON A THEME BY HANDEL   BRAHMS

ROSALYN TURECK, who played a recital of piano music last night in Town Hall, is an invigorating musician. We are not used to encountering in the same person a passionate temperament and a first-class mind. And we are certainly not used to finding in the same pianist a first-class technique and a correct sense of rhythm

Nothing Miss Tureck played last night was lacking in stimulation to the musical faculties except the Mozart C-major Sonata (K. 330). Even that was more interesting to listen to than the performances of it that one usually hears, though she misconstrued its sentiments, I think, broke the back of its rhythm, and utterly missed the fact that its slow movement is a minuet. The secret of her work, at its best, seems to be that her passionate nature finds its completest expression in works that demand by their own nature an objective approach.

Her playing of Bach, for instance, was vivid. And her execution of the Brahms-Handel Variations was a triumph of expressive variety. She warmed up these somewhat cold masters and made them stimulating, gave them high relief, projection, carrying power. The Beethoven "Appassionata" she is not quite so fully in command of yet. The shape of it is there and all its healthy violence of expression, but Miss Tureck seems to be not quite willing to let it play itself. She loses its relentless continuity by mooning over the soft passages and whipping up the loud ones.

The Aaron Copland Sonata is not quite her piece, either. It is a meditative, a lyrical, an improvisatory work. She lacks the lightness of touch, the spontaneity it requires. She gets excited by it and pounds. Its beauty is its ease, and Miss Tureck has no ease. She has intensity, both of feeling and of intelligence. But she works best in corseted music. Copland's neo-Romantic elegance of expression is almost as foreign to her temperament as Mozart's urbanity.

Many a contemporary pianist, especially among the younger American ones, is weak in Romantic repertory but completely at home with the moderns. Miss Tureck is quite good in Romantic works, not at all comfortable in modern ones, and amazingly, wonderfully exciting in the music of pre-Classic times. Indeed, the farther away she gets from contemporary life the more surefooted becomes her command, intellectual, technical, and passional, of the musical terrain.

She is a musician of high gifts, and she is maturing most satisfactorily. It was perfectly clear to last night's audience on the tenth anniversary of her Town Hall debut that she is an artist any country might be proud of. She has gone far in one decade, and she will go farther in another. Miss Tureck is not just an ordinary good pianist. She is invigorating; she is interesting; she is somebody.

November 13, 1945

Young but Not Romantic

SIDNEY FOSTER, pianist, in recital in Carnegie Hall last night.

ORGAN FANTASIA AND FUGUE, G MINOR	BACH-LISZT
VARIATIONS AND FUGUE ON A THEME OF HANDEL	BRAHMS
FIVE ÉTUDES, OP. 25	CHOPIN
VALSE from OP. 96 (First Performance); SUGGESTION DIABOLIQUE	
	PROKOFIEV
PRELUDE: "To a young musician"	DELLO JOIO
(First Performance)	
Two Mexican Dances:	
EL BUJOCO, EL INDIO	BOWLES
(First Performance)	
GNOMENREIGEN; WALDESRAUSCHEN; HUNGARIAN RHAPSODY No. 2	LISZT

SIDNEY FOSTER's piano recital in Carnegie Hall last night was honored by the first performance of a gracefully meditative piece by Norman Dello Joio and of two picturesque Mexican dances by Paul Bowles. Also by the American premiere of a waltz from one of Prokofiev's forthcoming operas, *War and Peace*, which turned out to be good routine Prokofiev of the noisy kind.

It is possible that Mr. Foster's noisy execution may have contributed to the routine effect of this work, as well as to that of the even noisier *Suggestion diabolique*, by the same author. Most pianists seem to think Prokofiev's music needs an iron touch, and this pianist is not one to spare the ends of his fingers.

He rattled quite as noisily and with no small violence through Liszt, Chopin, and Brahms. Only in the Liszt transcription of Bach's Fantasia and Fugue in G minor did he show a consistent nobility of tone and a delicate continuity in the feeling expressed. The works of his fellow Americans also drew from him care for the music's plain sense. In spite, however, of strong fingers and much dexterity, Mr. Foster seems not to perceive very exactly the subject matter of the great Romantics. No matter how different their notes are, the pieces all sound alike.

The phenomenon is one I have observed before among the most brilliantly gifted of our young Americans. They plow through the Romantic repertory because it is expected of them, but their hand is brutal with it. The eighteenth century and the twentieth they understand; they handle these with love and with a care for differences. But the history of music between 1790 and 1890 is their blind spot. They spend nine tenths of their working time practicing it, and it occupies at least that proportion of their concert playing-time. All the same, exactly as most Central Europeans of an older generation have no real understanding of any music but this, lots of our younger American musicians, in spite of elaborate instruction about it and of inveterate assiduity toward it, find themselves stymied by this very repertory. It escapes their comprehension; it is alien to their ways of feeling. And the sooner they find this out the better. In spite of the conservatism of the concert public, there is no future for a musician in anything he doesn't like, understand, take on with ease.

October 19, 1944

Perfect Host

MAXIM SCHAPIRO, pianist, recital in Town Hall last night.

SONATA IN C MAJOR, OP. 53 ("Waldstein")	BEETHOVEN
KREISLERIANA, OP. 16	SCHUMANN
IMPROVISATION (Theme and Variations)	MEDTNER
FIFTH BARCAROLLE, OP. 66	FAURÉ
TOCCATA	RAVEL
CHOROS NO. 5	VILLA-LOBOS
LA LIBERTADORA	MILHAUD
(First Performance)	
ANDANTE SPIANATO AND POLONAISE BRILLANTE, OP. 72	CHOPIN

MAXIM SCHAPIRO, who played his annual piano recital last night in Town Hall, is a gentlemanly musician in the best modern sense. Our preceding century knew the "gentleman musician" in another form, namely, that of the man whose distinguished bearing (and private fortune) gave his lack of professional execution a certain immunity to criticism.

This species of elegant amateur has largely disappeared from modern life, even in Boston. He has been replaced by thoroughly trained professionals who, nevertheless, approach music with a certain reserve. This reserve is neither an emotional one nor wholly intellectual. It is a kind of good manners toward composers and their works which expresses itself in a style of execution that, while neglecting no known device of clarity or of comprehension, still omits any irrevocable personal involvement with the goings on.

Thus it was that Mr. Schapiro, though an expert technician and an artist of no mean imagination, ended last night by presenting Beethoven and Schumann and Chopin along with the composers of our century as if they were all guests at a musical party of which he himself was the host. And, naturally, in such a gracious and democratic arrangement, it was the younger men who attracted most of the attention. The ancestral figures had their proper program precedence. But the host, being a man of our time, could not quite conceal the fact that he was more at ease with his contemporaries than with his elders. And so it turned out to be a young people's party in spite of the fact that the list of composers physically present on the program appeared to the eye as a catholic one.

This is not to say that Mr. Schapiro was in any way negligent in his attentions to the great Romantics. He gave them their due and a smile, handled them with care, and went on to have fun elsewhere. He had fun with Medtner, formerly his teacher, with Fauré and Ravel and Milhaud and Villa-Lobos. He handled them all with skill, with care, and with a perfect knowledge of what they were up to. The results could not have been more charming. Or more entertaining, either. Especially when it turned out that Milhaud's *La Libertadora*, in his own version of the Brazilian style, was, to us foreigners, more convincingly Brazilian in language than a Choros subtitled "The Brazilian Soul" by Villa-Lobos, Brazil's most determinedly nationalistic composer.

Fauré's Fifth Bacarolle was gracefully tossed. And the Ravel Toccata from *Le Tombeau de Couperin* was a joy for sound. Perhaps the fuller pleasure one derived from the modern works was due in part to the fact that they were being played on the instrument they were written for, namely, the modern pianoforte. Even so, they were admirably rendered, as was also the final Chopin Andante Spianato and Polonaise. The Beethoven "Waldstein" and the Schumann *Kreisleriana*, like all good chaperones, seemed at the end of the evening to have called little attention to themselves, to have bored no one, and to have cramped nobody's style.

November 10, 1945

Gershwin Black and Blue

PHILHARMONIC-SYMPHONY ORCHESTRA, *Artur Rodzinski*, conductor, Pension Fund benefit concert last night at Carnegie Hall, with *Anne Brown*, soprano, *Todd Duncan*, baritone, and *Oscar Levant*, pianist, as soloists in the following program of GEORGE GERSHWIN'S music:

AN AMERICAN IN PARIS
PIANO CONCERTO IN F
Excerpts from PORGY AND BESS: Buzzard Song, "Summertime," "I Got Plenty of Nuttin'," "My Man's Gone Now," "It Ain't Necessarily So," "Bess, You Is My Woman Now."
RHAPSODY IN BLUE

THE MUSIC was charming; the performance was first-class; and the audience enjoyed itself thoroughly at last night's Pension Fund Concert of the Philharmonic in Carnegie Hall. It is a pleasure to see an audience react so favorably to all the pieces on a program. It is a pleasure to find that audiences are still reacting favorably to Gershwin's music, that they love it and understand it, admire it, respect it, and communicate with it. It is a pleasure to observe how stylishly Artur Rodzinski conducts it, Anne Brown and Todd Duncan sing it, Oscar Levant plays it on the pianoforte. The impeccable Oscar, as a matter of fact, is a pretty fascinating spectacle, no matter what he does.

Miss Brown sings the *Porgy and Bess* airs in standard concert manner. Mr. Duncan sings them in the black-face comedian style. Both manners seemed equally acceptable to the audience as a whole. Your reviewer found more dignity in her performance than in his, however, and more real singing. He has never been wholly comfortable in the presence of Negroes interpreting Negro life through the conventions of the white black-face stage. The whole procedure seems to him unbecoming. Gershwin's music, moreover, is neither Negroid nor in any sense primitive, and it always comes out more humane in a straightforward rendering.

Mr. Levant's renderings of the Concerto in F and the *Rhapsody in Blue* are scholarly, in the sense that they are the product of thorough study. They are authoritative, in the sense that nobody else plays these pieces with quite that air of knowing exactly what they are all about. They are masterful, in the sense that technically they are both powerful and accurate. They are a little dead, too, because though they have every other quality of great musical execution, they lack spontaneity.

The works themselves, of course, especially the *Rhapsody*, are not so fresh to us, nor to him, as they once were. And it is not easy to toss lightly any piece that is so impressive at the box office as the latter one is. Also, Levant is too loyal a musician to traffic in the charm of youth when maturity comes upon him. He is a serious pianist nowadays and one of the most competent. And if he plays Gershwin with all the weight and prestige that the great Europeans lend to their own repertory, plus a natural platform impressiveness such as few possess, that is the beautiful and wise thing for him to have learned to do.

He could not have kept his spontaneity, anyway; nobody can who has such gifts and real ambition. Gershwin's music remains a music of youth and full of youth's sweetness and ease, like Schubert's music. But Levant has grown up and become a master. He rather overpowers Gershwin, in consequence, as all the great mature interpreters do to the music of those who died young.

April 19, 1946

Musical Badminton

VERA APPLETON and MICHAEL FIELD, duo-pianists, recital in Town Hall last night.

FANTASIA IN F MINOR	MOZART-FIELD
SONATA IN F MAJOR	W. F. BACH
MIKROKOSMOS (Ms.)	BARTÓK

(First Performance)

THREE ÉTUDES IN CANON FORM   SCHUMANN-DEBUSSY
TOCCATA   FULEIHAN
                        (First Performance)
THREE DANCES (Ms.)   KHACHATURIAN
SERENADE   R. STRAUSS-CHASINS
GRAND CONCERT VARIATIONS on a theme from THE PURITANS   LISZT
                (First Performance in America)

VERA APPLETON and Michael Field played a far from banal program of music for two pianos in the Town Hall last night. There
were unusual old pieces, brand new ones, and some pretty competent execution. The audience was grateful for all this and
most responsive. Your reviewer regrets that attendance at bouts
of duo-pianism is not his favorite form of spectator-sport.

Two pianists can play twice as many notes as one, and two
pianos can make twice as much noise. They do not ordinarily
make half as much music. The modern instrument, which is designed chiefly to hold its own against modern symphony orchestras in concerto playing, is inexpressive at all dynamic levels
louder than one f. Two of them can increase in volume up to five
or six f's. But there is no beauty in the sound and little variety.
It is too heavy for real brilliance, and the players are seated too
far apart to achieve fine adjustments of balance, delicate give-
and-take in rhythm. They take refuge inevitably in speed and in
too heavy accents. The whole business is a sort of musical bad-
minton, a game of crude energy rather than of refinement or of
studied skill.

Appleton and Field do not perform less charmingly, within
the limits of their medium, than most other duo-pianists. The
intellectual tone of their programs, if last night's is typical, is
higher than common. They have an awareness, evidently, of style,
too, of varied approaches to different kinds of music. I suspect
they are more interested in style, in fact, than in streamlining,
because they did get the style for each piece roughly right and
because they did not sacrifice this to the niceties of simultaneous
attack.

Their work does not have the commercial polish we are used
to in that of more famous teams. Its intentions are musical rather
than slick. Unfortunately, unless I am wrong about the nature of
the medium, duo-pianism has little to offer in the way of musical
returns for musical labor. It is too inflexible a setup. All the teams

go slick eventually. A smooth surfacing of the execution does not make their work any more interesting. But it does tend to conceal the paucity of expression.

November 9, 1944

Costume Party

PIERRE LUBOSHUTZ and GENIA NEMENOFF, duo-pianists, recital in Town Hall last night.

"NOW COMES THE GENTLE SAVIOUR"	BACH-LUBOSHUTZ
VARIATIONS ON A THEME BY HAYDN	BRAHMS
VALSES	SCHUBERT-PROKOFIEV
ALLEGRO BRILLANTE	MENDELSSOHN-LUBOSHUTZ
SONATINA FOR TWO PIANOS	KOUTZEN
(First Performance)	
"LARGO AL FACTOTUM"	ROSSINI-KOVACS
BERCEUSE	GRETCHANINOV
NEW DANCE	RIEGGER

PIERRE LUBOSHUTZ and Genia Nemenoff, duo-pianists, gave an evening of imitations last night at the Town Hall. Their arrangement of a Bach Chorale-Prelude imitated tastefully the rubato style that was considered appropriate in my youth for rendering the Brahms Chorale-Preludes, and their rendering of the Brahms Variations on a Theme by Haydn imitated the ruinous rigidity with which enlightened provincial music teachers sometimes still play Bach's "Goldberg" Variations. The Prokofiev arrangement of Schubert waltzes, which followed, transported us to a Tyrolean-style beer hall possessing a mechanical pianoforte. And Mr. Luboshutz's arrangement of the Mendelssohn Allegro Brillante sounded like nothing so much as a well-functioning coffee grinder.

The next masquerade, complete with scores and eyeglasses, represented a world-famous two-piano team being nice about modern music. Boris Koutzen's Sonatina for Two Pianos was the sacrificial offering, a hard and ugly tone being employed throughout so as to make it sound like some forgotten work from back in 1922, and a few (just a few) false notes being thrown in to show that the piece probably wasn't worth learning completely.

After that we had an arrangement of Rossini's baritone aria, *"Largo al factotum,"* from *The Barber of Seville,* an artistic equivalent of Leschetizky's once-popular transcription for left hand alone of the sextet from *Lucia di Lammermoor*. Gretchaninov's *Berceuse* which followed, is itself an imitation of the one by Chopin and of a music box at the same time. While Wallingford Riegger's *New Dance* is the finale of Stravinsky's *Sacre du printemps* with a couple of syncopated tunes added to make it sound American.

Consisting, as it did, almost entirely of transcriptions, the program as a whole was rather in the manner of those made popular in the last century by Liszt and Thalberg. I imagine we were all supposed to enter into the game, too, and applaud like mad. Indeed, many did. And indeed the precision with which Mr. and Mrs. Luboshutz imitated a single executant was no end impressive as a trick. If they had only imitated a rather more poetic executant, and if they had played, for that purpose, music of higher intellectual content, the evening, though it might have seemed less like a game, would have been more fun. It would also have been more worthy of the distinguished audience that it drew out.

Jaunary 27, 1945

New High

ARTHUR GOLD, ROBERT FIZDALE, duo-pianists, recital last night at Town Hall.

DUETTO IN F MAJOR	J. C. BACH
SONATA (1945)	PAUL BOWLES
(First Time in New York)	
TROIS MORCEAUX EN FORME DE POIRE	SATIE
SONATA (1945)	ALEXEI HAIEFF
(First Time in New York)	
FIVE INVENTIONS (1926)	VIRGIL THOMSON
SONATA (1944)	STRAVINSKY
DANCE, from THREE DANCES for prepared pianos	JOHN CAGE
THREE WALTZES, from SECOND AVENUE WALTZES	VITTORIO RIETI

DUO-PIANISM reaches heights technical and artistic in the work of Arthur Gold and Robert Fizdale, who gave a recital last night in Town Hall, hitherto unknown to the art. Such consistent beauty of tone and sweetness of sound, even in fortissimo passages, such refined precision of rhythm and grace of phraseology, such masterful penetration of the nature of music, of the differences between one piece and another, between one composer's thought and another's, such a thoroughly musical approach to music and to concert-giving produced an evening that left one elated, not tired of ear and mentally worn down, as is the common effect on this listener of two-piano recitals.

The program, save for a charming duet by Johann Christian Bach, which got the late comers to their seats, was strictly modern. The novelties were a sonata by Paul Bowles and one by Alexei Haieff. Mr. Bowles's piece consists of a lively and a slow movement in his most poetic early-Ravel vein and a finale in imitation of African drum sounds and rhythms. The effect of the whole is that of a strong musical work that is nowhere lacking in charm. Mr. Haieff's piece, though longer, is less serious and less forceful. Its textures are expert; but its thematic material wears thin under repetition, and its extended conservatory-style format (à la Anton Rubenstein) is inappropriate to the tight, modern-music-style angularity of its tune content.

Among the other modern works Satie's *Three Pieces in the Shape of a Pear* seemed to this observer the most richly packed with plums. Composed in 1903, these are still an unexhausted source of pleasure for listening and of lessons in musical composition. Seemingly unpretentious, they contain not one measure of banality, not a phrase that is not profoundly expressive and original. Beside their firm and gracious rightness, Stravinsky's Sonata for Two Pianos, also a work of gentle character, seemed lacking in concentration, though the latter is, compared to most contemporary works for that medium, expressively pretty compact. Its musical intention, if I mistake not, is to evoke Bach's "Goldberg" Variations.

John Cage's Dance for two prepared pianos is a rhythmic composition of tiny thudlike sounds that recalls Indonesian gamelang music. It is distinguished and beautiful and makes one feel good. Vittorio Rieti's *Second Avenue Waltzes*, of which three were played, are the original version of his ballet, *Waltz Acad-*

emy. They are graceful and melodious and not banal, even when they quote (knowingly) Verdi's *La Traviata* and Ravel's *La Valse*. There was a piece of mine on the program, too.

An audience of New York's best in music and letters applauded all this modernity with delight and discussed everything with vigor at the intermission. Opinions varied, as is natural, about the comparative value of the divers works played. That all were played to perfection was not questioned in my hearing. Nor was anything but gratitude expressed for the universal consideration shown by Messrs. Gold and Fizdale in offering so much music that can be enjoyed as a part of contemporary living.

February 16, 1946

Definitive Renderings

WANDA LANDOWSKA, harpsichordist-pianist, recital in Town Hall last night.

PASSACAILLE	COUPERIN
GAVOTE AND DOUBLES IN A MINOR	RAMEAU
FRENCH SUITE IN E MAJOR	BACH
SONATA IN D MAJOR (K. 311)	MOZART
(Played on the piano)	
CONCERTO IN D MAJOR	VIVALDI-BACH
ITALIAN CONCERTO IN F MAJOR	BACH

WANDA LANDOWSKA's playing of the harpsichord at Town Hall last night reminded one all over again that there is nothing else in the world like it. There does not exist in the world today, nor has there existed in my lifetime, another soloist of this or of any other instrument whose work is so dependable, so authoritative, and so thoroughly satisfactory. From all the points of view — historical knowledge, style, taste, understanding, and spontaneous musicality — her renderings of harpsichord repertory are, for our epoch, definitive. Criticism is unavailing against them, has been so, indeed, for thirty years.

Her piano playing is another story. She likes to play Mozart in evocation of the way Mozart himself must have, or might have, played on the early fortepiano. To this end she employs, as Mozart certainly employed, a high-fingered technique similar to that which gives the best result in harpsichord playing. She never plays louder than forte, not because she wishes to keep Mozart's music small, but because she wishes to keep it musical. The modern pianoforte gives another kind of sound, in many cases an ugly one, when played with arm weight. In any case, the extension of piano writing into the domain of modern power pianism, an extension that began only with Beethoven, seems inappropriate to her, as it does to many other modern musicians.

And so, limiting her dynamic range to approximately what was available to Mozart on the Stein fortepiano, she plays his solo sonatas for the musical contrasts that they unquestionably possess rather than for those for which they were never planned. As to rhythm, tempo, phrasing, and ornamentation — all the rendering of their basic musical content — her performance is matchless. She makes them large and alive and vivid, just as she does the harpsichord works of Couperin and Scarlatti and Rameau and Bach. Her conceptions and interpretations are a lesson to any musician. Pianistically, all the same, her execution is a little unsatisfactory.

It is not unsatisfactory because of any technical inefficiency. It is unsatisfactory because the modern pianoforte, a less brilliant instrument than Mozart's, does not yield what brilliance it has save by the exploitation of its full dynamic range. And Mozart's piano music, as we know, was of brilliance and virtuosity all compact. It need not glitter but it has to shine. Landowska gives us a photograph of it on the modern piano, very much as other pianists give us a photograph of Bach's harpsichord music.

Our instrument is closer to Mozart's than it is to the plucked instruments. But it is not the same instrument. That is why Mozart's symphonies and operas and chamber music always sound more vivid to us in execution than his piano music does. Fiddles, wind instruments, and voices do not have to walk through Mozart on tiptoes. The pianoforte, no matter how elegant its phrasing, inevitably sounds clumsy and a little meticulous.

I recommend Landowska's pianoforte Mozart, because I recommend any music she touches. It is the best piano Mozart I know. It is a model of understanding musically, as it is a tour de force technically. Nevertheless, by the very fact of being a translation — which her harpsichord playing, of course, is not — it is a slightly less authentic, less vigorous reconstitution.

November 20, 1944

Consort of Viols

SYLVIA MARLOWE, harpsichordist; BOSTON SOCIETY OF AN-CIENT INSTRUMENTS, *Alfred Zighera*, director; concert yesterday afternoon in the Carnegie Chamber Music Hall. *Paul Federowsky*, descant viol; *Albert Bernard*, treble viol; *Alfred Zighera*, viola da gamba; *Gaston Dufresne*, violone.

LA SULTANA, for four viols and harpsichord	FRANÇOIS COUPERIN
SONATA IN G, for viola da gamba alone	KARL F. ABEL
GAVOTTE AND VARIATIONS IN A MINOR, for harpsichord	J. P. RAMEAU
SONATA IN D MAJOR for viol da gamba, violone and harpsichord	
	DIETRICH BUXTEHUDE
TWO FANTASIAS, for four viols	ORLANDO GIBBONS
SONATAS FOR HARPSICHORD: No. 429, IN A MINOR, No. 433 IN F	
MAJOR, No. 461 IN D MAJOR, No. 257 IN E MAJOR, No. 232 IN	
G MAJOR (Longo Edition)	DOMENICO SCARLATTI
SUITE IN C MAJOR, for four viols and harpsichord	G. P. TELEMANN

SYLVIA MARLOWE, harpsichordist, and the Boston Society of Ancient Instruments gave yesterday afternoon in Carnegie Chamber Music Hall the first of three concerts devoted to the music of pre-Classical times. Miss Marlowe, an artist of the first quality, is well known to New York audiences, both as soloist and as participant in rare chamber music combinations. The Boston group, though certain of its members, such as Alfred Zighera, who plays the viola da gamba with a fine mastery, are familiar to local music lovers, has not previously appeared here manipulating a chest, or consort, of viols.

The program was of the most distinguished, the sweetest of all the works played being perhaps two Fantasias for quartet of viols by Orlando Gibbons. The whole afternoon, however, was rich in musical delights from a bygone age. Buxtehude and Telemann, Couperin and Rameau, Karl Abel, Gibbons, and Domenico

Scarlatti were all represented by major works; and the execution of these was in every way handsome.

To Miss Marlowe and Mr. Zighera must go the honors of the occasion for their virtuoso solo renderings of Scarlatti and Abel. The viol quartet, though better equilibrated in the Gibbons work than elsewhere, fell short of perfection through a certain heaviness and some inaccuracies of pitch on the part of the bass violone.

The viols, more limited in expressive scope than instruments of the violin family, have two extremely pleasant kinds of tone. One is a sweet, soft sound not unlike that of violins muted. The other is a nasal quality suggestive of the oboe or the English horn. The bass viol produces also a neutral tone that is ineffective for solo purposes because of its poverty in upper harmonics but that makes, for the same reason, an admirable bass in soft passages. Bowed too heavily, this instrument produces a boom, not unlike the boom of modern electronic instruments, that disrupts smooth ensemble effects.

Together, if the bass is played accurately and with dynamic discretion, viols produce a harmoniously blended tone more easily than a modern string quartet does. Taken separately, only the viola da gamba and the slightly larger viola bastarda, which was not played yesterday, offer sufficient variety in either tone color or volume to make proper solo instruments, though the viola d'amore, with its extra set of strings that add sympathetic vibrations to those produced by direct bowing, offers an inimitable timbre that is delicious in brief phrases.

One cannot be too grateful to Miss Marlowe and the Boston group for giving us great music from the past on instruments closely resembling those for which it was conceived. I say closely resembling because Miss Marlowe plays a modern harpsichord —a Pleyel, the finest in town, I should think—and the Boston viol players do use the modern bow. All the same, a concert like yesterday's gives us a closer idea of what instrumental chamber music by great masters sounded like in the sixteenth, seventeenth, and eighteenth centuries than it is currently our privilege to hear.

February 17, 1947

Variety without Loudness

SUZANNE BLOCH, singer and player of the lute, virginals, and recorders, concert of 16th, 17th, and 18th century music, last night at Times Hall. Assisting artists: *Eugene Morgan*, baritone; *Paul Smith*, recorders; *Monina Tavora, Margot Ramsay, Joseph Precker*, lutes; *Betty Martin*, virginals; *Nina Courant*, viola da gamba.

Music for lute:
POLISH DANCE	MATTHAUS WAISSEL
VOLTE	ROBERT DOWLAND
PADUANA	VINCENZO CAPIROLA
BRANLES	ANTOINE FRANCISQUE

(*Suzanne Bloch*)

Music for two lutes:
LE ROSSIGNOL; DREWIES ACCORDE	JANE PICKERING'S LUTE BOOK

(*Miss Bloch and Margot Ramsay*)

CONTRAPUNTO A DUE LIUTI	VINCENZO GALILEI

(*Miss Bloch and Monina Tavora*)

Consort of recorders, lute, virginals, viola da gamba:
TWO RICERCARI	PALESTRINA

Virginal Solos:
BONNIE SWEET ROBIN	JOHN MUNDAY
FANTASIA	GILES FARNABY
HUGH ASHTON'S GROUNDE	WILLIAM BYRD
THE KING'S HUNTING JIGG	JOHN BULL

(*Miss Bloch*)

Songs to the lute:
KOENNT ICH, SCHON REINES WERTES WEIB	HANS NEWSIDLER
CES FACHEUX SOTZ	PIERRE ATTAIGNANT
FALLAI MINA AMOR	LUYS MILAN
TROUBADOR SONG: "Ma viele veut vieler"	GAUTHIER DE COINCY

(*Miss Bloch*)

SONATA IN C FOR ALTO RECORDER	HANDEL

(*Paul Smith, Miss Bloch, Nina Courant*)

Songs for baritone and lute:
WANTON COME HITHER; DOWN IN A VALLEY	MICHAEL CAVENDISH
SAY LOVE!	JOHN DOWLAND
WHITHER RUNNETH MY SWEETHEART	JOHN BARTLETT

(*Eugene Morgan and Miss Bloch*)

Ensemble of lutes:
EN REVENANT DE SAINT NICOLAS; BRANLES DE VILLAGE	J. B. BISERDUS

SUZANNE BLOCH gave last night in Times Hall a concert of Renaissance music in strictly prebaroque instrumentation. There were solos for lute, duets for two lutes, music for a quartet of the same, vocal solos and duets accompanied by them, and divers compositions that included a recorder, a viola da gamba, and a pair of virginals, as well. There was also solo music for the virginals, for though the phrase seems self-contradictory (a pair of anything playing a solo), the virginals are, at least linguistically, a plural instrument, like scissors.

Gerald Hayes, an English writer about old music and old instruments, states in one of his books that there is in existence more first-class music for the lute than has ever been written for any other solo instrument. Certainly the music played last night was all first class and thoroughly delightful. And if Miss Bloch undertook none of the monumental Elizabethan fantasies that compare for length and variety with the Viennese piano sonatas of the classical period, she gave us a highly digestible selection of charm numbers from all over Europe.

The lute is a hand-plucked instrument related in sonority both to the mandolin (which is not hand-plucked) and to the Spanish guitar (which is). Like the mandolin, it plays melodies effectively and even counterpoint. Unlike the guitar, it cannot easily play chords across the board. It has too many strings to allow chord playing by any but selective means. Consequently, though the instrument resembles the guitar somewhat in sound, it has none of the latter's romantic abandon. It is a plain and noble instrument that lends itself to the execution of music of the highest complexity, rhythmic, harmonic, and contrapuntal. It sounds rather like a harpsichord without a keyboard mechanism.

Since wide variations of loudness as an expressive (and even rhetorical) device are an invention of the seventeenth century, no music written before that time counts on them for effect. The chamber music of Renaissance times was regularly and systematically quiet. Its interest is melodic, harmonic, contrapuntal, and rhythmic, but never dynamic. It can be played and sung for hours without any strain on the listener's nervous system, because loudness was never a part of its pattern.

The music making that Miss Bloch and her associate artists offered last night was like a cultivated conversation rather than like an exhortation of any kind. It was fanciful, instructive, intimate, gay, delicious, and vast for vistas opened. It was not emotionally portentous, but it was deeply refreshing.

The audience, a large and cultured one, took evident delight in it all; and Miss Bloch herself, an artist of no mean skill, seemed pleased to be communicating the things she has for so long studied to re-create. Let us hope that her clear success will encourage her and others to give us more frequent auditory access to a great musical repertory than has been our privilege of recent years. Contemporary life has need of music based on ingenuity and sentiment, music in which dynamic strain, however noble as mere sound, plays no part.

March 5, 1947

Strings Bowed; Strings Plucked

ALEXANDER SCHNEIDER, violinist; RALPH KIRKPATRICK, harpsichordist, joint recital at Kaufman Auditorium last night.

SONATA, F MAJOR (K. 377)	MOZART
SONATA NO. 2, A MAJOR	BACH
SONATA, G MAJOR (K. 379)	MOZART
SONATA NO. 4, C MINOR	BACH
SONATA, A MAJOR (K. 526)	MOZART

HARPSICHORD and violin certainly make a lovely duet. As played last night by Ralph Kirkpatrick and Alexander Schneider in a recital of sonatas by Mozart and Bach at the Y. M. H. A. in Lexington Avenue at Ninety-second Street, they produced one of the happiest musical evenings this critic has spent in a long time. Even when the detailed rendering was not fully to his taste the sound was always attractive to the ear. One could bear to listen to all the music all the time. And since at least two of the works played, the Mozart G and A major sonatas, are in themselves works of rare grandeur, one was grateful to the artists for giving them to us so nearly, so very nearly, intact.

By nearly intact I mean that there were rhythmic irregularities in the harpsichord playing and some imperfect cantilena on the violin. Tempo rubato, for instance, however slight, is scarcely appropriate to syncopated passages, as Mr. Kirkpatrick used it in the slow movement of the Mozart A-major sonata. And haste to get back to the nut of the bow will always produce a bumpy violin phrase. Both Kirkpatrick and Schneider are skilled technicians and experienced players of chamber music. Their work has ease, confidence, understanding, and some brilliance. What it lacks for full distinction and for the brio that it essays is equalized tension. It is clear but not wholly clean, highly presentable as reading but not very deeply thought.

Everything was played a little fast, as if speed were being used to conceal a want of exact rhythmic articulation. This procedure is less objectionable in Mozart than in Bach, because the Mozart last movements, at least, do demand a sort of demonic fury, though velocity is not necessarily the best means for achieving this. In Bach it only produces confusion. The attempt to make a show-off, à la Paganini, out of that most methodical of workmen is false stylistically, psychologically, and musically. The fury in Bach is the fury of complete control, a relentlessness of exactitude rather than of sweep. A too facile approach to his complexities captures no heavenly citadel; it is merely barnstorming.

Rather wonderful barnstorming the whole concert was. The music was recondite but not too much so for comprehension. The playing was adequate and pleasantly superficial. The sound of it all was delicious, spicy, eminently digestible. If nothing was played with penetration, neither was anything gravely violated. The evening was a revelation of how delightful music can be without a thumpy pianoforte or violin E strings of wire. Also, the Mozart A-major violin sonata is worth going some distance for.

November 2, 1944

An Evening of Delight

PHILHARMONIC-SYMPHONY ORCHESTRA, *Leopold Stokowski,* guest conductor, concert last night in Carnegie Hall with *Jacques Thibaud,* violinist, as soloist.

MOTET: JESUS, DULCIS MEMORIA   VICTORIA-STOKOWSKI
(First Performance)
OVERTURE TO DON GIOVANNI   MOZART
SYMPHONY NO. 1, IN E FLAT   HINDEMITH
SYMPHONIE ESPAGNOLE, FOR VIOLIN AND ORCHESTRA   LALO
(1st, 2nd, 4th and 5th Movements)
SAUDADES DO BRASIL: IPANEMA; BOTOFAGO   MILHAUD
(First Time by this Orchestra)
L'APRÈS-MIDI D'UN FAUNE   DEBUSSY

THE RETURN of Jacques Thibaud, violinist, to the American concert platform after a fifteen-year absence and some high-powered musical magic on the part of Leopold Stokowski, conductor, set apart as memorable last night's concert of the Philharmonic-Symphony Orchestra in Carnegie Hall. The program itself, moreover, was one of no mean distinction, containing, as it did, in addition to a familiar Mozart overture, a familiar violin concerto, and a popular Debussy tone-poem, two of Milhaud's seldom heard *Memories of Brazil* dances and the elegant but little known First (and only) Symphony by Hindemith, not to speak of a transcription by Mr. Stokowski of a ravishing Victoria motet.

Stokowski's transcription of the sixteenth-century *Jesu, Dulcis Memoria* was sonorous and in performance pleasantly atmospheric. But in conception it was less a direct translation of choral sound into orchestral than an organist's version of this turned into an ensemble piece. The Milhaud *Saudades do Brasil,* to dispose of the other small works, are ever a delight, vigorous in rhythm, gaily discordant in harmony, and poignantly nostalgic in their evocation of Brazilian song-and-dance poetry.

The Hindemith Symphony is a modernistic evocation of Brahms's Romantic evocation of Beethoven's middle period. It is not, however, a Romantic work. It is a neo-Classic (or neo-Romantic) work, concise, concentrated, buoyant, cheerful. It is agreeable to listen to rather for its masterful shipshapeness than for any especial eloquence or profundity. Its tonality is clear, if a little crowded, its counterpoint animated, its orchestral texture transparent. Rhythmically it is not very expressive, and its melodic content is far from striking. But it is an accomplished, a civilized work; it says what it says with authority, with dispatch, and with a certain amplitude. As to what it says, anybody's guess is as good as this reviewer's. In his opinion Mr. Hindemith has evoked a certain period in the history of the symphony rather than made up a really original piece.

Jacques Thibaud's performance of the solo part in Lalo's *Symphonie espagnole* was violin playing of the Franco-Belgian school at its most admirable and, for the present, most satisfactory. Accustomed as we are to the heavier-handed and more sentimental Russian style, it is no end refreshing to return to the smaller and finer but musically more ample manner of Ysaÿe and his pupils. Thibaud's tone, though not large, is beautiful; and his technical mastery has not diminished with the years. The ovations he received both before and after playing were witness of New York's loyalty to a great artist all too long missing from our platforms and of the fact that our taste in violin playing has not deteriorated in his absence.

As for Mr. Stokowski's conducting, it was pure miracle from beginning to end. Often in the past, critics, the present one included, have protested at errors of taste on this conductor's part. Last night there was none. Everything was played with a wondrous beauty of sound, with the noblest proportions, with the utmost grandeur of expression. The perfection of tonal rendering for which Stokowski and his Philadelphia Orchestra were so long famous was revived last night with the Philharmonic men in a performance of Debussy's *Afternoon of a Faun* that for both beauty and poetry has been unmatched for many years, if ever, in my experience.

January 3, 1947

Good Goods

ZINO FRANCESCATTI, violinist, recital last night at Carnegie Hall. Assisting pianist, *Artur Balsam.*

SONATA IN A MAJOR, OP. 13	FAURÉ
BERCEUSE (sur le nom de Fauré); TZIGANE	RAVEL
CHACONNE (violin alone)	BACH
DUO CONCERTANT	STRAVINSKY
SCHERZO-CAPRICE (violin alone); CAPRICE VIENNOIS; TAMBOURIN CHINOIS	KREISLER

ZINO FRANCESCATTI'S violin recital of last night in Carnegie Hall was a display of solid workmanship from beginning to end. By *workmanship* let us understand interpretation as well as technique. He not only played on pitch and correctly, but he gave musical readings of depth, breadth, and lucidity. Everything was powerful and plain to the understanding as well as shipshape to the ear. Nowhere in his work was there anything of bluff, of inadequacy, of vulgarity, of hesitation before any difficulty either of execution or of expression. Everywhere there was beauty, dignity, repose, and the authority of solid worth.

If violin playing is in the way of becoming a noble art again, after a generation of technical brilliancy used all too often for meretricious musical ends, this artist is one of those responsible for the change. So, also, of course, is the fact that the Auer pupils have mostly passed the peak of their powers without reproducing their kind. The classical Franco-Belgian school of string playing remains a lasting glory, while the cometlike Russian school seems about to fade from the sky.

Unique in contemporary music making is Francescatti's performance of Ravel's concert rhapsody, *Tzigane*. Nobody else has ever played the work so thoroughly. He has dug into its difficulties, mastered them, and come up with a repertory piece worthy of placement beside the best on any program. Last night he placed it beside the Bach unaccompanied Chaconne (no less), a juxtaposition dangerous to both works. Mr. Francescatti's thoroughness and sincerity made it of advantage to both and even to the Stravinsky *Duo Concertant*, which followed.

This reviewer does not remember a nobler or more powerfully sustained rendering of the Bach piece. Nor was the violin part of the Stravinsky work anywhere short of satisfying. Unfortunately the piano part was too ugly in tone and too subservient in volume to make of the whole a real duet. It was more like a beautiful and deeply expressive violin solo with a competent routine accompaniment of the kind the violinists don't seem to mind. The same infelicity of piano tone marred the Fauré Sonata. Mr. Francescatti's own modesty made of the Kreisler pieces at the end slightly dry marshmallows, though their accuracy of execution was far greater than what one is accustomed to hear.

April 9, 1947

Musical Satisfaction

JOSEPH FUCHS, violinist, recital last night at Carnegie Hall with *Artur Balsam* at the piano.

SONATA NO. 5	HANDEL
ROMANCE IN F, OP. 50	BEETHOVEN
SONATA IN A MAJOR, OP. 13	FAURÉ
SUITE	ALEXEI HAIEFF
(First Performance)	
CAPRICES NOS. 16, 9, 24	PAGANINI
CANTIGA LA DE LONGE (Song from Afar)	GUARNIERI
(First Performance)	
TANGO	ARBÓS

JOSEPH FUCHS, who gave a violin recital last night in Carnegie Hall, is ever a musical delight. He makes beautiful sounds, and he knows what the pieces he plays are about. His work never falls short of either beauty or distinction, and at its best it is unequaled by either test among the violin playing of our day.

It was at its best last night in the Fauré Sonata, Opus 13, in the Haieff Suite, and in the Paganini Caprices. The Fauré piece brought out his gift for a lyricism that soars without effort and without arrogance, a sweetness that is nowhere lacking in either grace or power but that seems to know no strain. The Haieff brought forth virility and rhythmic strength, the Paganini pieces a display of accurate acrobatics that left one gasping with admiration. All these works were read with a breadth of over-all planning, an awareness of their shape and progress that gave proof of intellectual powers in no way inferior to Mr. Fuchs's high skill of hand and accomplished musicianship.

Alexei Haieff's Suite, the chief novelty of the evening, is a broadly conceived work with lots of rhythmic drive. By broadly conceived I mean that it is neither short nor hesitant. It states its thought forcibly, amply, completely. It also states it with high finish; it is admirably, even brilliantly, written for the violin. Mr. Haieff has unquestionably a Russian taste for instrumentalism and no mean skill at exploiting it.

The fast movements are the most satisfactory, the slow ones

having a certain immobility that seems to reflect an emotional modesty that is becoming enough, heaven knows, but that provides him, at the present time of his life, with a less absorbing subject matter than frank displays of physical energy do. Certainly Haieff is a composer to watch, one of the brightest among our rising stars.

Camargo Guarnieri's *Song from Afar* was also a novelty. Guarnieri represents poetic Brazil, as contrasted with Villa-Lobos's travelogue Brazil and with the salon manner of Francisco Mignone. It is a really pretty piece. Arbós's *Tango*, which closed the concert (save for encores), is a set of variations on a Madrid-style popular song. It reminds one rather of the *Carnival of Venice* and is fun to hear once.

January 26, 1946

New Era

ROMAN TOTENBERG, violinist, recital in Carnegie Hall last night. Accompanist, *Artur Balsam*.

SONATA, E MINOR	BACH
CONCERTO, G MAJOR (K. 216)	MOZART
SONATA	DEBUSSY
EARLY SONG; DEDICATION; COMPOSER'S HOLIDAY	FOSS
(First Performance, composer at the piano)	
CHANSON POLONAISE	SZYMANOWSKI-KOCHANSKI
CAPRICE NO. 17	PAGANINI
MALAGUEÑA; ZAPATEADO	SARASATE

THE ENTHUSIASTIC reception that Roman Totenberg's violin recital got in Carnegie Hall last night is no doubt a sign of the times. Violin virtuosity has been the intellectual low point of the concert world for a good forty years now and maybe more. As smooth as an overgrown peach and about as tasteless, it has represented a maximum of surface appeal and a minimum of musical content. In just the last year, however, the recitals of Isaac Stern, of Joseph Fuchs, and of Mr. Totenberg have proved that there is a public for contemporary standards of musicianship, as well as of technique, in violin playing.

Technically speaking, Mr. Totenberg can play anything his predecessors could. He is, in fact, more expert than most of them. His is the smoothest bow arm of all and, in consequence, the most evenly sustained legato line. He plays on pitch, in time, and without bumpiness; and he has rhythm. He also has temperament, the ability to put himself inside a piece, which is valuable, and stylistic understanding, the knowledge of how one piece or period differs from another, which is indispensable. He has by gift, moreover, an awareness of music's continuing line that enables him to project a work as a single, whole thing, and to hold thus by sheer musical communication almost any musical person's interest.

If his execution has a major fault, it is a slight unevenness of color control. A shade acid is most of his work on the A and E strings. This does not appear when he plays high or in double stops, and it is quite lacking from his work on the G and D strings. It has to do, I presume, with the imperfect co-ordination of bow pressure with bow speed at a certain height of the arm. The sound produced is not ugly, but it is less beautiful than that produced in other registers. With this reserve, and with all admiration for his solid octaves, his clean harmonics, and his mastery of all the other difficulties usually troublesome to violinists, it seemed to me that Mr. Totenberg made remarkably lovely sounds and rich strong ones, too.

His Bach and his Debussy sonatas were musicianly performances of great breadth. The rhythm was right, as well as the pitch. His Mozart concerto was equally delightful as far as the solo part was concerned. Unfortunately the work as a whole was deformed by an imprecise and sloppy accompaniment that seemed to lack preparation. The Paganini and the Sarasate showpieces were not only brilliantly executed but interesting to listen to as well. Their musical content was exposed with such straightforward dignity that their bravura writing seemed to require no apology and, in consequence, to lower in no way the tone of the evening.

Lukas Foss's three pieces are the work of a skillful musician and a spontaneous one. They sound well; their sentiments are simple; and they are clearly expressed. They are not very original (the first one is an alternation of passages almost straight out of Copland with material that is recognizably imitated from the

Gymnopédies of Erik Satie). But they are not stale either, and they are never forced. The public's response to this direct and sincere music was as heartening as was its warm reception of Mr. Totenberg's solidly beautiful playing of the violin.

November 19, 1944

King of the Gypsies

TOSSY SPIVAKOVSKY, violinist, recital last night at Carnegie Hall. Assisting pianist, *Frank Glaser.*

ADAGIO AND ALLEGRO	BACH
PRELUDE AND FUGUE IN G MINOR (violin alone)	BACH
ADAGIO IN E MAJOR	VIOTTI
SONATA IN A MAJOR, OP. 47 ("Kreutzer")	BEETHOVEN
RUMANIAN FOLK DANCES	BARTÓK
THREE ÉTUDES	CHOPIN-SPIVAKOVSKY
UKULELE SERENADE	COPLAND
LA CAMPANELLA	PAGANINI-KOCHANSKY

TOSSY SPIVAKOVSKY, who played a recital last night in Carnegie Hall, is a sensationally effective violinist when he is effective and a major disappointment when he is not. The gypsy style is his meat; there he is forceful, varied, brilliant, and explosive. His classical violin playing has a certain grandeur, too, a hard nobility in slow passages. But it is so lacking in both flexibility of expression and, when he plays fast, accuracy of pitch that one cannot but regret the sacrifice he has made to achieve power in the other style.

The sacrifice has to do with his adoption of a right-hand position that is unique among reputable artists and, so the professionals tell me, heretical. He grasps the bow by bending his thumb clean round the nut and flexing the other fingers over it at the outer joints. In this position he has the full weight of his forearm available for bow pressure with small chance of producing an unsteady sound. Hence the nobility of his sustained cantilena. Hence also the unusual force he can put into off-center tonal effects, such as are produced by playing right on the bridge or way down on the fingerboard.

This strong but insensitive bow position, which lacks the cushion usually provided by a relaxed first finger, deprives him of two major expressive devices, the long light bow and the short light, or bouncing, bow. He is obliged, in legato playing, to alleviate the bad acoustical effects of excessive arm weight by drawing his bow too fast across the strings; and his wrist is too inflexible to allow him much play in the lighter qualities of spiccato and saltando playing. He changes the direction of his bow about twice as often as another good player needs to. He does it most skillfully, but he breaks up a phrase unnecessarily all the same. He also attempts to compensate for diminished phrasing interest by excessive vibrato.

A strong but indelicate bow arm, lots of vibrato, and an unusual mastery of off-center colorations, combined with the agilities and high pitches available to very long fingers, all go to make up the gypsy style of violin playing. Spivakovsky is admirable in works written for this style or in something resembling it. His performance, for instance, of Bartók's Violin Concerto several years back, with Artur Rodzinski and the Philharmonic, was a memorable performance of a memorable work. Last night he played with equal brio the same composer's Four Rumanian Folk Dances and Copland's entertaining *Ukulele Serenade*. Everything else, in spite of ocasional moments when slow sound was handsomely sustained, was disappointing.

The disappointment was all the greater from the contrast of the ineffective classical renderings with the extreme brilliance and power of the more fiery and picturesque pieces. Matters were not helped out by a toneless piano, a Baldwin this time, which merits certainly some kind of prize in a season already notable for its bumper crop of inferior instruments.

December 12, 1946

Great Quartet Playing

GUILET STRING QUARTET concert in Times Hall last night.

QUARTET, OP. 64, No. 5	HAYDN
QUARTET No. 1	R. THOMPSON
QUARTET	DEBUSSY

THE PRESTIGE of string quartet music is often a mystery to those who have never heard it played in the Great Tradition. But this normally recondite form of expression has never presented difficulties to any music lover when so played. In my lifetime the Kneisel Quartet from Boston, the Flonzaley from Lausanne, the Quatuors Capet of Paris and Pro Arte of Brussels, the Quartetto di Roma, perhaps, and the Kolisch Quartet from Budapest, and that is about all, have done the business right. Daniel Guilet is one of the great quartet leaders; and New York now has, in the Guilet Quartet, which has been playing together some three or four years already, and which played last night in Times Hall, one of the great string quartets of our century.

Believe me, the way they play is the way the great quartets in my time have always played. Such a group either holds the interest completely or puts one to sleep, and the Guilets last night certainly had the latter effect on no one in my neighborhood.

No other quartet now appearing before the American public has either the homogeneity of tone or the brightness of color that the Guilets have. And since sound pitch in ensemble playing is obtainable only when there is homogeneity of color, no similar group plays quite so harmoniously. Further elements of musical expression, such as amplitude of volume variation, coloristic contrast, and, most important of all, rhythmic freedom, are dependent on the same pitch security, which is in turn a function of the tonal blend. Having this last, the Guilets have, consequently, everything. Musical intelligibility goes without saying in such an ensemble, because only the most discerning and enlightened musicians are ever willing to go through the labor of attaining a clear blend of sounds, just as only the really great minds (and not all of them) ever master simple clarity in the art of writing music.

Last night's program contained a Haydn quartet and the now classical Debussy wonder piece in that form, as well as a contemporary work. This was Randall Thompson's gracious and songful Quartet No. 1, which it has been my joy to hear some three or more times in the last year. Each rehearing brings it closer to my heart, not only for its touching Appalachian Mountain Americanism but for its broader musical interest as well. It is one of the lovely pieces our country has produced, that any country, indeed, has produced in our century. And its reading last night by Mr. Guilet and his teammates — Louis Gralitzer, Frank Brieff, and Lucien K. Laporte — was a dream of sweetness and of poetry.

April 18, 1945

Soaring Unit

PASCAL STRING QUARTET (*Jacques Dumont,* first violin; *Maurice Crut,* second violin; *Leon Pascal,* viola; *Robert Salles,* cello), concert last night in Town Hall.

QUARTET NO. 17 ("Dissonant")	MOZART
QUARTET IN C MINOR, OP. 51, NO. 1	BRAHMS
QUARTET IN F MAJOR	RAVEL

THE PASCAL STRING QUARTET, newly arrived from Paris, is a pleasure and a refreshment. America has many excellent string teams but none that works with quite the technical precision and expressive freedom that this group manifested last night in Town Hall. The Flonzaleys used to work like that, but no other quartet appearing here now does. The Budapest at its best is musically handsome, but its accents are rougher; and the Guilet, for all its perfection of tone and balance, lacks breadth. Mr. Pascal and his colleagues play together, in tune, with thoroughly blended sound and in meter. Moreover, their music soars in both line and volume.

The soaring quality in ensemble playing is obtainable only when measure bars, a typographical device useful chiefly in rehearsals, are forgotten about in performance. I do not mean that simultaneity is not essential to good execution, for it is. I mean that in any final reading the phrase is the minimum unit of communication. Each must go through to its end without hesitation. When music is well written and reasonably well rehearsed, simultaneous articulation in performance is not hard to achieve. It is produced, indeed, most dependably as a by-product of common understanding among the players about the meaning of the expressive line.

Keeping the meaning, the expressive nature of the piece, always in full view of the audience is the chief preoccupation that has made French and Belgian string quartet playing the most musical, as well as the most intelligible, of our century. By this means the music not only comes out saying something; it also takes on beauty, since beauty in music is a by-product, too, a by-product of clarity. Beauty can exist sporadically, in detail, without there being any general clarity at all; but it can only exist throughout a rendering when the rhythmic and phraseological layout of the whole is firm and simple. Otherwise loveliness is mostly crowded out by bad planning.

The Pascal Quartet's work is full of lovely sound and gracious gesture, also of handsome loudnesses and of grand passion. I have never heard any Brahms quartet played with such warm romantic feeling as was the Opus 51, No. 1, last night. The Mozart No. 17 was lovely too, though it is not one of Mozart's most highly concentrated works. The Ravel quartet, though cleanly exposed with no scratching, was not so convincing as I have sometimes heard it. Possibly this piece needs a more luxurious sound than the Pascal instruments, which are not quite first-class, can produce. I had not, at any rate, so vividly missed expensive effects in the earlier works as I did in this. Mozart and Brahms, of course, do not require high coloration.

December 10, 1946

Jeritza's Return

MARIA JERITZA, soprano, recital last night at Carnegie Hall. Assisting pianist, *Paul Meyer.*

"Dich, teure Halle" from TANNHÄUSER	WAGNER
ZUEIGNUNG	STRAUSS
ERLKÖNIG	SCHUBERT
"Adieu, fôrets" from JEANNE D'ARC	TCHAIKOVSKY
BEAU SOIR	DEBUSSY
NIGHT	CHARLES
THIS DAY IS MINE	HARRIET WARE
WE TWO TOGETHER	KERNOCHAN
"Voi lo sapete" from CAVALLERIA RUSTICANA	MASCAGNI
Dance of the Seven Veils from SALOME (piano solo)	STRAUSS
Closing scene from SALOME	STRAUSS

MARIA JERITZA's return to the concert stage was cheered last night at Carnegie Hall by a capacity house that overflowed on the platform. Admirers stood to applaud her before she sang, in the middle of the program, and at the end. And like a schooled prima donna of the great tradition, Miss Jeritza was infallibly gracious of her person and generous with encores. All evening long she seemed to be bowing and singing encores, adding to a program of taxing songs and arias not only divers salon pieces but operatic numbers of the give-all type, such as the "Suicidio!" from *La Gioconda* and Brünnhilde's Cry from *Die Walküre*. When this reporter left, the public was calling for *La Tosca*.

As dramatic expression, nothing seemed last night to tax her. She is a great actress, always was, always will be. And she has the gift of glamour, a styled, a powerful projection elsewhere non-existent today. She has beauty, too, and dignity and grace and ease. Her rendering of the final scene from Strauss's *Salome*, fully clothed and with only a pianoforte accompaniment, was breath-taking in its expressive intensity. One forgot for a moment the vocal inefficiencies. There was a dramatico-musical creation the like of which we do not witness currently, nor shall, I imagine, till singing actors again find it worth while to master their art.

From a purely vocal point of view Miss Jeritza has lost most of the beauty that once was hers, and all of the accuracy. She can still sing very loud, amazingly loud, and very soft. But loud or soft, she sings flat; and her enunciation has become so obscure that one cannot half the time tell even what language she is singing. Power she has and confidence and a completely authorita-tive presence, but the beauty of sound is gone.

Neither is there in her work any unusual musical interest, intrinsically speaking. I don't suppose there ever was. In the old days she sang handsomely enough and accurately, but chiefly she was an actress. Nowadays the sounds she makes are neither hand-some nor accurate. But she is still an actress. And that is some-thing to stand up and cheer about in a decade of dearth. Miss Jeritza's particular personality, moreover, has long been dear to the New York public; and it was heart warming to see New York turned out in its best clothes and its happiest face to welcome her home with bravos and flowers.

April 30, 1946

France Delivers

MARTIAL SINGHER, baritone, in recital at Town Hall last night.

LA CHANSON DE ROLAND	*French XI Century*
EN VENANT DE LYON: L'AMOUR DE MOI	*French XV Century*
ARIA DE CARON, from ALCESTE	LULLY
ARIA DE THESÉE, from HIPPOLYTE ET ARICIE	RAMEAU
PLAISIR D'AMOUR	MARTINI
SERENADE DE DON GIOVANNI	MOZART
STÄNDCHEN	SCHUBERT
SERENATA DE MEPHISTOFELES	BERLIOZ
SERENATA	GOUNOD
SERENATA from SONGS AND DANCES OF DEATH	MUSSORGSKY
VERGEBLICHES STÄNDCHEN	BRAHMS
MANDOLINE	DEBUSSY
BALLADE DES GROS DINDONS; PASTORALE DES COCHONS ROSES;	
VILANELLE DES PETITS CANARDS	CHABRIER
DON QUICHOTTE A DULCINÉE	RAVEL

IN VIEW of all the gasping and sighing and good, solid hand clapping that received Martial Singher's recital last night in the Town Hall, it seems hardly necessary to add my humble testimonial. It is, neverthless, my privilege as well as my pleasure to report that everything went off elegantly, most elegantly, including the music.

Mr. Singher is a musician, a showman, and an artist to his fingertips, a French baritone in the great style. The perfect charm of his platform manner would be a little terrifying if it were not so clearly the buttonhole flower that merely sets off an artistic accouterment of the solidest stuff and tailoring. His singing and his gestures are neither studied nor natural. Schooled is nearer the word for them, schooled and stylish and free, all at the same time. They are frank, too, but about as spontaneous as the Maison Lanvin, in which establishment I should take a small bet his dress suit was cut and fitted.

One could use the word *taste* with considerable force with regard to Mr. Singher's work if that word really meant what the French word *goût* does. Unfortunately, our English word has chiefly negative connotations; it means mostly restraint, avoidance of the noticeable. Mr. Singher's quality is composed of high skill, sound knowledge, daring, confidence, and authority. He does not hesitate, for instance, to sing once in a while falsetto, provided this resonance is appropriate to the composition and provided also it is approached by a gradual transition of the vocal placement. He does not hesitate, either, to dramatize a song, because he knows how to dramatize music without throwing his personality at you. And he loyally gave his accompanist last night, Paul Ulanowsky, a bow every time the latter executed a piano part requiring especial precision or fluidity.

Mr. Singher's vocal gifts are great, though his voice is not one of unusual natural majesty. His vocal mastery is definitely unusual, especially around here, where baritones are likely either to imitate the barrel tone of a basso profundo or to affect a tearful tenor timbre. He sings squarely in the masque the whole time, in all ranges, at all volumes, and on all vowels. That is why his consonants could be so clearly projected that an English-speaking audience laughed, wept, and obviously understood what he was singing, though he sang only in French and in German (plus once in Italian, which he sings not quite so confidently).

A great singing style and a great musical understanding, assurance, dramatic power, and impeccable taste all go into his interpretations. But beneath everything, animating the grand line and sustaining his delicate phraseology, are a rhythmic tension and flexibility of rapier steel. A brief vocal fault here and there and a suggestion of fatigue toward the end of the concert were of no moment in a performance of such penetrating artistry and of such breath-taking elegance all round.

A spokesman for the artist informs me, for the benefit of many bothered by the problem, that the name is correctly pronounced Sang-gehr.

January 26, 1944

Pretty Singing

MURIEL RAHN, soprano, recital in Town Hall last night. Accompanist, *William Lawrence.*

ARIA from AGRIPPINA	HANDEL-BIBB
DIDO'S LAMENT, from DIDO AND AENEAS	PURCELL
DIVINITÉS DU STYX, from ALCESTE	GLUCK
DU BIST WIE EINE BLUME; WIDMUNG	SCHUMANN
VON EWIGER LIEBE	BRAHMS
LA PROCESSION	FRANCK
L'HEURE EXQUISE	HAHN
CARNAVAL	FOURDRAIN
RITORNA VINCITOR, from AÏDA	VERDI
BREATH OF A ROSE	STILL
WINTER'S APPROACH	STILL
EPITAPH TO A POET	COHEN
LET US BREAK BREAD TOGETHER	arr. RECKLING
JESUS, LAY YOUR HEAD IN DE WINDER	arr. H. JOHNSON
SONG OF THE HEART	J. R. JOHNSON
A DREAM	GRIEG
ARIA from TROUBLED ISLAND	STILL
AH, LOVE, BUT A DAY	BEACH
LET MY SONG FILL YOUR HEART	CHARLES

MURIEL RAHN, already well known to New York audiences as one of the two Carmens in *Carmen Jones,* gave a formal recital of songs and arias last night in Town Hall. There is no questioning the fact that Miss Rahn has a pretty voice and a charming personality and that she sings well. Whether she is better suited to the operatic or to the concert stage remains unsettled in your reviewer's mind, after having heard her work most effectively indeed in both circumstances.

In addition to excellent natural advantages both of voice and of person, Miss Rahn is a soundly trained singer. Excepting for the failure to bring the notes of her low register frankly forward (she swallows them a little bit), there is no fault in her vocalization. There is, indeed, much beauty and no mean skill in her handling of an organ that is by nature neither unusually wide in range nor of any arresting loudness. Vocal schooling and good musicianship marked all her work last night, and there were the additional graces of a pleasant personality and of easy dramatic projection.

A large part of this dramatic effectiveness, which she displayed in no manner inappropriate to recital conventions but merely as the natural mood of presentation for each song, is due to her verbal articulation. I doubt if one has ever before heard the words of a recital so completely. So clearly does Miss Rahn enunciate, and with so little apparent effort, that she was several songs along in her program before I realized that I was not having to listen for the words. They came at one with no explosive force; but they came infallibly, completely, correctly. If Miss Rahn were not an artist of other and fuller qualities, I should like to salute her for perfection in the rarely mastered art of singing words.

She can sing songs, too. The high point of her recital, according to this listener, was the rendering of six pieces by Negro composers, notable among these being the delicate and poetic *Breath of a Rose,* by William Grant Still. It was the easy projection of modern American songs that made me think Miss Rahn is possibly destined in the long run for a theatrical career. If our theater offered more roles for the dainty soubrette, and if it were not quite so indifferent to good singing, I should welcome such a future for her. Things being as they are, however, she is wise to "keep up her music," so to speak, by singing Town Hall recitals, too.

April 4, 1945

Folklore in Sunday Clothes

OLGA COELHO, soprano and guitarist, recital last night at Town Hall.

O CESSATE DI PIAGARMI	SCARLATTI
SE TU M'AMI	PERGOLESI
LA ROSE ET LE ROSSIGNOL	RIMSKY-KORSAKOV
EL MAJO TIMIDO	GRANADOS
ASTURIANA	DE FALLA
CANCIÓN ANDALUZA	SEGOVIA
MACUMBA SONG from Brazil	JAYME OVALLE

Folksongs:
  BAMBUCO (Columbia); INCA SONG (Peru); EL ESCONDIDO
  (Argentina); LOS FADRINS DE SAN BOY (Spain); STORNELLO
  ROMAGNUOLO (Italy); EMBOLADA (Brazil).
Brazilian Songs:

LINDU (folk songs)	*18th Century*
CASINHA PEQUENINA	*19th Century*
ACARAGE QUENTINHO	COELHO
CHORO	arr. ITIBERE
FUNERAL DE UM REI NAGO	TAVARES
QUEBRA O COCO, MENINA	GUARNIERI

OLGA COELHO, who sang a recital last night in Town Hall, accompanying herself on the guitar, is a folk-song artist of the drawing-room, rather than of the night club, type. Her voice is pretty, light, and clear; and her presentation is in every way refined. Even her repertory, which is extensive enough, including material from all the South American countries, as well as her native Brazil, seems, all the same, to have been chosen with the thought of keeping its subject matter well within the limits of what is appropriate to parlor entertainment before mixed company.

Everything she sings is innocent, virtuous, thoroughly washed behind the ears, combed, dressed up in the most stylish harmony (though never overdressed), and schooled for charm. The pieces she sings are all of the best quality, and their renderings are impeccable for breeding. They were even presented last night, every one, with a pedigree, recited in advance by the artist. These spoken program notes covered their origins, discovery, arrangement, and literary content, including, as well, translations of the words and explanations of all obscure references. If the furnishing of all this useful information was a shade relentless, consuming often more time than the rendering of the song in question, it was enlightening, all the same. One came away edified, instructed, and not without certain pleasant memories, even, of a strictly musical character.

One of the pleasantest of these, to your correspondent, was the admirable thoroughness with which Miss Coelho plays the guitar. No strummer she. She knows the instrument, plays tunes on it as well as chords, and is master of fifty varieties in tone and touch. This part of her musicianship, in fact, is more interesting to observe in action than her vocal interpretations, because it is more varied. The latter are a little too studied to be wholly convincing. They lack the improvisatory character that lends life to folklore. One feels she has worked them out too thoroughly.

When folk songs are interpreted as scholastically as that (for even charm and the affettuoso style can be scholastic), we are right back to the worst aspects of the lieder recital or caught up on the Wheel of Fate with Frank Sinatra. The whole point of any native idiom, its usefulness to the concert tradition, lies in its freshness. Miss Coelho is nice to look at, and she has the prettiest manners. She is an agreeable singer, too, and a good musician. But she does seem awfully determined that we should take the native music of South America on her terms. There are some who prefer it a shade less genteel.

February 22, 1947

The Concert Song

POVLA FRIJSH, soprano, first of three recitals at Town Hall yesterday afternoon. Accompanist, *Henri Deering.*

HIMMEL UND ERDE; VIEL GLUECK ZUR REISE; MEIN SCHOENER STERN; SCHOENE FREMDE	ROBERT SCHUMANN
ICH STAND IN DUNKLEN TRAEUME	CLARA SCHUMANN
DER SCHMETTERLING; AN SCHWAGER KRONOS	SCHUBERT
*LES PONTS DE C; AIR CHÂMPETRE; *HIER; *LES GARS QUI VONT À LA FÊTE; CHAMBRE D'HÔTEL; *CHANSON; *VIOLON; *VALSE CHANTÉE	POULENC
THE SEAL MAN	REBECCA CLARKE
*DIRGE	R. W. MORSE
*BELLS IN THE RAIN	JOHN DUKE
*3 A.M.	PAUL SARGENT
*CABARET	J. ALEXANDER
THE COMPLETE MISANTHROPIST	EMANUEL ROSENBERG
NORWEGIAN LOVE SONG (sung in Norwegian)	SINDING
DER GYNGER EN BAAD PAA BOELGE (sung in Danish)	GRIEG

* First Performance.

POVLA FRIJSH, who gave a song recital yesterday afternoon in the Town Hall, is a remarkable musician, an interpreter of intelligence and high temperament. The sound of her voice, which is neither fresh nor beautiful, is a little shocking for the first fifteen minutes. After that, one doesn't notice it at all, so skillfully does the artist use it as a means of revealing a song rather than for any intrinsic qualities it may formerly have possessed. She doesn't exactly sing a song, in the concert sense of singing; nor yet does she merely speak it. She shows you how it goes. And she gives a deep musical pleasure. She is mistress of her art.

The meat of yesterday's program was nine songs, all of them new, I think, by Francis Poulenc. This composer, though not always satisfactory in instrumental music, is without rival as world master of the concert song. The mantle, indeed, of Gabriel Fauré may well be said to have fallen upon his shoulders. No other composer, in fact, since Fauré has written for voice and piano so copiously, so authoritatively, with such freedom of musical thought, such variety of expression.

Poulenc is no child of Fauré, however; he is the musical offspring of Chabrier and of Erik Satie. His songs, in particular, derive directly from those of the Sage of Arceuil, from *Daphénéo* and *Le Chapelier* and *La Diva de l'Empire* and the waltz-songs, *Je te veux* and *Poudre d'Or*. They use musical materials objectively, for their customary associations rather than for possible subjective ones. Their romantic ancestor is therefore Schubert rather than Schumann, from whom both Fauré and Debussy stem. And their expressive variety is greater, from the very objectivity of their procedures, than is possible to any composer working by introspective methods.

The wit that points up many of Poulenc songs, just as it does so much of modern poetry, enjoys its newfound ease not because Satie, his master, was fond of fun, but because Satie's music has shown us all a way of admitting humor to musical expression on a basis of equality with sadness. By using all the musical materials, melodic, rhythmic, and harmonic, for their common rather than for their uncommon associations, he has made it possible to use formulas from folklore, from popular commercial music, from the classical masters, and from yesterday's little masters right along side of invented material, and without any vulgarity. The musical vocabulary that results is comparable in origin and in richness to that of Mozart and Haydn and Beethoven. Satie's working methods represent thus a renewal of the classic, the eighteenth-century Viennese tradition and a spectacular show-ing-up of the poverty of musical Romanticism.

Poulenc's songs are varied and rich and ample in expression because they treat music not as a kind of sorcery or as a form of prayer but as a means of straightforward human communication. They do not plot or yearn; they say things. And they say lots of things. Their vocal lines, their harmonic substructures, their pianoforte accompaniments, have freedom and variety because they are not afraid to be specific about what they mean.

The American songs on yesterday's program said little that was specific or that one had not heard before. John Duke's *Bells in the Rain* was the only one that stood up as workmanship be-side the Poulenc pieces. The others were all posey or cute. What stood up beautifully beside Poulenc's and Miss Frijsh's artistry was Henri Deering's piano playing. Twice in ten days now I have heard accompaniments of that intellectual and tech-nical quailty. The previous delight was George Reeves's playing for Maggie Teyte.

January 7, 1946

A Miracle and a Monument

MAGGIE TEYTE, soprano, recital last night at Town Hall. Accom-panist, *George Reeves.*

ADIEU, CHÈRE LOUISE	MONSIGNY
AIR DE ZERBINE, from LA SERVANTE MAITRESSE	PERGOLESI
OFFRANDE	DE SEVERAC
VEDRAI CARINO, from DON GIOVANNI	MOZART
UN MOTO DI GIOIA, from LE NOZZE DI FIGARO	MOZART
D'ANNE QUI ME JETA DE LA NEIGE; D'ANNE JOUANT DE L'ESPI-NETTE; NICOLETTE; LE MARTIN PECHEUR; L'INDIFFÉRENT, from SHEHERAZADE	RAVEL
IN THE SHADOWS	GOLDE
THE PLAYER QUEEN; SILHOUETTES	CARPENTER
THE TEARS OF ST. JOSEPH	VAN SOMEREN GODFREY
LOVE'S PHILOSOPHY	ROGER QUILTER
ICI-BAS; LYDIA; DANS LES RUINES D'UNE ABBAYE	FAURÉ
BEAU SOIR; JE TREMBLE EN VOYANT TON VISAGE	DEBUSSY
PSYCHÉ	PALADHILE

MAGGIE TEYTE, who gave her second Town Hall recital of the season last night, is both a miracle and a monument. To have retained both her beautiful singing voice and complete mastery of it over a period of some thirty-five years (I last heard her in 1912 at the Chicago Opera) is the miracle. The monumental nature of her work comes from the fact that she remains virtually alone today as an exponent of the French vocal style of the period that preceded the other war. If you want to hear the Debussy songs and the Ravel songs and Fauré sung by a vocalist who still knows what they sounded like in the epoch that saw their creation, there is no other living artist that can evoke them for you so authentically or so vividly. And if you want to hear the French singing style as Jean de Reszke invented it, as Muratore and Mary Garden practiced it, you will have to elbow your way into Town Hall the next time Miss Teyte gives a recital, though the house is already sold out, I believe.

That style is based technically on being able to sing any vowel in any color and at any degree of loudness or softness on any note of one's voice. It is based interpretatively on reading aloud. It is intoned elocution that uses so large a variety of vocal coloration that in no single piece is the gamut ever exhausted. Each song is a little drama, a slice of life that takes place in its own poetic climate, uses its own special and appropriate palette of sound. This vocal impressionism is of the utmost auditory richness, and also of the most intense poetic clarity. Such musical variety combined with ease of understanding, such apparent naturalism, is a summit of vocal art from which the singing of our epoch has long since declined. Miss Teyte alone has the key to it, the discipline of it, the workmanship and the knowledge to expose it before us.

It is a dramatic art. There is nothing personal or introspective about it, excepting that most of the repertory that shows it at its best is music of highly introspective subject matter. But introspective subject matter requires for its clear projection the most impersonal dramatic technique. Otherwise you get only obscurity. There is nothing inspirational about Miss Teyte's musical procedures. Her renderings are the product of discipline, reflection, and lots of rehearsal. Imagination and exactitude are what make them so dramatic. And naturally, they are not dramatic in any inappropriate sense. She projects poetry without getting theatrical.

It is as if somebody were singing very beautifully and reading very beautifully at the same time.

It would be hard to say which among the songs she sang offered the greatest revelation. Her Fauré was marked by a wonderfully unifying rhythm. Her Debussy had the real Debussy immobility, the rocklike reality of emotion that is the essence of Debussy. Her Ravel had a wiry delicacy that I have not heard applied to these songs since Eva Gauthier used to sing them for us with such fine awareness of their essential wit and parody.

Perhaps the grandest dramatic achievement of the evening was the letter scene from *Pelléas et Mélisande,* which Miss Teyte added at the close. This was so simple, so clear, and so relentless, so plain at the same time, that one was reminded of how touching *Pelléas* can be whenever anybody lets us hear the words of it.

In face of such thoroughly conscious workmanship it seems almost unnecessary to mention Miss Teyte's personal charm. But that charm is itself so deeply gracious, and Miss Teyte's schooled temperament as an actress and a musician is so wonderfully warmed by it, that the very sweetness and ease of her woman's personality becomes a valid part of her work as an artist. It is something of the kind, I am sure, that has made possible the miracle by which time has touched her singing so little.

December 29, 1945

THE OPERA

Singing Today

THE TECHNIQUE of singing, as practiced today in our concert halls and at the Metropolitan Opera House, is not the same technique that was employed by the masters and mistresses of vocal art thirty years ago. Many persons now alive, recalling the performances of that time and being able to verify the expert character of these through gramophone recordings, or even through listening to Maggie Teyte, who still sings that way, believe the art to be in decline. Judged by the standards that prevailed in 1910, it certainly is. But the standards of 1910 are not necessarily a unique summit. Singing style has changed several times in recent centuries, and I suspect that it is undergoing right now an evolution of some kind. That, as least, seems a legitimate presumption to make about any art that, being still copiously patronized by the public, in every way prosperous and prized, mysteriously loses contact with its most admired models in a time when these have in no grave way ceased to be accessible.

"Nothing changes from generation to generation," as Gertrude Stein once remarked, "except what people are looking at," which is to say, what they have their minds on. And certainly the human voice is a wind instrument of which the essential structure has not been altered, to my knowledge, within recorded history. Any wind instrument can be made to produce sound in various ways, and any generation defines as "correct" that method of production which produces the largest variety of sounds within the limits of what it finds, for reasons mysterious, "pleasing." Thus it is that the more pinched sounds, what we call commonly "nasal," were cultivated in Europe between 1650 and 1750, because velocity execution and altitudinous pitches, both of which are facilitated by a "nasal" production, were what the musical public had its mind on.

Round tones and chest registers were slow to be admitted as legitimate singing. Rameau and Gluck used basses for representing gods or priests, but their scores call for no baritones or altos. Human beings were supposed to be either high tenors or sopranos, sometimes very high tenors. The baritone came into glory with Mozart; but the female alto was a rarity on the operatic stage till the 1840's, when Bellini, Donizetti, and the young Verdi began using that chesty voice as a normally expressive kind of sound. Even today the lower part of the tenor voice is not expected to carry much weight, though it is perfectly capable of doing so if trained toward that end.

The most striking characteristic of today's vocalism in the field of popular music is the way it centers around the lower female ranges. If you write out what most lady night-club and radio artists really sing, you will find yourself using either the bass clef for it or constantly three, four, and five leger lines below the staff. Most of them have light voices, but almost none sings soprano. Few sing at all, of course, in the 1910 sense; they mostly croon. Even on the concert stage and at the opera one hears a good deal of crooning these days. It isn't at all effective in those acoustical setups; but singers, particularly young ones, will do it, because it is effective for microphone work; and the well-paying microphone is what they all have their little minds on, what they dream about, think about, and practice toward.

Naturally, they have to pretend to learn to sing, too, because classical concert and operatic repertory, being written for the last century's effective singing range, which was quite a large one, cannot be altogether crooned. And so they partly sing and partly croon. What none of them can do dependably is to sing, really sing, very loud or very soft. When they try to sing loud they either wobble or scream; and when they try to sing softly their voices change color all the time and fail to project. In both cases there is insufficient control of the throat muscles that determine pitch and color (neither of which should ever alter during the utterance of any single note) and of the abdominal muscles that regulate wind pressure.

In classical singing, the throat muscles are held firm during the projection of any note, while the abdominal muscles cause the lungs to supply a steady pressure of air across the vocal chords. The sole musical function of this controlled exhaling is to keep the vocal chords in vibration. In classical singing, projected singing, the wind pressure should be the maximum possible for steady vibration at the desired volume level. Excess pressure will make the sound louder or, if the throat muscles allow it to escape, breathy. Insufficient pressure will fail to produce a complete vibration of the still air in the mouth vault and the sinuses, which constitute the vocal soundbox.

Screaming is another process than singing. It uses excess wind pressure on a pinched throat. It is not "legitimate" singing, because its pitch is uncontrollable and because it is likely to make an irreparable tear in the vocal chords. Crooning, on the other hand, differs from classical singing by using a minimum of wind pressure. It makes a pretty sound; but it does not project well, because it is poor in upper harmonics. It is a limited kind of sound that "takes" well on the microphone (which has limited acoustical vibrations); but it is not very useful in halls, which mostly have unlimited acoustical vibrations. A classical pianissimo carries to the top gallery because it is a "rich" sound, a full harmony of overtones just like a fortissimo. Crooning carries about ten feet only, because it is a "pure" or "poor" sound. It is easier to produce, however, than a classical pianissimo, which requires a maximum of abdominal muscular control, more, even, than a fortissimo does.

If the music of the future and the chief market of the future are to be microphone music, young singers are wise to dabble in the techniques that are appropriate to that acoustical circumstance. Not knowing, or caring much, perhaps, about the future, but faced with the facts that today there is money to be made through both the processed and the nonprocessed musical operations and that for both operations they are obliged to use a repertory that was built entirely for public halls, they are right to compromise, to work on both sides of the fence. The price they pay is being not really first-class in either field. No concert or opera singer now working before the American public, at least none who is under forty, can match the classical workmanship, available on records and through living precept, of Eames or Melba or Nordica, on the one hand (not to mention the even fuller expressive ranges of Mary Garden and of Maggie Teyte), or Frank Sinatra's crooning, on the other. The two vocal techniques are wholly different and probably opposed. Nobody I know of has ever mastered them both. Coming to terms with both, however, whether by synthesis or by exclusion, is the vocal problem of our time. Till it is solved, one way or the other, singing is likely to remain unsatisfactory.

January 13, 1946

Voice Forum

Two weeks ago this column was devoted to a communication on the subject of voice fatigue from an elderly throat specialist who had cared for many singers in the course of his career and who included with his letter a chapter from a medical textbook. The theme of the letter and of the quoted article was that *myasthenia laryngis*, as distinguished from acute laryngitis (a mucosal condition), is a muscular condition due to overstrain and must be treated as such. Like all other conditions of muscular fatigue, said the author, that of the "phonatory muscles" imposes rest. Tired muscles can be restored to use by no other means. Consequently, to all persons who use these muscles professionally, whether they are hog callers or opera singers, "periods of silence" were recommended as a prophylactic measure; and these were prescribed, moreover, as an absolute necessity in cases where such fatigue has produced a vocal disability. The penalty, in the latter case, for laxity about following the silence regimen was stated by Dr. Chevalier M. Jackson to be permanent professional disability.

Whenever the subject of vocalism is brought up in this column readers write lots of letters. Most of them on this occasion express hearty applause. Echoing the doctor, another laryngologist says that he has "never been able to make any headway in saving young voices through 'prophylaxis.'" "Nobody seems to care," he adds, "or, at least, to care enough; hence the vocal cripples keep coming through this office. Anything you can do to help the voice physician will bring you great and deserved praise." He protests further that many managers and teachers "allow vocalization right through an attack of acute laryngitis, some even recommending it because it 'exercises the muscles.'"

Medical men are unanimous that muscular fatigue, however provoked, cannot be relieved without muscular repose. Not a few letters, however, expound the idea that voice fatigue is the product of a faulty singing technique. Most vocal teachers, of course, though convinced that their methods of training are perfectly designed to prevent fatigue, will admit that a great many singing voices are lost through "overstrain." It would be difficult to prove that any bodily action can be performed without the use of some muscle. A standard contention of singing teachers, nevertheless, is that the muscular effort involved in singing is so slight when a "proper," or efficient, use is made of the muscles involved, that serious fatigue can appear only from an "improper" use of these. The physicians reply that all singers, good, bad, or indifferent, are subject to voice fatigue and always have been, and that the more one uses the voice the more likely one is to strain it. The best swimmers do get cramps and the best leg men "Charley horses." "Form," classical medicine holds, though valuable to efficiency, is never foolproof; and excess is excess no matter who commits it.

The vocal teachers' argument savors of salesmanship. Certainly it is true that a schooled method of doing anything aids the doer. No one believes that naïve vocalism will get him through an opera, even, much less a career. Voice lessons are a prerequisite for high-class singing. And everybody knows that nowadays high-class singing is rare, though voice lessons can be bought in any block. The teachers maintain correctly that training, if efficiently accomplished, will enable a singer to sing higher, lower, faster, slower, louder, softer, and prettier than he did before. Also longer, both on any one evening and during a lifetime. There is no real argument about this, since all the voice-training methods in Christendom are designed with the same end in view.

Assuming that a given teacher is preferable to another because of his devotion to these aims merely eliminates the wholly unfit, since only the most ignorant and irresponsible have any other aim. Choosing a teacher by the evidence of successful pupils produced is sounder practice, but also risky, since all students do not work equally well with all teachers and vice versa. Besides, many of the best singers have had several teachers; and it is not always easy to judge which among them is responsible for the sound technics. The sense of well-being that many a vocalist experiences with a new teacher is no criterion at all, because it is practically universal. Everybody knows what the purpose of vocal training is; nevertheless, good singing is on the wane. Consequently, before we take any teacher's sales talk at face value in those cases, all too frequent, when he maintains that his teaching alone is capable of reversing the trend, we have to have more evidence in the way of sound singing by his pupils than any vocal teacher alive today can offer.

This article is no attack on singing teachers, for whom I have the highest respect, nor on singing students, toward whom I have the warmest feelings. I pity both, indeed, because neither is achieving what they both so passionately desire, namely, to make the world ring with beautiful song. I also wish to add to this forum my own opinion that when a good voice cracks up prematurely (that is to say, before the middle or late forties) the trainer of that voice is not necessarily at fault. The doctors tell me anybody can strain any muscle, and I believe them. The vocal teachers tell me a good "production" will help anybody to avoid the grosser forms of vocal strain, and I believe them, too. What I don't believe (nor has any doctor asked me to) is that medical care is a substitute for voice lessons. And neither do I believe (though many voice teachers have tried to persuade me of it) that any voice training, however sound, will eliminate the physiological effects of fatigue in the voice-producing apparatus, any more than it will prevent singers from catching cold. Moreover, everybody knows who has ever cheered at a football game that the voice-producing apparatus strains very easily.

There might be a way of getting around the present vocal impasse by pooling all the knowledge there is about the subject. Several of my correspondents have proposed in the past that a congress of singing teachers and throat doctors work out together a standard course of training for singers. If such a project were ever realized the assembly's first job would be, as a recent letter states, to agree on a vocabulary. Here I heartily applaud. No two singing specialists understand the same thing by "focus," "spread tones," "breath control," "breath support," "head resonance," "nasal resonance," "chest resonance," "throatiness," "pinched tone," "white voice," "brilliance," and so on. A standard set of words describing auditory vocal phenomena is necessary before the physiologists can even begin to list the conformations and positions of the vocal apparatus required for their production. A listing of these must precede any establishment of a standard method for eliminating the undesirable ones and for cultivating those considered appropriate to music.

The more I talk with singers and teachers the more I am convinced that words are their main trouble. It is not hard to recognize a faulty tone, but it is virtually impossible in any European language to describe it politely. As for correcting it, three fourths of the best instruction still depends on imitation. The other fourth uses up lots of time in talk, and at the end the pupil can only try everything till he makes some kind of sound his teacher doesn't veto. Neither of these classical systems is working very well today, and those that are advertised as based on "medical and scientific" knowledge are not doing one whit better. Maybe if the best of the old-line teachers and some medical men with a reasonably musical ear got together on the matter as a research job, something useful might be found out. If they merely got the terms defined they would have accomplished more than anybody has since Manuel García invented the laryngoscope.

December 1, 1946

Opera's Next Step

A FIRST-CLASS performance of anything is one in which the major element is first-class. Excellence among the subsidiary elements makes for glamour, but it cannot substitute satisfactorily for excellence in the major domain. A poetic tragedy is primarily poetry, and a good performance of it must consist first of all in elocution. It is nice to have scenery and costumes and incidental music that are appropriate, but first-rate declamation is more important. Sarah Bernhardt and Forbes-Robertson could play Racine or Shakespeare without any scenery at all, but the greatest scene designer in the world or the greatest director cannot make a worthy production of a classic work unless some pretty good readers are available.

The same applies to ballet, of course. Good music is not an essential; good dancing is. Ballet is not very glamorous without rich music and decorations; but it can be ballet and very good ballet indeed, as we have all seen recently in the performances of the Ballet Theater.

The opera, at its best, should please the eye as well as the ear; but when sacrifice is necessary (and some always is) visual beauty can always be sacrificed to the auditory elements without the performance ceasing to be first-class. For though the opera, like poetic tragedy, can be, at its grandest, a complete art form, with a whole universe of entertainment on the stage, it can still be great opera though there be nothing more to look at than a conductor and an orchestra and some singers in street clothes.

Even musically, however, it is pretty rare to find everything perfect. The greatest music, the greatest singers, the greatest conductors, and an impeccable orchestra are not always obtainable cheap. Excepting for the operas of Mozart and Wagner and Strauss and for isolated works like *Fidelio* or *Pelléas et Mélisande,* most operatic repertory has always sounded quite well enough with second-class orchestral support, provided the singing was tops. Even Wagner, in recent years, seems to be acceptable on that basis; and Mozart used to be, though nowadays a good conductor seems to be as necessary to the Mozart operas as good vocalism.

Most musicians agree that there are not available anywhere in the world today enough vocalists to supply the opera houses of the world with singing such as was available in all the great houses in 1900, say, or 1910. Neither has the decay of the bravura style been accompanied by any noticeable improvements in diction or in dramatic interpretation. Mary Gardens are even rarer than Melbas these days. For it is the tradition itself of great singing that is lying fallow. There are plenty of voices, but it seems hardly worth while for the possessors of them to go through a complete vocal discipline in an epoch when the public doesn't care so much about great singing as it used to.

The public cares a lot these days about great conducting. In consequence of this, there are more good conductors available in the world than there ever were before. And there are so many first-class instrumentalists around that it is far from rare to encounter them among the ranks of the unemployed. A goodly number of these fine leaders and players are in the United States. As a consequence of this, our orchestral and chamber music organizations have attained a degree of excellence that leaves little to be desired as far as execution is concerned. And the orchestra of the Metropolitan Opera House is so capable these days that it doesn't seem to make very much difference who conducts it, at least among the second-string conductors.

A first-string conductor makes considerable difference, as we have all noticed since Bruno Walter has been appearing there occasionally as guest, because first-class orchestral interpretation is way ahead of second-class in style and power. Still, any night at the Met is a pretty good night orchestrally.

Most nights are good vocally, too, and some quite fine. Because there are lots of good voices around. There are more good voices than good vocalism, in fact, and more good vocalism than good musical or dramatic style. And there is far more good style than there is star quality. All this is due, I think, to a change that has taken place in the comprehension of music. Singers no longer expect conducting to be subservient to their whims. They want good direction and need it. That is the extraordinary and noticeable difference between the singing stars of our day and those of thirty or more years ago. They have neither the prestige nor the vanity that used to make them so glamorous and musically so hard to handle. Even they have come to understand that musical architectonics are the order of the day and that a firm foundation of these is the prime requisite for the success of serious music. Universal acquaintance by means of records and radio with the symphonic style of musical interpretation has made that style, which is primarily occupied with unity, proportion, and emphasis, more popular than the old-fashioned way of merely producing as often as possible a momentary enthusiasm by the effective rendering of single pieces, single phrases, even single notes.

As I have listened to the Metropolitan performances this winter and fondled over many of them in recollection afterward, I am astonished at the amount of good singing there has been in them in minor as well as in major roles. I am astonished because that singing, except in the Wagner operas, which have become for our time the vehicles of vocalism that the operas of Verdi and Donizetti were for a previous epoch, is somehow not played up in performance by the singers themselves to the extent it would have been thirty and more years ago. There are singers with fine voices and good schooling, all doing excellent vocal work but somehow doing it passively, as if they were waiting for somebody to put their show over for them, as if they were counting on the conductor to animate their conception. I have also noticed that, lacking such directorial domination, the tendency to try animating the performance from the stage itself by taking every occasion that presents itself for sticking in a bit of ham comedy and even for running around in circles is growing and is at present nearing the point where it makes the whole cast look a little silly.

I feel a certain lack of authority in most of the Metropolitan performances, and I've an idea the next move in opera everywhere (for this lack of authority is not merely a local phenomenon) will be to put in star conductors in order to give the performances the authoritative accent that the singers are no longer able to provide by themselves. The public of our century loves conductorial rhetoric and adores good teamwork. It is suspicious of personal display and confused by anything that is not streamlined. Streamlining a theatrical or a musical production is a dictatorial job. Diffuse direction makes for hodgepodge in an epoch when the performers themselves don't really believe in personal display and have not been trained in its traditional techniques. The old-time vocal stars sang handsomely no matter who conducted or how inefficient the orchestra was. They often made their biggest successes with a self-effacing accompaniment. Today they actually sing better under a conductor like Toscanini or Walter or Reiner or Rodzinski than under the modern second-class leader, who is neither wholly authoritative, like the great ones, nor wholly subservient, like his predecessors.

Wagner performances do not follow this rule, because they have become chiefly vehicles to display vocal mastery. For seventy-five years Wagner has been a conductor's fief. Today the *Tristan und Isolde* orchestra is being led (and quite satisfactorily) by Kirsten Flagstad's personal accompanist, while the Verdi operas languish everywhere unless animated by a masterful hand.

Flagstad herself is a unique survival. Singers of that quality are rare, of course, in any epoch, though there has always been the legend that at some former time they were more common. But the prima donna who, with superb assurance and knowing exactly what she wants, can take command of her own performance and put it over to everybody's satisfaction, even that of musicians, does not exist, to my knowledge, elsewhere in the world today.

Singers used to be the gods of the opera house. Today they are mostly at best just good executant musicians like those in the pit. They need direction; they want it; they beg for it. To the conductor they offer the kingdom and the power and glory that once were theirs. It is my prophecy that when our operatic establishments shall have finally placed thus all musical authority in his hands, as the contemporary public has long since placed there its worship and confidence, a new era of operatic grandeur will ensue.

That era may not be of long duration. Indeed, I cannot imagine it as other than brief, because no amount of fancy conducting can ever very long take the place of living music. And what the opera lacks most of all in our century is a satisfactory contemporary repertory. But it will be brilliant while it does last, as Salzburg was. And at the end of it the opera will either have transformed itself into a contemporary medium of expression (as it has always done at about the middle of the century) or have passed over into Valhalla midst the iridescent glories of its own Götterdämmerung.

March 9, 1941

Reconverting Opera

WHETHER an operatic repertory theater like the Metropolitan — and its artistic equivalents in other countries — is engaged in public instruction or in the entertainment business is not always clearly understood, I think, by those directing the enterprise. The public, curiously enough, knows what it wants and what it should be getting. It expects education, culture, contact with beauty and with the history of spiritual values. It demands of its subsidized opera companies exactly what it demands of its symphony orchestras, its art museums, and its universities, namely, a true and disinterested representation of the cultural past. But managements, though they know this, do, in penurious epochs, tend to diminish their spiritual, like their financial, largesse and to drain the excess quality off their performances down to a mere money's-worth level.

Wartime restrictions being now loosened up about raising money for what we may call nonmilitary objectives (restrictions that were none the less firm for being chiefly a matter of taste), it would seem only natural that subsidized opera should be getting back to its normal way of life. That way is to operate as a successful money-spending enterprise rather than as an unsuccessful money-making one. In other words, the dissemination of real culture and education is the proper business of the Metropolitan Opera, no matter what that costs.

A reasonable amount of showmanship is no hindrance to the educational function. On the contrary, gracious, charming, or impressive presentation has long been considered valuable, even in university circles. Indeed, our national talents for showmanship and for giving one another a good time have often made American educational methods seem superficial to Europeans who haven't looked at what really goes on beneath the musical-comedy exterior. Similarly, our art museums and our symphony orchestras use every device known to psychology, to business, and to religion for rendering their programs attractive. One almost wishes sometimes that our cultural presentations were less oppressively luxurious, so closely does their high finish — as at the Museum of Modern Art, for instance, or at a concert of any of our major orchestras — resemble a merely commercial patina, a luxury packaging.

But all that is really unimportant when the matter put out is first-class. It is the excess of a proud and culture-conscious nation. And it expresses a general will that where culture is concerned no care must be spared. We do not expect culture to show a profit; we expect of it spiritual and intellectual benefits, which are without price. As a nation we are intellectually ambitious, devoted to self-improvement of all kinds, insatiable consumers of books, music, and drama. Also we are rich. There is no reason in the world why we should not have the finest opera money can buy, and I don't mean just showmanship. I mean Classical, Romantic, and modern repertory correctly and beautifully sung, thoroughly rehearsed on the stage and luxuriously accompanied in the pit, stylishly presented all round, with magnificence the standard. The show behind the footlights has got to live up to the solid values, both financial and cultural, that the audience itself represents in all parts of the house.

Plenty of living citizens remember this kind of opera in Chicago, in Boston, and in New York, not to speak of memorable moments in Milan, in Paris, Vienna, London, Munich, St. Petersburg, and Berlin. It can be produced again if anybody wants it, and I think that America does want it. I think she wants it for the simple reason that she wants everything she uses, particularly the art she patronizes and most particularly her music, to be of the best. Not just the best there is around, but the best that anybody anywhere knows how to make. And there are certainly lots of people in the world who know how to produce better opera performances than anybody in the world is producing just now.

The chief thing required for good opera production is the same thing that it takes to make a symphony orchestra: money. Money has to be spent on every detail, the top price paid for every workman. Otherwise one can't have top quality. Grandeur and penury make bad bedfellows. You can't be magnificent and economical at once. And believe me, for what the Metropolitan pays its artists you couldn't cast a Broadway operetta. It takes more than talent to sing Wagner and Verdi or to play the oboe. It takes brains and sacrifice and years of expensive preparation. It takes leisure, too, and rest and good food and a comfortable house and vacations for study and the ability to put one's mind on the problem in hand without having to worry about the years when one won't be able any longer to sing Wagner and Verdi or to play the oboe.

Any community can have a first-class opera company that will spend the money it costs. Artists are available, plenty of them. And you don't have to make prices prohibitive, either. There is always a price level that brings in the maximum of receipts, but in no field of cultural endeavor are box-office receipts sufficient to pay for top quality. Extra money must be found through state subsidy, private philanthropy, or popular subscription. We raise lots of money in these days for colleges, hospitals, scientific research, and symphonic foundations. I know of no reason why it can't be raised for opera. America is a rich country or it isn't, and the war is over or it isn't. I believe America to be a rich country, perfectly capable of having the finest opera anybody ever heard; and I think we all consider anything less to be unworthy of us. Also, I suspect, though none of the victorious countries has admitted the fact yet, that the war is over and that it is time to start getting our cultural institutions back to peacetime standards and to operating them on the only method known to history that has ever produced first-class cultural results, namely, an economy of abundance.

In other words, let's start spending some real money on our opera. It is not important whether the present directors be entrusted with this spending. If our musical and civic leaders have confidence in these directors, let us keep them. If not, let's thank them prettily and get new ones. Or start a new opera project from scratch and let the old one worry along with its real-estate mortgages. Whether to work through the present setup or to walk out on it is a delicate decision, with many cultural advantages to be gained and lost either way. But it is not an impossible decision. What is important is that we start acting toward opera like the rich, cultivated, ambitious, proud people that we are. We have first-class symphony orchestras. There is no reason why we shouldn't have one opera company, or even several, upholding comparable standards.

December 9, 1945

English at the Met

THERE is no doubt that the performance of opera in English to an English-speaking audience brings enormous benefits in the way of general understanding. There is also no question but that such performance presents unusual difficulties to an organization like the Metropolitan Opera Company, which was long ago set up for another purpose. Ideally, and naïvely, viewed, this troupe has usually been considered a polygot repertory theater, prepared to offer a proper performance of almost any known opera in its original tongue. Actually it has rarely been convincing in any languages but the Italian and the German. It still has enough good Italian singers to cast and render Italian opera correctly and enough German-speaking Central Europeans (mostly of Swedish or Hungarian birth) to give a reasonably satisfying performance of Wagner. French opera rarely sounds like French opera at the Met; and English, though the mother tongue of many of the artists, more often than not leaves much to be desired in the way of clarity.

Russian opera, when performed there, is offered in translations more or less fortuitously chosen. Mussorgsky's *Boris Godunov* is currently given in Italian, that being the native language of Ezio Pinza, who sings the title role. Rimsky-Korsakov's *Golden Cockerel,* formerly given in French, has been heard of late years in a language that might be described as Basic Bromide English. Similarly, the Czechish *Bartered Bride,* by Smetana, has been moved from the German in which it used to be given over to our own vernacular, and none too effectively, I may add.

The Metropolitan is lucky to have a chorus capable of singing German, Italian, French, and English and enough soloists to cast any opera with moderate effectiveness in those languages. To offer the Slavic ones as well, though not at all out of the question in New York City, would require firing most of the present Italo-German chorus and hiring a Russo-Polish one with Western language accomplishments. Even the giving of *Boris* in Italian is condonable on the ground that it leaves the excellent Mr. Pinza in the cast, though why this artist should not, in his more than twenty years' American residence, have learned, even accidentally, to speak and sing our language passes my comprehension. One would have thought that simple curiosity might have led him somewhere in that direction.[1]

The same slow progress that has got all the Slavic operas but *Boris* into English at the Metropolitan has begun now to work on the production in translation, one every two or so years, of operas from the more familiar European repertory, chiefly, so far, from the German. Mozart's *Magic Flute* and *Abduction from the Seraglio* and Humperdinck's *Hansel and Gretel* are now given in an English that, if not exactly of the highest literary distinction, is perfectly clear and for the most part inoffensive. Little by little, if present trends continue, the Met will go on augmenting its in-English list, though the Italian wing of the company, as Italian wings have always done everywhere, will no doubt oppose

---

[1] Pinza sings English in concert.

progress in this direction by every means in its power. Since one of these means is the refusal to co-operate, to sing in English on any stage, the in-English productions will, of course, be deprived of all the best acting talent in the company, which is, to a man, Italian.

Articulating the English language clearly in a house of that size, though this has not always in the past been accomplished impeccably, is not an insoluble problem. The present production of Mozart's *Seraglio* is highly presentable in that regard, and that of Bernard Rogers's *The Warrior* is well nigh perfect. Opera in English for an English-speaking audience requires a good initial fitting of words to music by the composer, if the opera is composed in English; a good literary and prosodic translation, if it is a foreign work; and a clear projection of the verbal text by all the singers on the stage, including the chorus. Without these elements the show is bound to be second-class and to disappoint any audience that expects a first-class entertainment for its seven dollars. But both are in the long run, with patience on everybody's part, obtainable, as current productions prove.

What is going to give trouble from now on is acting. Acting in English to music has no local tradition; and one must be formed, in however elementary a fashion, right away. So far the Metropolitan management has tried to side-step the problem by giving in English only comedies and fairy-tale fantasies. The acting in Humperdinck's *Hansel and Gretel* will do. That in Mozart's *Seraglio* will not. I do not believe, moreover, that a proper technique of rendering grown-up comedy is available among the Met's English-singing artists. Neither do I believe that bad acting is more nearly acceptable in the comic style than in the tragic. On the contrary, an amateur *Hamlet* or *Macbeth* is far easier to listen to than an amateur *Twelfth Night* or *Tempest*. Anybody can act *Il Trovatore*, and the popular Puccini operas — *La Tosca*, *La Bohème* and *Madama Butterfly* — are foolproof in any language. Tears need no timing, only insistence. Farce and fantasy are a monopoly of the great stage technicians.

Here, I think, is the reason why Mozart's *Seraglio*, for all its sound musical execution, has not yet caught public favor at the Metropolitan. It has a silly plot that does not lend itself to easy rendering. *Figaro*, on the other hand, which makes sense as a play, is rarely ineffective in any language, played by no matter whom. Even Debussy's *Pelléas et Mélisande,* for all its intimate French tone and its thoroughly French vocal line, can be convincing in English, as the Philadelphia Opera Company demonstrated several years back. But silly plots and silly jokes are all the sillier when one can understand them. Those are the operatic elements that profit best from being left in a foreign tongue.

To the Metropolitan management, therefore, the writer suggests that the next time an opera is to be translated and refurbished, one with a serious story be chosen. If our English-speaking singing actors and actresses are going to learn to act, which they must do eventually, they must be given, for their early efforts in that enterprise, something that is capable of being acted. *Seraglio, The Magic Flute,* and *The Golden Cockerel* are hard jobs for the most expert and imaginative comedians. For average singing actors they are hopelessly difficult. We must give our American singers every facility. Give them young love, irate parenthood, sexy seduction, the royal mien, maternal sentiments, jealousies, noble friendships, priesthoods, vendettas, tears, and tuberculosis. And if the Met must do farce comedy, let some insistence be made that Baccaloni learn to sing English. Or, failing that, how would it do if a stand-by sang the bass solos while somebody like Bobby Clark did some real clowning?

January 26, 1947

Fairy Tale about Music

DIE MEISTERSINGER, opera in three acts, book and music by WAGNER, revival at the Metropolitan Opera House last night.

Eva	*Eleanor Steber*
Magdalene	*Kerstin Thorborg*
Walther von Stolzing	*Charles Kullman*
Hans Sachs	*Herbert Janssen*
Beckmesser	*Gerhard Pechner*
Pogner	*Emanuel List*
Kothner	*Mack Harrell*
Vogelsang	*Donald Dame*
Zorn	*Richard Manning*
Moser	*Lodovico Oliviero*

Eisslinger	*Karl Laufkoetter*
Nachtigall	*Hugh Thompson*
Ortel	*Osie Hawkins*
Foltz	*Lorenzo Alvary*
Schwartz	*John Gurney*
David	*John Garris*
A Night Watchman	*Louis D'Angelo*

Conductor, *George Szell*. Stage Director, *Herbert Graf*. Chorus Master, *Konrad Neuger*.

RICHARD WAGNER's *Die Meistersinger von Nürnberg*, which was given again at the Metropolitan Opera House last night after an interval of five years, is the most enchanting of all the fairy-tale operas. It is about a never-never land where shoemakers give vocal lessons, where presidents of musical societies offer their daughters as prizes in musical contests, and where music critics believe in rules of composition and get mobbed for preferring young girls to young composers.

It is enchanting musically because there is no enchantment, literally speaking, in it. It is all direct and human and warm and sentimental and down to earth. It is unique among Wagner's theatrical works in that none of the characters takes drugs or gets mixed up with magic. And nobody gets redeemed according to the usual Wagnerian pattern, which a German critic once described as "around the mountain and through the woman." There is no metaphysics at all. The hero merely gives a successful debut recital and marries the girl of his heart.

And Wagner without his erotico-metaphysical paraphernalia is a better composer than with it. He pays more attention to holding interest by musical means, wastes less time predicting doom, describing weather, soul states, and ecstatic experiences. He writes better voice leading and orchestrates more transparently, too. *Die Meistersinger* is virtually without the hubbub string-writing that dilutes all his other operas, and the music's pacing is reasonable in terms of the play. The whole score is reasonable. It is also rich and witty and romantic, full of interest and of human expression.

The first of the successful operatic comedies for gigantic orchestra, like Verdi's *Falstaff* and Strauss's *Rosenkavalier*, it is the least elephantine of them all, the sweetest, the cleanest, the most graceful. For the preservation of these qualities in performance George Szell, the conductor, and Herbert Graf, the stage director, are presumably responsible. For the loan of some new scenery, which enhanced the final tableau, the Chicago Civic Opera Company merits our thanks. For careful singing and general musical good behaviour all the artists deserve a modest palm.

Charles Kullmann, who sang the tenor lead, did the most responsible and satisfactory work, I should say. John Garris, as David; Herbert Janssen, as Hans Sachs, and Gerhard Pechner, as Beckmesser (and he didn't ham this role, either) were highly agreeable. Eleanor Steber's Eva was pretty to look at but vocally satisfactory only at the difficult moments. Elsewhere there was a careless buzz in her voice. Emanuel List, as Pogner, sang well but a little stiffly, keeping his voice down to match the others, who are all small-volume vocalists. Mr. Szell kept the orchestra down, too, so that everybody could be heard. The performance all through was charming, intelligible, and a pleasure to this usually anti-Wagnerian opera fan.

January 13, 1945

Good Singing

NORMA, opera in two acts, text by ROMANI, music by BELLINI. First performance of the season at the Metropolitan Opera House last night.

Pollione	*Frederick Jagel*
Oroveso	*Norman Cordon*
Norma	*Zinka Milanov*
Clothilde	*Thelma Votipka*
Adalgisa	*Jennie Tourel*
Flavio	*Alessio De Paolis*

Conductor, *Cesare Sodero*. Stage Director, *Lothar Wallerstein*. Chorus Master, *Giacomo Spadoni*.

BELLINI's *Norma*, as given last night at the Metropolitan Opera House, was a distinguished performance. Jennie Tourel, who made her first appearance of the season in the role of Adalgisa, proved to us all over again that the human voice is a first-class musical instrument. Zinka Milanov, who sang the title role, did some beautiful work in her great *"Casta diva"* air and in the three duets with Miss Tourel. Otherwise she showed us, as she so often does, that the bravura style cannot be produced by mere courage without skill.

Miss Tourel is a great pleasure to hear. She is very short and she doesn't wear quite the right clothes, but every phrase she sings is a musical act. And everybody who sings with her sings better than usual. Miss Milanov, always erratic from lack of technique, reserved her vocal risks for her own solos. When the two ladies sang together, she sang securely and right. Their duets contained some of the best singing heard here this winter. I do hope there will be more performances of this opera with the same artists, because, working well together, they are certain to profit by repetition and to give much pleasure to the lovers of song.

I wish Miss Milanov would practice more at home. She has a beautiful voice and a taste for the bravura style. Unfortunately, bravura singing is always a failure unless based on the daily exercise of scales and arpeggios. Overconfident and underexercised, Miss Milanov invariably in moments of temperamental enthusiasm sings off pitch and with ugly tone. This is not only unfortunate but unnecessary. An artist of her abundant natural gifts is foolish not to acquire a mastery over them. She would be a great singer if she could bring herself to accept the necessary routine of perfection and if she could refrain from getting excited. If more sure of her throat muscles and of her breath, she would probably not need to get excited.

The rest of the cast was good, and Cesare Sodero conducted with delicacy and animation. The Metropolitan has given some incredibly bad performances this year, but *Norma* is not among them. It is not among those memorable in any year, either, for dramatic conviction. But it contains a great deal of very beautiful singing, and Bellini's melody is always a delight for its instinctive elegance and its sustained complexity. The artist chiefly responsible for the vocal distinction of the whole thing is Jennie Tourel. May we hear more of her, please, and often!

December 16, 1944

Two New Stars

LA TRAVIATA, opera in four acts, book by *F. M. Piave*, music by
GIUSEPPE VERDI, fourth performance of the season at the Metropolitan
Opera House last night.

Violetta	*Dorothy Kirsten*
Flora Bervoix	*Thelma Votipka*
Annina	*Thelma Altman*
Alfredo	*Armand Tokatyan*
Giorgio Germont	*Robert Merrill*
Gastone	*Alessio De Paolis*
Baron Douphol	*George Cehanovsky*
Marquis d'Obigny	*William Hargrave*
Doctor Grenvil	*Louis D'Angelo*

Conductor, *Cesare Sodero*. Stage Director, *Désiré Defrère*. Chorus
Master, *Kurt Adler*. Solo dancers, *Marina Svetlova* and *Peggy Smithers*.

VERDI's *La Traviata*, as sung last night at the Metropolitan Opera
House, presented for the first time in those premises the admirable Dorothy Kirsten as Violetta. Miss Kirsten's handling of the
role, already favorably known from last season at the City Center,
brought liveliness and beauty in no lesser degree to the grander
establishment. Backed up by a first-class orchestra and chorus,
with Cesare Sodero conducting, and surrounded by such excellent singers as Robert Merrill and Armand Tokatyan, she appeared to this observer as definitely a singer and a singing actress
of the first category.

Miss Kirsten is still young, of course; and her star quality is
almost brutally brilliant. But she is not afraid of her voice, which
is big, beautiful, and well trained, or of her person, which she
projects dramatically with confidence not only in herself, which
is common enough these days, but in the reality of her role, which
is all too rare on the operatic stage. She seems to have all the
material, vocal, personal, and intellectual, for a great operatic
career. If she has any vocal disadvantage (and this is not grave),
it lies in her singing the closed vowels, the Italian e and i, less
perfectly than she does the darker, open ones, the a and o. Her
range is wide; her scales are clean, her marksmanship impeccable.

And whether she is uttering a musical line or crossing the stage, she means it.

Robert Merrill is also a fine singing actor. His noble baritone voice and his intensely dignified bearing gave a pathos to the parental role of Germont that was in no way forced and in no way sentimental. To be as moving as that in a frock coat is evidence of mental power, as well as of vocal skill. For two singers of such well-matched equipment as Mr. Merrill and Miss Kirsten, and of such mutually complementary vocal color, to have had almost a whole act, the third, to themselves is a bit of luck all round. Their work together was not only handsome to hear; it was deeply, wonderfully, quite unexpectedly, expressive.

La Traviata has long been one of the Metropolitan's pleasanter evenings, thanks to Mr. Sodero, who leads it to perfection. There have been some good Violettas, too, in late years, notably Licia Albanese. With Miss Kirsten and Mr. Merrill in the cast and Mr. Sodero conducting, it is one of the few genuinely sweet and animated performances in the repertory. Armand Tokatyan, who sang Alfred, adds distinction to the cast, though last night he was not always vocally at ease.

March 8, 1946

First-Class Thriller

LA GIOCONDA, opera in four acts, book by *Arrigo Boïto*, music by AMILCARE PONCHIELLI, first performance of the season at the Metropolitan Opera House last night.

La Gioconda	*Zinka Milanov*
Laura Adorno	*Risë Stevens*
Alvise Badoero	*Ezio Pinza*
La Cieca	*Margaret Harshaw*
Enzio Grimaldo	*Richard Tucker*
Barnaba	*Leonard Warren*
Zuane	*Osie Hawkins*
First Singer	*Wellington Ezekiel*
Second Singer	*Richard Manning*
Iseppo	*Lodovico Oliviero*

A Monk *William Hargrave*
A Steersman *John Baker*
Conductor, *Emil Cooper*. Stage Director, *Désiré Defrère*. Chorus Master, *Kurt Adler*. Ballet soloists, *Marina Svetlova, Leon Varkas*, and *Josef Carmassi*.

THERE is no denying that Ponchielli's *La Gioconda* makes a good show when they really sing it. It is tommyrot from beginning to end, skillfully varied, exciting hokum. But since hokum is chiefly what makes a good show anyhow, and since the musical part of this particular hokum was written for tiptop show-off, the piece is capable of producing shivers no end when the musical execution is a bang-up one. And that is exactly what Emil Cooper, who conducted, and a brilliant cast of singers gave us last night at the Metropolitan Opera House.

Lush-throated Zinka Milanov, who sang the title role, has never been in better voice. Risë Stevens, who sang Laura, has never in my hearing sung half so well. And her voice, when she does sing well, is one of rare beauty. Ezio Pinza, as the Doge of Venice, could not have been more distinguished, both vocally and dramatically. Richard Tucker did his tenor stuff most handsomely. Leonard Warren articulated his baritone villainies with all power and elegance, though it did take him an act and a half to get the meal out of his voice. Margaret Harshaw, as the Blind Woman, sounded rich in the concerted numbers. And even the ballet troupe put on a Dance of the Hours that was more than merely presentable.

Mr. Cooper is the only conductor on the Metropolitan's present staff for whom the orchestra plays invariably in tune. And since his readings are always intelligent and warm, his work rarely fails to give pleasure 'all round. Last night the pleasure began a little quietly, as if the musical elements were all in place but as if some final Italian oomph were missing. This tranquility turned out to be just more showmanship on Mr. Cooper's part, because when the third act had got going and built up through the ballet to its choral production-number finale, one realized that saving the excitement had all along been the better part of wisdom.

That excitement was the most prodigious theatrical climax I have ever witnessed in that house. It wasn't about anything, because Victor Hugo's play and Arrigo Boïto's libretto and Amilcare

Ponchielli's music are not about anything, unless one counts the provoking of applause sufficient motivation for an opera. But the moment was thrilling and the applause wholehearted; and we were all, I think, grateful for an experience so rare at the Metropolitan. Besides, hokum properly performed has a purity about it that is refreshing. It makes one feel good, like a shower bath, leaves a clean taste in the mouth the way a good murder story does. From that point of view Ponchielli's opera is one of the best, and last night's brilliant performance was more than worthy of it.

December 22, 1945

Aggressive but Harmonious

OTELLO, lyric drama in four acts founded on Shakespeare's tragedy; music by GIUSEPPE VERDI, book by *Arrigo Boïto;* revival yesterday afternoon at the Metropolitan Opera House.

Otello	*Torsten Ralf*
Iago	*Leonard Warren*
Cassio	*Alessio De Paolis*
Roderigo	*Anthony Marlowe*
Lodovico	*Nicola Moscona*
Montano	*Kenneth Schon*
A herald	*Wellington Ezekiel*
Desdemona	*Stella Roman*
Emilia	*Martha Lipton*

Conductor, *George Szell.* Production staged by *Herbert Graf.* Chorus Master, *Kurt Adler.*

VERDI's *Otello,* which was revived yesterday afternoon at the Metropolitan Opera House after a four-year interval, is an "effective" musico-theatrical work very much in the vein of Ponchielli's *La Gioconda.* Indeed, the latter piece, which preceded *Otello* in composition and in production by eleven years, is probably responsible, along with the revised (and theatrically successful) version of Boïto's *Mefistofele,* which appeared a year before that, in 1875, for the violent theatricalism of this particular work, of which Boïto himself was the librettist.

The word "violence" comes constantly to tongue in speaking

of *Otello*. And yet, as Italian opera plots of the late nineteenth century go, there is not much visible violence in this one. The spectacle is, on the whole, statuesque. But violence is present, nevertheless. It is present in the attitude of the composer toward his audience, which for three acts is allowed no respite from aggression. Every remark is exaggerated, every sentiment blown up into a passion. And since the passions, however they may differ in origin and in social reference, all have exactly the same amount of emotional content (the maximum) and a virtually identical (at that intensity) expressive content, the first three acts of *Otello*, for all their masterful orchestral detail, are as monotonous in their insistence on applause-at-any-price as any Broadway musical or floor show.

The fourth act is less wearing. It takes its time, makes its points one by one, and allows, in consequence, a certain awareness of the actors as characters in a play. It allows one time to feel sorry for them, even. If Verdi, at seventy-four, had not lost the abundance of melodic invention that flowed throughout his early and middle years, the last act of *Otello* might well be as deeply touching as those of *La Traviata* and *Il Trovatore*. The repose and the leisurely timing are there, the whole shape and progress of a noble act; but its "*Ave Maria*" is a far cry from the great "*Miserere*."

Yesterday's performance under George Szell was orchestrally a delight for precision and for variety. Vocally it was a delight for the handsome sounds uttered by Torsten Ralf, as Otello, by Leonard Warren, as Iago, and by Stella Roman, who sang Desdemona. The others sang agreeably, too, even the chorus. And everybody moved about with style. The only serious fault in the vocal rendering was the forced sounds that came from the three principals every time an overloud orchestral climax threatened to submerge their efforts. The performance on the whole was one of the most satisfactory to the ear that this announcer has lately had the pleasure of attending.

February 24, 1946

A Happy Return

MADAMA BUTTERFLY, opera in three acts, book by *L. Illica* and *G. Giacosa*, music by GIACOMO PUCCINI; revival yesterday afternoon at the Metropolitan Opera House.

Cio-Cio-San	*Licia Albanese*
Suzuki	*Lucielle Browning*
Kate Pinkerton	*Maxine Stellman*
B. F. Pinkerton	*James Melton*
U. S. Consul Sharpless	*John Brownlee*
Goro	*Alessio De Paolis*
Yamadori	*George Cehanovsky*
The Uncle-Priest	*Osie Hawkins*
The Imperial Commissary	*John Baker*

Conductor, *Pietro Cimara*. Stage Director, *Désiré Defrère*. Chorus Master, *Kurt Adler*.

PUCCINI's *Madama Butterfly* came back to the Metropolitan yesterday afternoon. The war had caused it to be put in storage, apparently because it shows Japanese behaving more or less properly and a United States naval officer behaving (with consular benediction) improperly. The work seems to have been extremely popular in Italy during our occupation of that country, Italian families loving to point out to their daughters the unfortunate results of becoming seriously attached to members of our armed forces. It will probably be popular here too now, though less for moralistic reasons than for the fact that it is a beautiful and touching opera.

The present production, though not a world-beater, is good. Licia Albanese sings the title role with full vocal beauty and acts it with style. Her power of vocal projection is somewhat weak in the lower passages, but her top voice sails out admirably. James Melton sings Pinkerton most pleasantly, except for the inability to project with resonance any note above A flat. The notes are in his voice; he merely doesn't know how to make them carry. John Brownlee's work, as Sharpless, is distinguished, if a bit tame. Lucielle Browning sings Suzuki with handsome sounds. Osie Hawkins, as the Uncle-Priest, does the most striking bit of acting in the whole show.

Mechanically, too, yesterday's performance was well adjusted and quite reasonably pleasing. Pietro Cimara, who conducted, began nervously and too fast; but after Butterfly's entrance, some ten or fifteen minutes later, he settled down to a normal pacing and got music out of the orchestra. It was regrettable that somebody had not noted in rehearsal the injurious effect on the love duet of a scenic device that might well, in more appropriate circumstances, have been any electrician's pride. The moment was a tender one, and the two principals labored admirably. But a garden background full of fireflies was no help to them. Nobody should be asked to sing a difficult and romantic number against an animated lighting effect that cannot fail to distract the audience's attention.

It was refreshing to discover, after not hearing *Madama Butterfly* for some years, what a fine piece of music it is. Every phrase has meaning, and the texture is admirably economical. It is not padded anywhere. A well-made play with simply drawn characters is explained by music of the most ample clarity. Not once does the composer lose interest in the plot and start writing hubbub. The score is full of apt invention that all serves the play. Since the play, even unaccompanied, is an unfailing tear-jerker, with music of pointed expressivity and masterful cut it becomes a work of great power and no inconsiderable charm, in spite of its lack of even the most elementary intellectual content, or thoughtful tone. *Madama Butterfly* is not a work of art in the class with *Pelléas et Mélisande* or *Don Giovanni*, but it is a masterpiece of effective musical theater. It is a pleasure to have it back in repertory, especially with Albanese singing it.

January 20, 1946

Glamorous Evening

LA BOHÈME, opera in four acts, libretto by *Giuseppe Giacosa* and *Luigi Illica;* music by GIACOMO PUCCINI; second performance of the season at the Metropolitan Opera House last night.

Rodolfo	*Ferruccio Tagliavini* (debut)
Schaunard	*George Cehanovsky*

Benoit; Alcindoro	*Gerhard Pechner*
Mimi	*Licia Albanese*
Parpignol	*Lodovico Oliviero*
Marcello	*Francesco Valentino*
Colline	*Giacomo Vaghi*
Musetta	*Mimi Benzell*
A sergeant	*John Baker*

Conductor, *Cesare Sodero*. Stage Director, *Désiré Defrère*. Chorus Master, *Kurt Adler*.

FERRUCCIO TAGLIAVINI's debut at the Metropolitan Opera House last night brought out an unusually large and enthusiastic audience. Such unrestrained applause has not been heard in that house for some years. It was heart-warming. It was merited, too, for Mr. Tagliavini has a handsome voice and sings better than merely well. With Licia Albanese, as Mimi, and Francesco Valentino, as Marcello, supporting him in first-class style, Puccini's *La Bohème* took on an animation that was in every way enjoyable. Cesare Sodero and these principal artists gave the work, moreover, a genuinely Italianate reading. It was warm, and it did not drag. I suspect, moreover, that the artists responded to the audience's wideawakeness and gave a better show for solid appreciation shown at the outset.

Mr. Tagliavini has a lyric tenor voice, fresh in timbre and not without power. It is a typical Italian voice, frank and not very subtle, but smooth of scale. His singing style is typically Italian, too, though without the ostentation one is accustomed to associate with Italian tenors of an older generation. Mr. Tagliavini sings high and loud with perfect adequacy and no inconsiderable brilliance, but he does not gulp or gasp or gargle salt tears. He is a competent artist, thoroughly straightforward, quite without airs of genius and a little lacking in variety of coloristic vocal effect. To the eye he is plump but manly and a perfectly good actor. He has a pleasing personality, a temperament of no unusual projection.

The dominating quality of his work, besides its genuine competence, both vocal and dramatic, is its youthfulness. He sings like a young man who enjoys singing and who is neither afraid of high notes nor especially proud of them. He has reserves of energy and a great naturalness. Not in a very long time have we heard tenor singing at once so easy and so adequate. He makes no attempt to sing like a baritone, and neither does he croon. At least he did not last night. He even at one point sang a genuine open-throated pianissimo, the first I have heard in Thirty-ninth Street since I started reviewing opera six years ago. So sound an artist could go far. Without going any farther than he has, he can give great pleasure to anybody who likes singing.

Mimi Benzell's Musetta was good to look at, if a little buzzy to the ear. Mr. Valentino sang well, looked well, acted well. His beautiful baritone voice was nicely matched for size with Mr. Tagliavini's and with that of the ever-lovely Miss Albanese. And last night the wonderful thing took place that happens all too rarely these days. Italian singing actors, working under an Italian conductor before an audience that was pretty largely Mediterranean, gave us real Italian opera. Not ham Italian opera, but the real thing, the kind in which the play and music come alive because the cast knows what the show is all about and is singing, every one of them, the same piece. Genuine enjoyment all round was the note of the evening, the glamorous, incandescent kind of enjoyment that makes audiences listen better and artists work better. The performance, for once, seemed unusually short, in consequence.

January 11, 1947

Charade with Music

THE GOLDEN COCKEREL, opera in three acts, music by *Rimsky-Korsakov*, given at the Metropolitan Opera House for the first time last night in the English version of Tatiana Balkoff Drowne of *Bielsky's* original Russian text.

The Queen of Shemakha	*Patrice Munsel*
King Dodon	*Norman Cordon*
General Polkan	*John Gurney*
Prince Guidon	*Richard Manning*
Prince Aphron	*John Baker*
Amelfa	*Margaret Harshaw*
The Astrologer	*Anthony Marlowe*
The Voice of the Golden Cockerel	*Thelma Votipka*

Conductor, *Emil Cooper*. Stage Director, *Désiré Defrère*. Chorus Master, *Konrad Neuger*. Ballet Master, *Laurent Novikoff*.

THE GOLDEN COCKEREL, which was produced last night at the Metropolitan Opera House, is Bielsky's (after Pushkin) *Le Coq d'or* in nursery-rhyme English text and with Donald Duck stage direction. Fortunately it is also Rimsky-Korsakov's lascivious and sparkling score directed by Emil Cooper, who conducted the premières of the work in Moscow in 1909 and later in Paris and in London. Orchestrally the performance is a delight for its animation, clarity, and general authority. Vocally some of it is pretty good, too, especially the work of Patrice Munsel as the Queen of Shemakha. As a piece of sexual and political satire, which I gather its authors intended it to be, the play makes no more sense, as here directed and performed, than a children's performance of *Salome* might.

Miss Munsel is a little young for Oriental seduction scenes. Her acquaintance with such matters, like that of many another young Miss of today, seems to be derived from the burlesque stage by way of the films. She even did a sort of strip tease in the second act with no end of fetching Hollywood vivacity. But she sang like an angel, like a not quite mature angel, still a very, very gifted one.

Her voice has grown in volume since last year. The middle part of it is louder now and quite beautiful. The very top of it, everything above high C, has always been firm and richly brilliant. There is still a region, most of the octave just below high C, the one where coloraturas spend the best part of their singing time, that is wavery. She is far from being mistress of her instrument; but it is a great instrument, or seems to be growing into one. And she has a natural talent for making music with it.

Norman Cordon and Margaret Harshaw sang their parts pleasantly but acted them absurdly, just bouncing about. Mr. Cordon might have been playing Foxy Grandpa. Both showed up to advantage singing in English, however, because with the vowels of their own language to vocalize on, they were quite free of the hot-potato effect that has marred the work of both recently in foreign languages. They sang right out through the face, instead of through the top of the head; and they projected their consonants. The effect was most agreeable.

Miss Munsel's enunciation was excellent, too. So excellent that she nearly brought down the house when in the last act she came forth in her stentorian middle voice with the following literary gem:

"That old man has surely push;
He doesn't beat about the bush!"

March 2, 1945

Lurching and Mugging

SALOME, opera in one act, music by RICHARD STRAUSS, libretto by *Oscar Wilde* in *Hedwig Lachmann's* German version, produced by the New York City Opera Company last night at the New York City Center.

Salome	*Brenda Lewis*
Herodias	*Terese Gerson*
Herod	*Frederick Jagel*
Jochanaan	*Ralph Herbert*
Narraboth	*William Horne*
The page	*Rosalind Nadell*

Five Jews:
   Nathaniel Sprinzena, Frank Murray, Grant Garnell, Allen Stewart, and *Paul Dennis*

Cappadocian	*Edwin Dunning*
A slave	*Frank Mandile*

Two Nazarenes:
   Desire Ligeti and *Lawrence Harwood*
Two soldiers:
   Manfred Hecht and *Arthur Newman*
   Conductor, *Laszlo Halasz.* Stage Director, *Leopold Sachse.* Scenic Designer, *H. A. Condell.*

RICHARD STRAUSS's *Salome,* a musical version of Oscar Wilde's play, was produced last night at the City Center of Music and Drama. The orchestral version used is one for slightly reduced forces, reported to have been made by the composer. The musical execution was shipshape and most agreeable to the ear. The visual production, though no more absurd than most, was a hodgepodge of stylistic elements, running from Assyrian architecture to Hollywood kimonos split down the front and gilt leather G-strings. There were pasteboard goblets aplenty, too, and artificial peaches that got thrown about like pincushions, and for once a realistic head of the prophet. That helped, though Brenda Lewis, who sang the title role, didn't seem to know quite what to do with it when she had got it.

Miss Lewis is a skilled vocalist with a pretty voice. Her singing, save for a few forced moments, was excellent. So was that of Terese Gerson, the Herodias; of Frederick Jagel, the Herod; of Ralph Herbert, the Jochanaan; and of William Horne, as the young Captain who kills himself. The orchestra sounded well, too; and Laszlo Halasz conducted with spirit and an admirable clarity. The whole opera would probably have been a pleasure over the air. But as a stage spectacle it was consistently inept. This is unfortunate, because *Salome* is a highly dramatic piece, lurid, outrageous and thoroughly gripping.

Somebody should teach opera singers not to lurch. This movement is never graceful and rarely convincing. Mr. Jagel did it oftenest last night, though the others indulged when they couldn't think of anything else to do. He suggested Soglow's Little King played by Mr. Zero Mostel, rather than a figure in an erotic tragedy. Miss Lewis did a good deal of lurching, too, and lots of leaning backwards. The constant projecting forward of the pelvis may be a sexy movement, but it is not a sensuous one. It is a concomitant rather of commercialized vice than of seduction. In a role of this kind it betrays, indeed, a certain innocence, a child's concept of the lascivious. And it can easily be comic.

Miss Lewis's Dance of the Seven Veils was full of good will and not wholly lacking in charm, though real style it had none. Where she failed as an actress most gravely was in the final scene with the head. She might have been singing it a lullaby. And she took her last lines standing and looking upward, as if she were playing Joan of Arc. Her miming of this sensational scene was not in any sense puritanical. It was sexy enough, as I said before; but it gave no suggestion of sensuality. No small part of its ineffectiveness came also from her constant attempt to act with the face, a procedure known commonly as "mugging" and one that has no place in opera. In opera the face is used for singing. One acts with the body. It would be interesting to hear this excellent singer in a role more becoming to her age and temperament.

April 17, 1947

After Thirty Years

ARIADNE AUF NAXOS, opera in one act, preceded by a prologue; German text by *Hugo von Hofmannsthal*, music by RICHARD STRAUSS, performed by the New York City Opera Company at the New York City Center. Prologue sung in *Lewis Sydenham's* English translation.

Major-Domo	*Gene Greenwell*
Music Master	*James Pease*
Composer	*Polyna Stoska*
The Tenor; Bacchus	*Vasso Argyris*
An Officer	*Lawrence Harwood*
Dancing Master	*Allen Stewart*
Wigmaker	*Grant Garnell*
Lackey	*Arthur Newman*
Zerbinetta	*Virginia MacWatters*
Prima Donna; **Ariadne**	*Ella Flesch*
Harlequin	*Ralph Herbert*
Scaramuccio	*Hubert Norville*
Truffaldin	*Paul Dennis*
Brighella	*Nathaniel Sprinzena*
Naiad	*Lillian Fawcett*
Dryad	*Rosalind Nadell*
Echo	*Lenore Portnoy*

Conductor, *Laszlo Halasz*. Stage Director, *Leopold Sachse*. Scenic Designer, *H. A. Condell*.

RICHARD STRAUSS's *Ariadne on the Isle of Naxos*, which was given its first professional New York performance last night at the City Center of Music and Drama, is considered by many Strauss fanciers to be its composer's masterpiece. That it is the work of a master there is no doubt. If it lacks, perhaps, the lurid vigor of *Elektra* and *Salome* or the straight sex appeal of *Der Rosenkavalier*, it has a clarity of musical texture that is missing from these earlier works. It is indeed a pleasure to hear Strauss's music pruned of the 10,000 useless notes per act with which he was so long accustomed to clutter up his scores. *Ariadne*, though thin, perhaps, of expressive substance, has great charm, both melodic and harmonic; and its small, clean orchestra is a perpetual delight.

Last night's performance of the work under Laszlo Halasz was a pleasure all round. The orchestra was lovely; the singers sang with style; the staging, if not especially chic, was at the same time neither dull nor clownish. The work was not played for laughs or for easy applause; it was presented as a serious piece of theater. And the audience responded with gratitude to the compliment paid its intelligence.

It responded most of all to Virginia MacWatters, who sang the difficult coloratura aria with a purity of style and an accuracy of pitch unmatched in New York City by any other coloratura soprano during my reviewing years. Second in audience favor was Polyna Stoska, who sang the role of the Composer. Ella Flesch, curiously, did not work at her best as Ariadne. She is a schooled artist, and her voice is a commanding one. But she mostly just stood around looking like the Statue of Liberty and sang flat. The three ladies who waited on her in exile — Lillian Fawcett, Rosalind Nadell, and Lenore Portnoy sang their trios with skill and beauty. James Pease, as the Music Master, was first class in every way.

The work itself, from both the literary and the musical points of view, is what the Marxians would probably call "decadent capitalist art." It is shallow of substance and utterly sophisticated in style. It is a masterful display of learning, skill, and deliberate charm, all luxury and no meat. It evokes the eighteenth century through the conventions of the Reinhardt baroque. It aims, one learns from the librettist Hofmannsthal's own publicity, at a certain profundity, which this writer finds scant, and at a humor which he finds facile. Musically it is an elaborate joke about how much fun it is to play around with the classical techniques.

From any point of view it is good to listen to, because it is in its own way a completely successful work. About what its place in musical history will be a century from now I have no guess. But for thirty years it has had a unique place in the contemporary world of music, and the City Center has contributed to New York's intellectual life by making us acquainted with it. Whether in all those thirty years the Metropolitan Opera, upon whom the responsibility for our operatic culture has chiefly rested, could ever have produced it I do not know. Their setup is, of course, almost unbelievably inefficient; and the work requires skill and lots of rehearsal. In any case, the fact remains that

Ariadne auf Naxos is New York news this morning and its City Center performance musically good news.

October 11, 1946

Carolina *Carmen*

CARMEN JONES, it is agreed by press and public, is a good musical show. But not a few sincere persons, accustomed to hearing Bizet's *Carmen* given by operatic repertory companies in mammoth houses and being a little surprised at the vigor it has when given in the vernacular with a properly rehearsed troupe in a place of reasonable size, are asking themselves, with an excess of scruple, "Is the new version *Carmen?*" and "Is it grand opera?"

This writer's answer to the first question is an enthusiastic yes. The plot is there and the music is there; the whole shape and sequence of the musico-dramatic work are intact. The landscape has been altered from Spain to Carolina, but that is standard operatic procedure. Verdi's *Un Ballo in Maschera* has shuttled back and forth for years between Sweden and Massachusetts. Spain's gypsies have in this case become Carolina's Negro proletariat, and the bull fighter is pugilist. The social parallel is really surprisingly close. And when one considers that the Negroes are here speaking their own language (or at least what passes up North for Negro English) the verisimilitude is even closer than that of Spanish gypsies singing in French. The music is cut some, but that is nothing new in opera. What is new is that the translation has wit, makes sense, and fits the music. It is superior to anything of the kind that I know in English, excepting only the musical translations of Marion Farquhar. All things considered, it seems to me that *Carmen Jones* has at least as much of Bizet's *Carmen* in it, dramatically and musically speaking, as the current production by the Metropolitan Opera Company has, for all that the latter boasts a bigger and better orchestra plus Sir Thomas Beecham to conduct it.

The answer to the other question is no. *Carmen Jones* is not grand opera. Neither is the Bizet work. The transformations that have been operated on the French piece have been mostly in the way of restoring to it its original style and dimensions. *Carmen* is no more grand opera than *The Daughter of the Regiment* is. It is *opéra-comique,* differing from the *opéras-comiques* of Grétry and Boïeldieu and Auber only by the literary genre of its libretto, which is that of realistic proletarian melodrama. This genre had never been used previously with any success in either light opera or grand. There had been romantic melodrama operas of the cape-and-dagger school and proletarian idylls in pastoral vein; but lust and murder among the workers and hijackers was Bizet's revolutionary contribution to the musical theater. Wagner's return to gods and goddesses was reactionary by comparison. The French proletarian operas of Bruneau and Charpentier, the *Lady Macbeth* of Shostakovich, and the whole of Italian *verismo* — the works of Mascagni and Leoncavallo — as well as Gershwin's *Porgy and Bess,* are all Bizet's progeny. The works of Puccini and Montemezzi and Alfano, too, derive from him rather than from Verdi their musical technique of direct dramatic impact, though their subject matter involves a certain return to high Romanticism in the fact that their melodramas mostly take place among persons of some economic substance. Bizet's *Carmen* is a realistic proletarian melodramatic *opéra-comique* with lots of spoken dialogue, and so is Billy Rose's *Carmen Jones.* The Metropolitan production, though orchestrally and even vocally, for the most part, superior, is less true to the genre of the original piece and far less convincingly presented.

This does not mean that the new production is a masterpiece. I think it suffers a little from New York theater disease, a nervous habit of building up excitement too quickly. Most of our musicals are less interesting after the intermission than before. There is a pretty tasteless Brazilian ballet, too, in the second part, in which Negroes who can really dance well are required to dance badly because somebody thought that would be funny. Or perhaps because it was considered that they couldn't really carry off the Brazilian style, though what Brazilian dancing is if not Negroid I wouldn't know. Some of the solo singing, though no doubt the best available, is less expert than the ensemble work. The show has its disappointments; but taken all round, it is the kind of musical show I wish there were more of and the kind of opera we certainly need lots and lots more of.

The production has two elements of authenticity. One is Oscar Hammerstein's translation, and the other is the Negro company. All the rest is Broadway, good Broadway, but nothing very powerful. The fitting of new words to old music, however, as Mr. Hammerstein has done it, is ingenious, neat, and wholly triumphant. It should serve as a model, or at least as a minimum standard of excellence, for other efforts of the kind. It certainly makes the *Magic Flute* translation used at the Metropolitan sound silly, though this latter is not by current operatic standards a bad piece of work.

The Negro singers, as always, make opera credible. And, as always, they make music shine. They have physical beauty of movement, natural distinction, and grace. Musically they have rhythm, real resonance, excellent pitch, perfect enunciation, and full understanding of the operatic convention. They never look bored or out of place on a stage or seem inappropriately cast for any musical style. I had thought in advance that the Spanish coloring of Bizet's score might prove to be the intractable element in this adaptation of it to American Negro life. Not at all. It swears less with its Negro subject than the Viennese and Broadway elements do in Gershwin's *Porgy*. The people on the stage might very credibly have Caribbean blood in them, so naturally does this Spanish half-caste music (written by a Frenchman) espouse Negro rhythmic firmness and Negro vocal *melisma*. This is not the first Negro opera production Broadway has seen nor the most distinguished. But it is a contribution to the repertory of that permanent Negro opera company that is going to provide the solution one day for all our opera problems.

December 5, 1943

Farce and Melodrama

THE BALLET SOCIETY, new productions of two chamber operas with book and music by GIAN-CARLO MENOTTI, The Telephone (or L'Amour à Trois), opera-buffa in one act (world premiere), and The Medium, tragedy in two acts, last night at the Heckscher Theatre.

THE TELEPHONE

| Lucy | Marilyn Cotlow |
| Ben | Paul Kwartin |

THE MEDIUM

Monica	Evelyn Keller
Toby, a mute	Leo Coleman
Madame Flora (Baba)	Marie Powers
Mrs. Gobineau	Beverly Dame
Mr. Gobineau	Paul Kwartin
Mrs. Nolan	Virginia Beeler

Conductor, *Leon Barzin*. Stage direction by the composer. Scenery and costumes by *Horace Armistead*. Musicians from Ballet Society Orchestra.

THE BALLET SOCIETY produced last night at the Heckscher Theater two operas by Gian-Carlo Menotti, one of them, *The Telephone*, a world première. The other, *The Medium*, had been given for the first time last May at the Brander Mathews Theater in Columbia University by the Columbia Theater Associates. Both are first-class musico-theatrical works. The first is an opera buffa, light and full of laughter. The second is a tragedy in melodramatic vein that is the most gripping operatic narrative this reviewer has witnessed in many a year.

The Medium is about the private life of a woman who evokes by trickery, for paying customers, visions and voices of the dead. Caught up in her own psychic ambience, and aided by alcohol, she imagines she feels a hand on her throat. Terrified by the experience, she renounces her racket and exposes it to her clients. They refuse to believe that what they had wanted to believe in was false. At this point, the medium goes hysterical and murders a dumb boy who was previously part of her household and an aid in her trickery setup.

No such reduction of the plot can give an idea of how absorbing this work is. I have heard it three times and it never fails to hold me enthralled. Mr. Menotti's libretto, which he wrote himself, and his music form a unit that is deeply touching and terrifying. And if the second act is a little reminiscent as theater (though not as music) of the second act of Puccini's *La Tosca*, the piece in no way suffers by comparison with that infallible piece of stage craft. The play wrings every heart string, and so does the music. I cannot conceive the whole work otherwise than as destined for a long and successful career.

The Telephone, or *L'Amour à Trois*, is a skit about a young man whose girl friend is so busy talking to people on the telephone that the only way he can get her attention for a proposal of marriage is to go out to the corner drugstore and call her up himself. It is gay and funny and completely humane. Both operas, indeed, are infused with a straightforward humanity that is a welcome note of sincerity in contemporary operatic composition. Their librettos are skillfully made, and their music is skillfully composed. But that is not the main point. Their unusual efficacy as operas comes from their frankly Italianate treatment of ordinary human beings as thoroughly interesting.

The visual production of *The Medium* was one of unusual distinction. The casting of both operas was excellent. Particularly notable for both singing and acting were Marie Powers, who sang the title role in *The Medium* (her predecessor, Claramae Turner, was immediately engaged by the Metropolitan Opera), and Evelyn Keller, who sang the part of her daughter. Leo Coleman, who mimed the mute, was admirable also. Both operas were decorated and costumed more than prettily by Horace Armistead. Mr. Menotti, who directed them, in addition to having written both words and music, proved himself no less an expert in this domain than in the others. The musical direction of Leon Barzin was, as usual, impeccable.

Evviva Menotti!

February 19, 1947

Acting to Song

WHEN Americans speak words on a stage they act them out in one way, and when they sing they mostly act them out in another. It seems to be considered normal procedure, especially among our women actors, to play down the dramatic characterization of any singing role and to play up at the same time their personal charms in a way that is not considered proper at all by European stage folk. For these latter tragedy, comedy, farce, realistic drama, the poetic recital, opera, operetta, musical comedy, fantasy, vaudeville, torch singing, and even the cinema, however much the cadence of their verbal articulation and the style

of their pantomime may vary (for each has its manner of elocution and its repertory of appropriate gesture), are all branches of
the mummer's art, since they all involve impersonation.

Now the first rule of convincing impersonation is that one
must not try to impersonate more than one character at a time.
American singing actors, however, like American film actors,
seem more and more to be dealing in double characterization.
This is effective in films, because the films, especially the American films, do not aim much at creating an illusion of reality but
rather at creating a dream, with all that that implies of obscurity
as to what it is really about. (A film, like a dream, takes place in
the dark, and for the most part in black and white, whereas live
theater plays in a gamut of light and of color.) Miss Helen
Hayes, for instance, does nothing in *Harriet* except to present
as clearly and convincingly as she is able (and she is very able)
the character of Harriet Beecher Stowe. Miss Gertrude Lawrence,
on the other hand, though an able actress, too, of spoken parts,
played *Lady in the Dark* as a double role. Only part of the time
did she impersonate an editress in need of psychoanalysis; she
also played Gertrude Lawrence up to the hilt. Not Gertrude
Lawrence as she is in private life, either, but a fictitious Gertrude
Lawrence, a personality of pure glamour.

In the course, one evening last week, of a genteel pub crawl,
it came into my reflections that double characterization has probably crept into American singing by way of advertising, where
everything, from lollipops to laxatives, is described in the language of love. In any case, it is pretty common among American
singers and quite rare among the Europeans. At an establishment called "Paris qui Chante," which cultivates the French
style, I found the *chanteuses* no less charming from the fact that
the songs they sang were the songs they acted. At "The Blue
Angel" I found the American style in flower. One young woman
sang a straightforward sentimental song while her face and body
acted the role of Delilah. Then she sang about a tough gold-
digger. But to the deaf she could only have been impersonating
somebody pretty hoity-toity, say a suburban hostess bidding
good-by to tea guests.

At "Casablanca" the style was frank again. There was a pair
of ballroom exhibition dancers that did ballroom exhibition dancing. And Miss Muriel Rahn, from *Carmen Jones*, sang a series of

opera solos absolutely straight, very beautifully indeed, and without electrical amplification. She sang the three great airs from *Carmen* in the Hammerstein translation and one from *Martha* in a not dissimilar literary revision. At a later show she sang the "*Vissi d'arte*" from *La Tosca* in Italian and a piece from *Porgy and Bess*. Not only was it a pleasure to hear really expert vocalism (which is rare enough anywhere) in a night club, but it was deeply comforting to encounter a young American actress who does not seem to feel that the musical medium justifies an indirect style of character presentation.

Our singing actresses would do well to observe more carefully the work of the European *chanteuses* and other musical entertainers, as well as of the great European opera singers, of whom we still have several among us. The force of the impersonations that these artists project is due to the fact that, whatever the musical style or the dramatic medium may be, a single, complete characterization is the thing that is being projected. Half the trouble with our younger singers at the Metropolitan Opera, for instance, is that nobody seems to have told them that they do not have to do anything on a stage but the role they are doing. The art of acting is not especially recondite. The chief techniques involved are speaking and singing, and those can be perfected by study. For the rest, a simple understanding of the motives and sentiments implied by the text will do wonders toward creating a convincing impersonation. But any assertion, conscious or otherwise, of one's own personality and still more the attempt to add a fabricated platform charm to dramatic characterization will diminish the force of dramatic impact and destroy the illusion that is the basic reality of the stage.

January 24, 1944

RESPECTING COMPOSERS

Choral Effectives

CHORAL music almost never sounds well in performance. Chamber music, orchestral music, even the opera, can be produced efficiently and satisfactorily, given experienced workmen and enough rehearsal. That is because everybody involved knows the purpose of the enterprise, which is to produce the music in hand efficiently and satisfactorily. In choruses this purpose is only a part of the business, the other part, probably the more exigent one, being to provide musical exercise for the participants.

Amateurism, in other words, is inherent to the present setup. There are professional choruses, of course, though not many. And they perform less well, for the most part, than the amateur ones. In the instrumental field, in recital repertory, in the theater, though there is much good amateur music making, the standards of execution that prevail are those established by professionals. And by professionals I mean exactly what is meant by professionals in any activity; I mean they receive money. But in choral singing, and this is true all over the world, the highest standards of efficiency are those set by amateurs, by societies in which the members pay for the privilege of participating.

The advantages of amateurism in the choral field are well known. Nothing is so lifeless as a professional chorus. Amateurs put passion into their work; they will rehearse indefinitely; they adore their conductor. They love the whole business. Indeed, there are few greater sources of lasting satisfaction than the practice of communal singing. It is the very richness of the experience that produces both the virtues and the defects of our great choral organizations.

The chief trouble with these is that they have no standard size. The modern world has never arrived at any agreement about what number of choral executants makes for maximum musical efficiency, for the very simple reason that in our best choral societies, all of which are amateur, the privilege of participation is recognized as of such great value, culturally and humanly, that it is not considered loyal to refuse it to anyone who can meet the technical requirements. Since these do not need, for the best execution, to be very high, all our societies tend toward hypertrophy; they get too big for efficiency. They begin small; and as long as they have only fifty or sixty members, they do beautiful work. Then they start growing, overflowing on every stage; and nothing stops that growth but the architecture of Carnegie Hall, the limits of how many can be crowded on the platform behind a symphony orchestra.

By this time they have lost their flexibility and most of their effective repertory. They look very impressive in their robes as they sit there waiting through three movements of Beethoven's Ninth Symphony just to stand up in the last and force their voices. Gone by now are the days when they could sing the great choral literature of pre-Baroque and modern times. They go through a certain amount of it, even reducing their number for an occasional work that just won't let itself be sung by 250 people. But once they have become 250 people, their chief work is serving as an adjunct to symphony orchestras. They cannot deflate. And since at that size nothing sounds well but shouting and whispering, they lose first their beauty of tone, next their variety of tone, next their diction, with which goes all rhythm and preciseness of attack, and finally their ability to sing on pitch, leaving to the orchestral musicians the responsibility of making clear to the audience the harmony of any piece. They just shout and whisper and stand there looking impressive in cassocks or gowns or in dark suits and maidenly white dresses.

These thoughts occurred to me the other evening at a concert in Carnegie Hall of the Collegiate Chorale. This excellent organization is just beginning its downward path. All it has lost so far is tonal beauty. Our next best outfit, the Westminster Choir, a semiprofessional organization made up from students of the Westminster Choir School in Princeton, has gone one step farther; it has had no diction for five years. The New York Oratorio Society, once, I am told, musically high class, has nothing left but a medium pitch average. The Harvard Glee Club, twenty-five years ago a virtuoso group in its own right, is now, so far as musical values are concerned, only an occasional tail to the Boston Symphony Orchestra's kite. The Dessoff Choirs have gone symphonic too. They have not much tone left; but their pitch, rhythm, and diction are still good.

The truth is that almost none of the great choral literature, ancient or modern, will stand blowing up. It is chamber music of personalized expression and high coloristic refinement. This applies to all liturgical music and also to the choral works of J. S. Bach, though we have become so accustomed to hearing these sung by depersonalized armies, like the Schola Cantorum and the Bach Choir of Bethlehem, Pennsylvania, that few living musicians know the brilliance and real power they can have when produced with limited effectives. The only part of great choral literature, as something over and beyond orchestral works with choral interpolations, that can stand numbers is the oratorio. Handel can be blown up both chorally and orchestrally and still sound well. It doesn't have to be, but it can. That is because it is broadly dramatic in conception. It is theater music, the theater's only first-class contribution to choral art.

If music were the only aim in choral singing, we could standardize the procedures and improve the sound of it. Unfortunately the social, the religious, the cultural purposes served are no less valuable. And so we have a whole literature of the most sensitive music in the world shouted at us by a football cheering section. There is nothing to be done about it. One cannot argue with a social custom. Nor would one wish to hamper the functioning of one so rich. But as a reviewer attending concerts regularly and listening, as George Antheil used to say, not so much *to* music as *for* it, I am more often than not, at choral ceremonies, reminded of one of the season's classical sentiments. I salute you with it, choral devotees, even as I wish that we critics might perhaps, just for Christmas, occasionally be greeted so. "God rest you merry, gentlemen! Let nothing you dismay."

December 23, 1945

Majestic but Inefficient

BACH CHOIR, OF BETHLEHEM, *Ifor Jones* conductor, performance of Bach's Mass in B minor last night at Carnegie Hall, with members of the Philadelphia Orchestra and the following assisting artists: *Ruth Diehl*, soprano; *Lilian Knowles*, contralto; *Lucius Metz*, tenor; *Calvin Marsh*, baritone; *Edwin Steffe*, bass; and *E. Power Biggs*, organist.

THE BACH CHOIR OF BETHLEHEM, Pennsylvania, which has not visited New York in twenty-five years, brought its full effectives to Carnegie Hall last night. These consist nowadays of about two hundred choristers, trained and directed by Ifor Jones; some sixty members of the Philadelphia Orchestra; E. Power Biggs, organist; and the necessary vocal soloists, these last varying from season to season. The evening's music was the work that music lovers have long traveled in May to Bethlehem for hearing sung by this choir, Bach's Mass in B minor.

Let us praise last night's performance right off as the best of its kind this Bach lover has ever heard. Its kind is that invented by Mendelssohn, namely, a transformation, or distortion, or, if you like, transfiguration of Bach's intricate music for small forces into a massive Romantic oratorio like Mendelssohn's own *Elijah* or *Saint Paul*. The appropriateness of the operation need not be questioned, since for a century now it has been considered acceptable by music lovers all over the world. It has been recognized, however, for forty or more years as a distortion, and a grave one. This writer, for one, considers it unfortunate that so much devotion, sound musical skill, and publicity should be mobilized for the preserving of a tradition that has long been known to be historically and esthetically false.

The falsity lies in the inability of that number of executants to render this particular music, which is full of linear complexity, with a reasonable degree of exactitude. Any chorus of two hundred can make a majestic noise; and Mr. Jones's chorus makes the most agreeable, the most brilliant and bright-sounding choral fortissimo I have ever heard. But when they get to the intricate and rapid passages they go fuzzy, just like any other group of that size. Moreover, the very grandeur and power with which they sing the choral numbers inevitably makes the solos sound puny.

Faced with this prospect, the soloists attempt to sing their arias louder than they can do correctly. Nobody living can sing those solos with power vocalism. They are fluid, florid, and melismatic; the only possible way to make them expressive, to stay on pitch, and to blend the vocal line with the instrumental obbligato that accompanies it is to sing lightly, with a marked nasal resonance. But this produces chamber music and makes the massive choir sound coarse. So the choral conductor cannot let them do it. Thus a full half of the Mass, the solo half, ends by sounding strained, incompetent, and foolish. Since a good half of the choral numbers are already overstuffed and not sounding at their best, this leaves only about one fourth of the work making the kind of musical clarity that we all know Bach's music should make.

Hearing the work at all, of course, is a major musical experience. And hearing even so much as a quarter of it sound forth so frankly and so confidently as the Bethlehem group makes it do is reason for throwing anybody's hat in air. But how much richer and grander it would be if Mr. Jones would cut his chorus down about eighty per cent and his orchestra by half, spend more time and thought on the soloists, and move the whole thing to Town Hall. The benefit to Bach would be enormous.

February 19, 1946

In the Royal Style

COLLEGIATE CHORALE, *Robert Shaw,* conductor, performance of Bach's Mass in B minor last night in the Hunter College Auditorium, with chorus of sixty and chamber orchestra. Soloists: *Ann McKnight,* and *June Gardner,* sopranos; *Lydia Summers,* contralto; *Lucius Metz,* tenor; and *Paul Matthen,* baritone. Harpsichordist, *Ernst Victor Wolf;* organist *Ernest White;* solo trumpet, *William Vacchiano.*

THE COLLEGIATE CHORALE, conducted by Robert Shaw, gave last night in the Hunter College Auditorium an uncut performance of Bach's B-minor Mass. Though this lasted nigh on to three hours, your reporter experienced no fatigue and observed no sleepers. Indeed, it has not previously been his privilege to hear so thoroughly delightful a reading of this majestic work, though he has attended many. How Mr. Shaw worked his miracle on this most recalcitrant of pieces is the subject of this morning's sermon.

He started by organizing his musical effectives in proportions not unlike those available in the German eighteenth-century courts, for one of which the work was originally planned. A chorus of sixty mixed voices (American amateur female sopranos are not as loud as trained German boys), an orchestra of strictly chamber proportions, a harpsichord, an organ used with extreme discretion, and the necessary soloists were quite sufficient for volume and not excessive for the florid style. He further reduced the orchestral effectives in accompanying the solos and duets to single instruments or, in the case of string backgrounds, to two on a part. And then he rehearsed the choruses for lightness and clarity, the vocal soloists for harmonious blending with the instrumental soloists that accompany them.

As a result, the accompanied solos, in reality small chamber ensembles, took their place in the choral framework very much as the concertino group in a concerto grosso is set off against the larger instrumental body. The work became thus a dialogue, an antiphony, each kind of music being beautiful in its own way, the two kinds giving amplitude and perspective to the whole.

That whole turns out to be, as one might have expected, not at all a giant Lutheran cantata, nor yet a liturgical Mass, but a grand and sumptuous court oratorio on the subject of the Mass. Its grandeur lies in its vast proportions and in its completely simple expressivity, its sumptuousness in the extreme and formal floridity of the musical texture. Its layout is huge but perfectly clear; its style is the ultimate in ornateness. It is at once enormous and graceful, like the palace architecture of its time, complete with gardens, ponds, statues, and vistas.

Mr. Shaw preserved these proportions and all their grace by simply limiting his forces to a size capable of achieving grace. He added, moreover, a grace of his own in the firm lilt of his beat. His rhythmic alacrity evoked a court ballet. The *"Cum sancto spiritu"* that ends the Gloria was as gay as a hornpipe; and the bass aria, *"Et in spiritum sanctum,"* from the Credo, tripped along none the less reverently for being light on its feet. Just as the alto Agnus Dei might easily have rocked a cradle.

Rhythmic courage, tonal exactitude, pretty balances, and sweetness all round allowed the proportions of the work to take on full majesty without any heaviness. If Mr. Shaw and his admirable colleagues will give us such a performance annually, Bach's choral masterpieces will cease in short order to be merely edifying and become humane, as I am sure, from last night's performance of the Mass, they were conceived to be. The sacred music of the great masters is not designed to shake humanity; that is a function of the theater. It is made to please God by fine workmanship. This one was planned, as well, to get its author a job at the Saxon court.

January 29, 1947

Beethoven's Fifth

BEETHOVEN's C-minor Symphony is the most famous piece of orchestral music in the world. Everybody knows it; everybody loves it; everybody admires it. Other pieces have their special charms and their devoted publics, but this one is accepted by all as the world masterpiece of monumental abstract, or "absolute," music. For the grandeur and simplicity of its melodic materials, the nobility of its formal proportions, and the forthrightness of its expression it has been esteemed throughout the Western world for over a century now as a sort of Parthenon among symphonies. Yet what it means nobody really knows. It has been as much argued about as *Hamlet,* and it remains to this day as movingly obscure a work.

The Germans long ago associated its opening phrases with their favorite idea of Fate Knocking at the Door. The French have always taken the work as a whole to be connected in some way with political liberalism. It was so completely appropriated as a theme song, in fact, by French socialists of the Second International that adherents of the Third and Fourth have tended rather to keep quiet about its possible political significance. Of late more conservative politicians have taken it over as the slogan, or symbol, of military victory, specifically the victory of the United Nations.

The Germans were clumsy not to think of this first; the victory idea would have fitted perfectly with their already popular interpretation of the piece as having to do with fate. It could have become thus a forecast of their "manifest destiny." Perhaps they felt its author was not quite the right man to put forward as the advocate of unbridled submission to authority. In any case, their propagandists have pretty much let the work alone. Whether ours would have done well to let it alone, too, was the subject of considerable reflection on your reviewer's part week before last, when George Szell conducted the Philharmonic-Symphony Orchestra through a thoroughly demagogic and militarized version of it.

If thinking of the work as embodying faith and hope has helped conquered nations to resist tyranny, that is all to the good. An energizing moral result is more valuable than any misreading of the composer's specific thought is dangerous. Besides, the piece will recover from its present military service just as easily as it has from its past metaphysical and political associations. But as a musician I was interested to observe the amount of distortion that Mr. Szell was obliged to impose on the work in order to make it seem to be representing military struggle and final victory.

There is no intrinsic reason, in this work or in any other, for considering contrast to mean conflict. The expression of strength, even of rudeness, in one chief theme of a piece and of pathos or tenderness in another does not mean that there is a war going on between the two sentiments. The highly contrasted materials of the Fifth Symphony have always seemed to me as complementary rather than conflicting. They make it whole and humane, the complete picture of a man. And I cannot find in the last movement of it, for all its triumphal trumpets, any representation, thematic or otherwise, of the victory of either sentiment. I find, rather, an apotheosis, in which the two are transformed into a third expression, which is one of optimism and confidence, a glorious but still dynamic serenity. Neither assertiveness nor lyricism wins; they simply decide to co-operate.

This is no picture of military victory. It is the purest Hegelian dialectic, by which thesis and antithesis unite to form a third element, or synthesis. It may be an enlightened way of resolving contrasts, or even of conflicts, this using of them as complementary floodlights toward a general luminosity. And it may be an enlightened way of envisaging postwar problems, including Germany itself, though I am suspicious of the Hegelian dialectic, which lends itself to much trickiness in handling. Like most other philosophic methods, it can be made to give any result the handler desires. But in no case is it involved with anybody's unconditional surrender. It offers exactly the opposite kind of solution to a military victory. It is a peace proposition all round. Nowhere in Beethoven's Fifth Symphony, moreover, is there any suggestion of military operations, though other works of his portray them plentifully.

In order to throw the symphony into a key of direct action, Mr. Szell has been obliged to emphasize the assertiveness of the masculine material and to sort of slip over the significance of its tender and gentle passages. He made the strings play loud and rough, with that fierce impact that the Philharmonic strings achieve so admirably. He managed to keep the horns, with some difficulty, up to a reasonable balance with these for three movements. With the appearance of the trombones, at the beginning of the last movement, the horns appeared as hopelessly outclassed in the weight-throwing contest as the woodwinds had been from the beginning. The whole disequilibrium made Beethoven sound no end authoritative and didactic as a composer, which he certainly was, but hopelessly incompetent as an orchestrator, which he was not. And it is exactly the musical ineffectiveness of the orchestral contrasts that proved, in spite of the moral impressiveness of the rendering, that violence was being done to the spirit of the work, whatever one may consider this to be.

Lots of people don't mind that sort of thing at any time; it rather amuses them. And nobody at all minds when it serves a national emergency. We were all interested, I think, to hear this piece played right up to the hilt as a sword of psychological warfare, as the symbol of military victory that it has come to represent in Allied strategy. I doubt if a more thoroughgoing job of the kind could be done on it; certainly none has. And now that military victory seems to be imminent in the European theater, where the Fifth Symphony has its chief psychological utility, it is hardly to be expected that other conductors will attempt to carry it much farther in this direction. It is always a satisfaction to have visited the ultimate outpost of anything; and it is a pleasure to have viewed once this O, so familiar piece in a new light, however false. But the expedition is about over now, and I imagine that all the conductors, including Mr. Szell, will be getting back to Beethoven's plain markings, or else inventing a new distortion of them to please other times.

March 18, 1945

Brahms without Bathos

PHILADELPHIA ORCHESTRA, *Eugene Ormandy*, conductor, last New York concert of the season last night in Carnegie Hall.

ACADEMIC FESTIVAL OVERTURE	BRAHMS
SYMPHONY NO. 3, IN F MAJOR	BRAHMS
SYMPHONY NO. 2, IN D MAJOR	BRAHMS

"BRAHMS is so dependable," said a musician's wife at last night's concert of the Philadelphia Orchestra. Certainly he filled Carnegie Hall at the beginning with customers and at the end with cheers. For the latter, Eugene Ormandy and his orchestra were, of course, in part responsible, because they read the all-Brahms program with a sweetness and an alacrity all too rare in current performances of this master's work. Nothing was soggy or heavy in their lyricism. Two symphonies, the Second and the Third, had wind in their sails from beginning to end. The *Academic Festival Overture*, which presents no problem of animation, was no less a delight for being by nature a piece easy to infuse with spirit.

The Brahms symphonies do not support becomingly much dalliance. Richly impregnated with sentiment, they are nevertheless works of predominantly rhetorical structure and require a continuous forward movement if they are to be apprehended as whole pieces, and not merely as plum cakes from which one picks out for immediate enjoyment the juicier morsels. Their structure is loose but real. Excessive lingering over the vast outlay of expressive detail that accompanies it is as injurious to their noble proportions as insufficient care for the rounded execution of that detail can be. They need loving care, a light hand, and a dreamlike continuity. Otherwise they bog down and have to be rescued at the climactic moments by an overinsistence that destroys the natural emphasis of their grand but leisurely build-up.

Just such care and such a hand were Mr. Ormandy's last night. Seldom has the length of the Brahms symphonies seemed less insistent to this listener, their present public favor more deserved. The Second and Third were not only beautiful, as they have always been. They were easy to listen to. A just balance between expeditious tempos and expressivity of detail, aided by orchestral balances of perfect transparency, gave them a clarity and a luminosity all unusual to them.

That luminosity was Eugene Ormandy's achievement. It is not in Brahms's scoring, which is neither bright in color nor entirely limpid. Excessive doubling of woodwinds in octaves and insufficient uncovering of expressive clarinet or bassoon phrases are characteristic of Brahms's orchestral style. These habits are not necessarily inefficient, for they have an undeniable charm. But they do make it difficult for a conductor to keep the predominantly grayish texture of Brahms's woodwind writing from going muddy. Mr. Ormandy's success in avoiding this sonorous pitfall was as notable last night as his triumph in achieving through reasonable tempos and a forward-moving rhythm eloquence without bathos, song without sobbing, magniloquence and authority without any bluster or bluff.

April 2, 1947

Bruckner

PHILHARMONIC-SYMPHONY ORCHESTRA, *Artur Rodzinski,* conductor, concert in Carnegie Hall last night. Assisting pianist, *Rudolf Serkin.*

OVERTURE, "CORIOLANUS	BEETHOVEN
SYMPHONY No. 7	BRUCKNER
PIANO CONCERTO No. 3	BEETHOVEN

ANTON BRUCKNER, whose Seventh Symphony was played last night in Carnegie Hall by the Philharmonic-Symphony Orchestra under Artur Rodzinski, became a cause in his own lifetime and has remained one ever since. The public has never either accepted or rejected him. Musicians have always loved or hated his music; they have never quite classified it. And yet its virtues and its weaknesses are admitted by all.

A high songfulness in the melody of it is one of its charms. A great suavity of harmonic figuration (one can scarcely call it counterpoint) is another. A real seriousness of thought and a certain amount of purity of spirit it undoubtedly has. There is nothing vulgar, cheap, or meretricious about it. And it sounds extremely well; it is graciously written.

On the other hand, the eight symphonies, which constitute the major body of Bruckner's work, are none of them well integrated formally; they barely hang together. And their unvarying pattern of four-measure phrases, brings them, like Cesar Franck's two-measure monotony, dangerously close to a doggerel meter. Also, their melodic material, for all its grace, is derivative. Schubert, Brahms, and Wagner are never wholly absent from the memory as one listens. The music is intended, I think, to feel like Brahms and to sound like Wagner; and unfortunately it more often than not does just that.

It does another thing, however, which is probably not intentional but which gives it what personal flavor it has. It imitates, by orchestral means, organ registration. Bruckner uses his brasses exactly as an organist uses the reed stops; and he uses the woodwind more often than not as a choir-organ, or *positif.* His masterful cleanliness in the antiphonal deployment of the different kinds of sound is the work of a great organ player, which he was. The looseness of his formal structures is due, no doubt, to the same professional formation, as is certainly his unvarying use of the apocalypatic climax to finish off his longer works.

There is a pious theatricality about all Bruckner's symphonies that, combined with his constant reverence toward his masters, makes them most attractive. They represent esthetically a philosophy of quietism, musically the ultimate of humility. They rest one; they are perfect to daydream to. Of real originality they have, I think, very little to offer.

April 6, 1945

MacDowell's Music

REVISITING the music of Edward MacDowell, through copies found in a borrowed house, was one of the pleasures of your reviewer's late summer vacation. What the larger works would sound like nowadays — the two Suites for Orchestra, the two piano concertos, and the four piano sonatas — he does not know, because he has not for many years handled their scores; and they have almost disappeared from our metropolitan programs. But the shorter piano works — the *Woodland Sketches,* the *New England Sketches,* and the *Sea Pieces* — have kept an extraordinary freshness through the years. Rereading them brought the reflection that although no living American would have written them in just that way (the Wagnerian harmonic texture having passed out of vogue), no living American quite *could* have written them, either.

Let us take them for what they are, not for what they are not. They are landscapes mostly, landscapes with and without figures, literary or historical evocations, *morceaux de genre.* The test of such pieces is their power of evocation. Couperin, Mendelssohn, Schumann, and Debussy are the great masters of genre painting in music, Grieg, Smetana, and possibly Albéniz or Villa-Lobos its lesser luminaries. MacDowell might well rank with these last if he had had access to a body of folklore comparable in extent to theirs, an access that Americans do have, in fact, now. He divined the problems of style that face American composers, but he was not able to solve them singlehanded. So he borrowed more from German sources than he would have liked, I think, and more than anybody has to do today.

Nevertheless, the scenes he describes are vivid. His rhythmic contours evoke the stated subject quickly, accurately. No other American composer has painted a wild rose or an iceberg, a water lily or a deserted farmhouse so neatly. The rendering is concise, the outline definite. No piece is a rewriting of any other. Each is itself, economical, elegant, clearly projected. The impersonality of the procedure is proof of the author's sincerity; its evocative power is proof of his high skill as a craftsman. MacDowell did not leave his mark on music as a stylist; he left us merely a repertory of unforgettable pieces, all different from one another and all charming. And he left to American composers an example of clear thought and objective workmanship that has been an inspiration to us all.

There is a movement on foot toward influencing the American Academy of Arts and Sciences to place his bust in the Hall of Fame at New York University. Stephen Foster is the only writer of music there honored at present. MacDowell could not be in better company, because his music, like that of Foster, is part of every American's culture who has any musical culture. Everybody has played it, loved it, remembered it. Just as no student who ever attended MacDowell's classes at Columbia University ever forgot the master's penetrating observations about music, no musician or no music lover has ever forgotten the delicate firmness of MacDowell's melody, the exactitude with which his rhythm (and his piano figuration, too) depicts the picturesque. To have become, whether by sheer genius for music making, as in Foster's case, or, as in MacDowell's, by the professional exercise of a fully trained gift and by an integrity of attitude unequaled in our musical history, part and parcel of every musical American's musical thought is, in any meaning of the term, it seems to me, immortality.

November 5, 1944

The American Song

ENGLISH-SPEAKING singers are trained and grow to maturity on one of the most curious musical literatures in the world. German vocalists cut their professional teeth on the lieder of Romantic masters and, if the voice is strong, on airs from Weber and Wagner. The Italians, to a man (or woman), sing Puccini and Verdi and very little else. The French have their Fauré, their Gounod, and their fragments from Massenet. All this is perfectly reputable music. The Continent has its popular religious pieces, too, like Faure's *The Palms,* Adam's *Minuit Chrétien,* and Bach's *My Heart Ever Faithful,* and its glorified folklore like Irish mother songs and Italian boat pieces.

But just cross the Channel, and you find that the basic vocal repertory is not either the classics or the indigenous folk lyric. It is a commercial product known variously as "ballads" or "art songs" or just "songs," though it is not in a proper sense any of these things. You hear it in homes, at banquets, in recitals, and over the BBC. In its manlier forms it is a hearty baritone number about how "when we were young and I went down to Rio." Its tender mood deals with gardens and somebody referred to as "YOUUU." For a light touch children are introduced who resist medicine or dislike the cook, though they never go so far as to refuse spinach. The American version of this vast Anglo-Saxon musical literature admires trees and sunsets, believes that marriages are made in heaven, faces the future with confidence, and enjoys playing cowboy.

There is nothing wrong, of course, about any of these ideas. They represent ethnic aspirations and touch infallibly the English-speaking heart. What is curious about the musical literature in which they are embodied is its stylistic vulgarity, its technical and esthetic ineptitude. The literary aspect of it, though often banal in verbiage, is as to sentiment perfectly sound and humane. But take a look, I ask you, at the musical settings; or listen to them at recitals. A sunrise is described in the idiom of *Tristan und Isolde,* trout fishing in that of *Pelléas et Mélisande.* A nursery incident may be blown up till it suggests *The Sorcerer's Appren-*

tice. As for mating, you would imagine the whole population sex-starved if you believed in the amorous intensity of our "art-song" harmonizations. The musical vulgarity of the literature I am describing is due, as a matter of fact, not only to its exaggerated passional make-believe but to its practice of describing everything, literally everything, in the musical language of love.

The stuff needs only comparison with the Continental equivalent for the technical ineptitude to be patent. The rhythmic inflections of the English language are more often than not correctly observed and neatly dramatized. But vowel quantities are handled with as complete disregard for their exigence as could well be imagined. An otherwise skillful song by the late Carl Engel asks that three beats of slowish time, plus a retard, be occupied to pronounce the word *stop.* And one by Bainbridge Crist, quoted in this composer's far from uninteresting brochure, *The Art of Setting Words to Music,* asks that the word *kiss* be held on a high F for something like five seconds. If you think my criticism finicky, just try this trick out; and you will discover that the result is neither English nor music.

The esthetic fault most commonly committed in American vocal music is the confusion of genres. Setting a simple love lyric as if it were an operatic aria removes all poignancy from the poem. Dramatic expression in music requires a dramatic situation in the text. The Continental song literature from Mozart through the German Romantics to Fauré, Debussy, Ravel, Sauguet, and Poulenc deals, in any one piece, with a single person in an unequivocal mood. No event, inner or outer, takes place; and no logical conclusion is arrived at, though the sense of the whole may be summed up in a final couplet. These are the classical limits of lyric poetry. The ballad form, as in *Der Erlkönig,* is equally set and stylized by its stanza construction. Epic recitation and dramatic narrative demand still another musical form. I accuse the English and American composers (especially the Americans) of having hopelessly confused one kind of poetic expression with another in their vocal concert music. I am not naming any names, because they are practically all guilty. Just listen, if you want examples, to the American group of any singer's recital program. Or take a look at what your kid sister is given by her vocal teacher.

Is it any wonder that our American singers are not masters and mistresses of their art, when the repertory they all learn music through is so incompetently composed? They don't know that English vowel lengths, like Continental ones, are immutable. They don't know that poetic expression, no matter what its subject, falls into four or five styles, or genres rather, and no more. They don't know that lyric poetry does not permit an aggressive mood, that impersonation of the poet by the interpreter is unbecoming to it, that it can be recited or sung but never acted, though the ballad style can, on the contrary, be dramatized up to the hilt.

How can they know these things when the composers of the music that is virtually their whole fare write as if they didn't know them either, and when singing teachers, for lack of a better repertory, give them for study year after year pieces that nobody can vocalize correctly or interpret convincingly because they are incorrectly composed? They are incorrect as to vowel quantities, false to the known esthetics of poetry, and irresponsible in their misapplication of a climactic and passionate musical style to virtually any subject, even the sacred. America is full of beautiful young voices and high musical temperaments. The singing teachers are not bad either, on the whole. Students often learn from them to vocalize the long vowels quite prettily. After that they commit every fault. What about our composers' sitting down and writing them something that can be sung without fault? Our playwrights write plays that can be acted. Our painters paint pictures that can be hung, looked at, lived with. Our better composers write fair symphonies and thrilling ballets. But the human voice they have left in second-rate hands. There are probably not twenty American "art songs" that can be sung in Town Hall with dignity or listened to there without shame. Nor are there five American "art composers" who can be compared, as song writers, for either technical skill or artistic responsibility with Irving Berlin.

February 16, 1947

American Conservatives

PHILHARMONIC-SYMPHONY ORCHESTRA, *Howard Hanson,* guest conductor, concert last night at Carnegie Hall.

SUITE from THE INCREDIBLE FLUTIST	WALTER PISTON
(First time by the Philharmonic)	
THE WHITE PEACOCK, OP. 7, NO. 1	CHARLES T. GRIFFES
A PAGAN POEM (after Virgil), OP. 14	C. M. LOEFFLER
Piano, *Walter Hendl;* English Horn, *M. Nazzi;* Trumpets, *W. Vacchiano,*	
N. Prager, J. Smith	
MUSIC ON A QUIET THEME	WILLIAM BERGSMA
SYMPHONY NO. 2, "ROMANTIC," OP. 30	HOWARD HANSON

HOWARD HANSON, who conducted the Philharmonic-Symphony Orchestra last night in Carnegie Hall, is a thoroughly competent conductor, particularly of American music. The program of American music that he played was more than a shade on the conservative side, but the fact that it was played at all leads one to hope that the Philharmonic Society may be finally, in its own conservative way, taking up America. If this is true, and one American program is not just a brush-off to the whole problem (or to Mr. Hanson), it is equally to be hoped that so adequate a protagonist of the struggle will be asked again to lead the home-front forces.

The conservatism of last night's problem might be taken for reactionary if one did not know the passive resistance to American composition that exists among subscription audiences, long duped on this subject by unfavorable propaganda of German origin. It was sagacious of Mr. Hanson to select works of known audience appeal. Piston's *Incredible Flutist,* Griffes's *White Peacock,* Loeffler's *Pagan Poem,* and Hanson's own "Romantic" Symphony are pieces of tested popularity; they will carry anything, cushion the fall of anything.

They carried last night, or cushioned, a short work by William Bergsma entitled, *Music on a Quiet Theme.* Still far from mature as a writing personality, Mr. Bergsma has not yet shaken off the vices of his teacher, Mr. Hanson. These are chiefly a tendency to belabor his thematic material and a habit of working anything, literally anything, up to a feverlike climax and then letting it fall with a gasp. This procedure turns any short piece into a *Liebestraum* and any long one into a series of *Liebestraüme*. Let us hope that Mr. Bergsma, who is clearly a musician of high natural gifts, will start now to forget about his schooling and to write music in his own way. His schooling is no worse than anybody else's, better, indeed, than most. But all schoolings have to be got round. That is the way one becomes a real creator.

Mr. Hanson, though long a successful pedagogue, has never been, in my judgment, a very real creator. He has written lots of music that lots of poeple have enjoyed listening to, and that makes him a real composer. But I have never yet found in any work of his a single phrase or turn of harmony that did not sound familiar. His "Romantic" Symphony is no exception; it is as standardized in expression as it is eclectic in style. Not a surprise from beginning to end, nor any adventure. Unless the attempt to construct melodies by the constant repetition, or "riffing," of short motives and the attempt to substitute ostinato accompaniment for inner contrapuntal life in symphonic writing be considered a noble experiment. Riffing procedures have the advantage of making musical composition easy, but no amount of bombastic orchestration can conceal their expressive poverty. Their abuse by Mr. Hanson limits, I am convinced, his possible achievement as a musical creator.

January 18, 1946

Annual Gesture

NBC SYMPHONY ORCHESTRA, *Arturo Toscanini,* conductor, concert in Studio 8-H, Radio City, yesterday afternoon.

OVERTURE TO A FAIRY TALE	CASTELNUOVO-TEDESCO
SINFONÌA TRIPARTITA	RIETI
FRONTIERS	CRESTON
WESTERN SUITE	SIEGMEISTER

ARTURO TOSCANINI paid his annual compliment to living composers yesterday afternoon at the weekly concert of the NBC

Symphony Orchestra in Studio 8-H at Radio City. Of the four works played three were fairly negligible in substance, though one was not without style. The fourth was more robust.

The Castelnuovo-Tedesco *Overture to a Fairy Tale* is an inoffensive repetition of an inoffensive theme lightly, though not very fancifully, orchestrated. Vittorio Rieti's *Sinfonìa Tripartita* is a neoclassic work, diatonic in material and straightforward of manner. It could be made into a ballet, perhaps. As a concert work it has more style than intensity. It is modest and a little empty, but it is well made.

Paul Creston's *Frontiers* is unclear to me in subject. I could not tell whether it referred to the kind of frontiers that get pushed back or to the kind one crosses. Its musical material, which was as varied in origin as what collects in any customs warehouse, rather suggested the latter. Its chief interest to this listener was its successful handling of the problem of keeping opposed masses of orchestral sound opposed.

Elie Siegmeister's *Western Suite* is livelier stuff. Its material, cowboy folklore, is of the highest beauty; and its treatment is full of sound sense, as well as skill. Its moods run from the tenderest sentiment to the roughest roughhouse, and all are convincing. It is outdoor music with air in it and horses around. It is written with love and with gusto. Also with an experienced folklorist's judgment. The tunes are put through their paces without any timidity but equally without any misunderstanding of their nature and habits. Mr. Siegmeister's suite is a real rodeo.

The orchestral execution of all these works was of the utmost clarity under the maestro's impeccable (and even prudent) hand. It has long been a matter of regret to this concertgoer that Mr. Toscanini does not oftener put his admirable lucidity at the disposal of contemporary music.

November 26, 1945

Melodious and Skillful

ERNST BACON, concert of his music presented by Syracuse University last night at Times Hall, with the following participants: Madrigal Singers of Syracuse University; *Claire Harper*, violinist; *Elizabeth Mulfinger, Elena Irish*, and *Ernst Bacon*, pianists; *Priscilla Gillette*, soprano; and *Raymond di Giacomo*, baritone.

FOUR SONGS FROM EMILY DICKINSON: The Grass; O Friend; Velvet People; The Heart Asks Pleasure First.
Miss Gillette
Buncombe County; The Flower of Night; The Purple Land.
Miss Harper
FROM EMILY'S DIARY, a cantata for women on poems of Emily Dickinson, *Beverly Hess, Vera Ford, Stephanie Karageorge*, and *Anna Little*, sopranos; *Mary Samuel*, alto; *Elena Irish*, pianist.
FROM THE APPALACHIANS: The Lonesome Grove; Night and Day; Pretty Little Horsey; The Story of Adam and Eve; Cripple Creek.
Miss Gillette
BEARWALLA; THE RIVER QUEEN; THE COAL-SCUTTLE BLUES (jointly composed with Otto Luening).
Miss Mulfinger and *Mr. Bacon*

A PROGRAM of music all by one composer, such as that of works by Ernest Bacon which was given last night in Times Hall, is a good way to exhibit any good composer's music. A mood is established, a temperament made clear, mastery demonstrated through a variety of subjects. Since Mr. Bacon is a very good composer indeed, one of America's best, last night's concert was both an interesting and a pleasant experience.

The mood and temper of Mr. Bacon's work are chiefly a meditation on nineteenth-century rural America. He is full of our Scotch-Irish folklore, knows it from the inside, speaks and writes it as his own musical language. Mr. Bacon also has a modern musician's knowledge of American speech cadences. Few living composers prosodize to music so accurately. His piano accompaniments, too, carefully plain of harmony and never note-heavy, are most ingeniously evocative of our back-country musical style. They do not imitate ignorance or assume a naïve air; but they are poetical and reflective in an atavistic direction.

The violin pieces played last night showed a less original approach to that instrument, a less confident mastery of its expressive possibilities than the writing for voices or for the piano. A two-piano piece called *The River Queen,* all about President Lincoln's stern-wheel yacht, was in every way charming and picturesque. All the works performed, with the exception of a *Coal-Scuttle Blues,* jointly composed with Otto Luening, eschewed effects of dynamism for its own sake. The music was mostly soft and pretty in sound, deriving its interest from melodic, rhythmic and prosodic design rather than from oratory or from any kind of punch.

Mr. Bacon's work is remarkably pure in its expressive intent. It communicates its meaning with a straightforward and touching humanity. It is not got up with chromium-plated cadenzas or lace-curtainlike instrumental figurations, and it poses in no passionate attitude. But it is full of melody and variety; it makes, so far as it goes, complete sense. If it doesn't go very far forward, in the way of technical or expressive originality, it at least looks backward toward an ideal and primitive America without snobbery, self-deception, or truculence. It is honest and skillful and beautiful. One is grateful to Syracuse University, where Mr. Bacon professes his art, for presenting us with a whole evening of it, executed under the composer's direction by a bevy of personable young women.

March 4, 1946

New and Good

LEAGUE OF COMPOSERS, last concert of its twenty-fourth season, yesterday evening at the Museum of Modern Art. Participating artists: *Carolyn Blakeslee* and *Helen Boatwright,* sopranos; *Andor Foldes* and *Alvin Bauman,* pianists; *Werner Lywen* and *Barnett Gardelle,* violinists; *Walter Trampler* and *Emanuel Vardi,* violists; *Jesse Ehrlich,* cellist; *Helmut Baerwald* and *Edmund Haines,* accompanists.

PIANO SONATA NO. 3, OP. 13   PAUL KADOSA
          (First New York Performance: *Mr. Foldes*)
SONGS: Voyage; Warble for Lilac Time   ELLIOTT CARTER
     (First New York Performances; *Miss Boatwright* and *Mr. Baerwald*)

PIANO SONATA NO. 2　　　　　　　　　　　　　ROGER SESSIONS
　　　　　　(First Performance; *Mr. Foldes*)
SONATINA for Viola and Piano　　　　　　JACOB AVSHALOMOFF
　　　　　(First Peformance; *Messrs. Vardi* and *Bauman*)
SONGS: Quel est ton nom; Il n'y avait que de troncs dechirés
　　　　　　　　　　　　　　　　　　　　YVES BAUDRIER
　　　　　　(First American Performances)
THE FLIGHT　　　　　　　　　　　　　　THEODORE CHANLER
　　　　　　Miss Blakeslee and *Mr. Haines*
ISTHMUS TONALIS FOR STRING QUARTET, OP. 9　　　KURT LIST
THIRD STRING QUARTET (First Performance)　　DAVID DIAMOND
　　　Messrs. Lywen, Gardelle, Trampler, and *Ehrlich*

THE LEAGUE OF COMPOSERS, which has been giving unusually agreeable concerts this winter, presented a charmingly varied and admirably executed program last night at the Museum of Modern Art. There were works in all the modern styles — the neo-Classic, the neo-Romantic, the twelve-tone technique, and the new French neo-Impressionism. All were interesting and many were lovely, but the nugget of the evening was a brand-new piano sonata by Roger Sessions.

Roger Sessions, in spite of considerable renown as a talked-about composer and a long history of success as a pedagogue, is little known through his music. His production is small; and the few works available are seldom performed, because they are difficult to play and not easy to listen to. They are learned, laborious, complex, and withal not strikingly original. They pass for professor's music, and the term is not wholly unjustified. Because the complexity and elaboration of their manner is out of all proportion to the matter expressed. Nevertheless, they are impressive both for the seriousness of their thought and for the ingenuity of their workmanship. They are hard to take and even harder to reject. They represent the most embarrassing problem in American music, because though they have unquestionably quality, they have just as certainly almost no charm at all. And we have no place in our vast system of musical distribution for music without charm.

The piano sonata played last night by Andor Foldes (and dedicated to him) is Mr. Session's second. The first dates from nearly twenty years back. Like the first, it is composed in a consistently dissonant but tonal style. Unlike the first, it is in melodic style largely chromatic. Like all of this composer's music, it bears no clear marks of its national or local origins. It could have been written anywhere in the world — in Leningrad, Shanghai, Paris, Buenos Aires, Vienna, Rome, or Melbourne — as easily as in Berkeley, California, where it actually was composed, and by a man of any race and clime as easily as by a one-hundred-per-cent New Englander. Its speech represents the international neo-Classic style at its most complete and eclectic, though the feelings expressed in the work are derived from the violence-and-meditation contrast beloved of the German Late Romantics.

It is not music of direct melodic or harmonic appeal for the uninitiated; nor yet has it great stimulus value for modernists, who have already heard elsewhere practically everything in it. All the same, it is interesting to listen to, because it is wonderfully, thoroughly sophisticated. The slow movement, moreover, is almost atmospheric. Operating in a small range of pitch, with little variety of rhythm and, for once, no great variety of musical device employed, Sessions has achieved here a completely absorbing tranquility. The work is not likely to be popular, I should think, either soon or ever. But it is not a negligible composition, and Roger Sessions has reminded us through it that his very existence as a musician is a far from negligible contribution to the history of America.

Space forbids my reviewing in detail, as I should like to do, the other works presented. Notable, however, were the half-Jewish, half-Chinese, Sonatina for Viola and Piano, by Jacob Avshalomoff, a sweet and lyrical piece; some luminous French recitative songs by Yves Baudrier; the far from banal twelve-tone *Isthmus Tonalis* for string quartet, by Kurt List; and a pretty *Flight Into Egypt*, by Theodore Chanler. Elliott Carter's long songs on texts by Whitman and Hart Crane were weakened in impact by the composer's insistence in treating short vowels as if they were long ones. David Diamond's Third String Quartet, which closed the concert, though a shade facile in sentiment and far too easygoing about length, is string writing of the first quality, varied, precise, graceful, and free.

March 17, 1947

Schuman's *Undertow*

WILLIAM SCHUMAN's ballet, *Undertow*, which will be played again tonight at Ballet Theater's closing performance of the season, has enlarged our acquaintance with this composer's personality; and I suspect it may be about to add something to the repertory of his concert works. It is the first narrative instrumental piece by him that many have had occasion to hear, possibly the first he has composed, though he has worked successfully in most of the other musical forms both vocal and instrumental. Whatever may be the future of Antony Tudor's ballet, there is probably an effective concert piece to be derived from this score.

There is no question, I think, that American composers by and large, at least those of the presently mature and maturing generation, have done their most striking work in the theater. Also that the best training available for serious musico-theatrical work is practice in the concert forms. Interestingness of texture and soundness of continuity are the minimal requirements of concert music, and a composer cannot hold the attention of concert audiences without mastery of these qualities. On the other hand, concentration on a specific subject, the depicting of it without expansion or digression, which is the minimal requirement of any music destined for theatrical collaboration, is exactly where American concert composition tends to fall down. It is weak in specific expressivity, partly because our American training in composition is formalistic, seeking abstract perfection, even at the expense of direct speech, and partly because our concert audiences are not sufficiently accomplished at seizing the meanings in music to require of musical composition the kind of coherence that they demand, for instance, of literature.

Formed entirely by American teachers and American audiences, William Schuman is a product of the American musical scene. He has written symphonies, string quartets, overtures, band pieces, and lots of choral works; and they have all been performed by major musical organizations. His workmanship is skillful, individual, striking. His expressivity has always been tenuous, timid, conventional. His serious works have shown a respectable seriousness of attitude without much private or particular passion, while his gayer ones have expressed either a standard American cheerfulness or the comforting bumptiousness of middle-quality comic-strip humor. He has written easily, abundantly, and, in a technical sense, well; but his music has been, on the whole, reticent, has communicated to the public little about himself or about anything else.

Undertow has a sounder proportion of matter to means. The story of this particular ballet has required, to begin with, vivid rather than formalistic treatment. That story, or plot, for all its inefficiencies as dramatic literature (it has a realistic but nonessential beginning and a nonrealistic, quite unbelievable ending; with all that public opinion around, the young man would certainly have been arrested for murder if he had committed one), has a serious subject, namely, the pathos of sexual initiation. The music is full of frustration and violence. It has a static intensity in the passages of pure feeling and a spastic muscular energy in the passages that depict physical action that are completely appropriate to the subject and completely interesting. The climactic *pas de deux* is the most realistic piece about sexual intercourse we have had since Shostakovich's *Lady Macbeth of Mzensk*. And the contrapuntal accompaniment to the scene of ganged-up lovemaking between one girl and four men is both exciting and convincing.

Whether Schuman has a real theatrical gift or merely certain qualities that are useful in the theater, I am not sure. The whole score does not accompany the ballet as consistently as certain passages underline it strikingly. If Schuman were a born man of the theater, he ought to have given to the choreographer, or secured from him, a closer communion. But Tudor, who likes to work from ready-made music, may not be easy to do a duo with. Further dramatic works from Schuman will no doubt reveal further his qualities. For the present he has shown a gift for expressing the lurid; and the lurid has afforded him a more ample field for exploiting his full powers as an artist than the formalistic, middleground modernism of his concert style and the boisterous-but-not-much-else Americanism of his assumed concert personality have done. Also, his gift for massive orchestration, which lends so easily a merely demagogic air to his concert works, becomes an element of magnificent emphasis when applied to a melodramatic subject in a theater.

And so, viewed freshly through his new-found medium, Schuman turns out to be not at all the composer of small expressive range and assumed monumental proportions that his concert music has long led one to consider him, but a man of high, of spectacular expressive gifts who has been constricted by the elegant abstractions of the American concert style—and a little bit, too, perhaps, by his youth. The concert forms have been good schooling for him, but he has never expressed himself in them with any freedom. The theater gives him elbow room. His mind can move around in it. And his feeling-content, his compassion, as well as his inveterate love for depicting physical movement, take on an unexpected strength under the theater's channelization of them to purposes of specific meaning. *Undertow* is not a masterpiece of music, any more than it is of choreography. But it is full of music that says something. It speaks. It can even be listened to. I think it will be remembered. And the man who wrote it, whether he cares to exploit the achievement further or not, has become visible to us through it as a stronger, a bigger, and a more generous personality than he had appeared before.

April 29, 1945

Good Music, Poor Literature

NEW YORK CITY SYMPHONY, *Leonard Bernstein,* conductor, concert last night at the New York City Center. Assisting artists: Collegiate Chorale, *Robert Shaw,* director; *Werner Lywen,* violinist; *Orson Welles,* speaker; *Charles Holland,* tenor; and *Walter Scheff,* baritone.

OVERTURE TO THE ABDUCTION FROM THE SERAGLIO	MOZART
VIOLIN CONCERTO IN D MAJOR (K. 218)	MOZART
THE AIRBORNE SYMPHONY, for orchestra, chorus, speaker, and soloists	BLITZSTEIN

(First Performance)

MARC BLITZSTEIN's *The Airborne,* which was heard last night for the first time anywhere at a concert of the City Symphony in the

City Center of Music and Drama, is an ingenious piece of musical work and far from uninspired. Its ingenuity consists in the composer's having managed to inject a high degree of musical interest into an entertainment formula that has hitherto been musically pretty sterile. I refer to the kind of broadcast perfected at the Columbia Workshop and made famous by Norman Corwin, the patriotic poem about current events that mobilizes for its recitation actors, vocal soloists, a chorus or two, a symphony orchestra, and any number of microphones. The inspiration of the present piece consists in the more than merely ingenious use of contrasted musical styles for purposes of specific expression. There is detailed invention in it, a real musico-dramatic texture that is communicative.

Whether there is much real communication in Mr. Blitzstein's poem I doubt. It is a pæan of praise to aviation in general, and to military aviation in particular, that smacks more of directed publicity than of original thought. Actually it says little that is not already a commonplace of the sentimental press, and its folksy language is both facile and affected. With such a text it was inevitable that any musical setting designed to throw the words into relief should have difficulty rising above the banality of these. For that reason the most distinguished music in the work is that of the purely instrumental interludes, which are less earthbound than the choral and recitative passages. Only two of these last seemed to this listener musically adequate at all, a piece for speaker and chorus called *The Enemy* and a sentimental song in which a young bombardier writes a letter to his girl back home. These have continuity and musical progress, just as the orchestral intermezzi do.

They do not, however, have quite the originality and the forceful musical texture of the instrumental sections. Mr. Blitzstein's musical style in these is diatonic, dissonant without the use of chromatics, and highly melodious. His tunes are both distinguished and singable. His whole invention, melodic, contrapuntal, and orchestral, has a higher degree of specific expressivity, a clearer way of saying what it means, than we are accustomed to encounter in the work of American composers.

He sets stylistic formulas against one another in much the same way that a stage director will turn on his scene spotlights, floodlights, footlights, and borders, composing these for specific expressivity rather than for any mere display of his equipment. That is why, beyond its straightforward diatonicism, there is little in the Blitzstein musical style that is strikingly personal or consciously characteristic. Blitzstein has, however, the more valuable power to call on a large repertory of varied stylistic conventions and to use these as a musical vocabulary, making thus, as scene designers do, a language out of the history of styles and an expressive syntax out of constant stylistic cross reference.

The execution of this masterful but not entirely satisfactory work under the direction of Leonard Bernstein was a triumph of efficiency. Orson Welles, who spoke; Charles Holland and Walter Scheff, who sang; and a male chorus from the Collegiate Chorale were impeccable. And the City Symphony played its orchestral passages, which are not easy, with full clarity. Previously Mr. Bernstein and the orchestra had given a lively and careful reading of Mozart's *Seraglio* overture and, with Werner Lywen, the concertmaster, as soloist, as sweet and sensible a performance of Mozart's Violin Concerto in D major (K. 218) as any of us is likely to hear in many a day. Mr. Blitzstein's *The Airborne*, I may add, was more than warmly received by the audience both for its handsome execution and for the unquestioned merits of its composition.

April 2, 1946

Two Ballets

THE POSTSEASONAL week of ballet, if that is the proper term for it, that Martha Graham and her dance company have been offering at the National Theater has given New York finally a hearing of Aaron Copland's *Appalachian Spring* and of Paul Hindemith's *Hérodiade*. Crowning a season that had already offered (through the Monte Carlo company) Stravinsky's *Danses Concertantes* and Richard Strauss's *Le Bourgeois Gentilhomme*, (through Billy Rose) Stravinsky's *Scènes de Ballet*, (through Ballet International) Paul Bowles's *Colloques Sentimentales* and Menotti's *Sebastian*, and (through Ballet Theater) Rieti's *Waltz Academy* and William Schuman's *Undertow*, not to speak of John Cage's strange and delicate scores for altered pianoforte which Merce Cunningham presented in recital, one of which, *Strange Adventure,* was heard again at Miss Graham's recent festivities, these two latest musical works have made it clear to all, even, we hope, to dancing's "modern" wing, that terpsichoric entertainment can be something more than cavorting to a scenario with sound effects.

Miss Graham has given us in the past music by reputable living composers, notably Paul Nordoff and Hunter Johnson; but none of this has ever been strong or memorable. It has all been little music, well meaning but agitated and unsure. And Charles Mills's *John Brown,* heard twice last week, is of the same subservient tweedle-dee-bang-bang school that has long been cultivated by nonclassical dance troupes. The Copland and Hindemith scores are another line of musical country, I assure you, higher and more commanding and incredibly more adequate both to the support of a choreographic line and to the evocation of their stated subjects.

The Copland subject is marriage preliminaries in nineteenth-century rural America. The style is pastoral, the tone, as is appropriate to the pastoral style, blythe and beatific. The material is folklore, some of it vocal, some violinistic. The harmonic treatment, based chiefly on open fourths and fifths, evokes our sparse and dissonant rural tradition rather than the thick suavities of our urban manner. The instrumentation is plain, clean-colored, deeply imaginative. It is designed not only to express the moods of the story but to amplify the characteristics of the dramatis personae. It is both poetically effective and theatrically functional. It is also musically interesting; it has style.

Every aspect of the work is musically interesting, though all of it is not equally intense as expression. If there is by moments, even in energetic passages, a static quality that does not seem to be advancing the story, that same immobility, when it comes off right, gives us both the very particular Copland miracle and that blythe Elysian-Fields note that is ideally the pastoral manner. Specifically, this effect seemed to me on first hearing to be more intense at the beginning and at the end of the work than in its middle sections. A second hearing revealed it at somewhere near its best in the second, as well as in the first, number and in the central (country-fiddle style) *pas de deux.* Elsewhere the expressivity seemed less powerful, though the musical texture was always interesting and the adequacy of the poetic and theatrical treatment, even at its least intense, of great help to those on the stage.

Aided as little, in the past, by her musical as by her pictorial collaborators, and devoted, by temperament and by preconception, to the rendering of emotion (specifically, feminist emotion) rather than of character, Miss Graham's work has long leaned toward the introspective and the psychologically lurid. Copland, in *Appalachian Spring*, has, by the inflexibility of his pastoral landscape mood, kept her away from the violence of solitary meditation and drawn her toward awareness of persons and the sweetness of manners. Paul Hindemith, long acquainted with the traps that Miss Graham's Germanic approach to the theater presents, has led her away from them by another means. He has given her a subject that is lurid enough for any taste but that is objectively rather than subjectively so. By this simple device he has forced her to represent a real and visible person rather than a state of mind about one. And, of course, in such a situation, she turns out to be, as one has long suspected, not only an expressive dancer but a great actress, one of the very great among living actresses, in fact.

The piece, called *Hérodiade* (though the English form *Herodias* would have been preferable), is derived from Mallarmé's French poem of that title. It represents the boudoir afternoon of a woman who is beautiful, sensual, intellectual, proud, passionate, rich, and middle-aged. She consults her mirror and converses with her maid, frankly, without illusion and without despair. And then she dresses for the evening. The music is sumptuously evocative, rich, complex, civilized. Also solidly sustained architecturally. If it is reminiscent, in the central portion, of Strauss's *Salomé*, with its characteristic jumping-all-about-the-place melodic line, who is to say that that hypertrophied and decadent manner is inappropriate to the Herod family? Mallarmé's conception is stiffer and more concentratedly sumptuous, and so is Miss Graham's. But the Hindemith score, though not completely distinguished, is a fine piece of music. And it has inspired Miss Graham to the creation, for once, of a character that is real enough, I should think, for other dancers to undertake.

The music has more ease in it than Copland's and a higher

level of picturesque and dramatic fulfillment. At no time, however, does it touch the poignancy of certain moments in the other, those special Copland moments when the whole musical texture reaches an ultimate of thinness and of translucency. It is not my purpose here to weigh the works against each other, but rather to show how they set each other off. Both are sound theater and beautiful music. And both can be heard, along with *Letter to the World*, the well-known ballet about Emily Dickinson, at tonight's final performance of Miss Graham's all too brief New York season.

May 20, 1945

Expressive Percussion

JOHN CAGE, program of compositions for the prepared piano at the New School for Social Research yesterday afternoon. Assisting duo-pianists, *Arthur Gold, Robert Fizdale.*

THE PERILOUS NIGHT (six solos); A BOOK OF MUSIC FOR TWO PIANOS; THREE DANCES

JOHN CAGE, whose recent compositions made up the program of a concert given yesterday afternoon at the New School for Social Research, is already famous as a specialist in the use of percussive sounds. Two years ago the Museum of Modern Art presented pieces by him for a large group of players, using flowerpots, brake bands, electric buzzers, drums, and similar objects not primarily musical but capable of producing a wide variety of interesting sounds all the same. The works offered yesterday included an even greater variety of sounds, all prepared by inserting bits of metal, wood, rubber, or leather at carefully studied points and distances between the strings of an ordinary pianoforte.

The effect in general is slightly reminiscent, on first hearing, of the Balinese gamelang orchestras, though the interior structure of Mr. Cage's music is not Oriental at all. His work attaches itself, in fact, to two different traditions of Western modernism. One is the percussive experiments begun by Marinetti's Futurist Noisemakers and continued in the music of Edgar Varèse, Henry Cowell, and George Antheil, all of which, though made in full awareness of Oriental methods, is thoroughly Western in its expression. The other is, curiously enough, the atonal music of Arnold Schönberg and his school.

Mr. Cage has carried Schönberg's twelve-tone harmonic maneuvers to their logical conclusion. He has produced atonal music not by causing the twelve tones of the chromatic scale to contradict one another consistently, but by eliminating, to start with, all sounds of precise pitch. He substitutes for the classical chromatic scale a gamut of pings, plucks, and delicate thuds that is both varied and expressive and that is different in each piece. By thus getting rid, at the beginning, of the constricting element in atonal writing — which is the necessity of taking constant care to avoid making classical harmony with a standardized palette of instrumental sounds and pitches that exists primarily for the purpose of producing such harmony — Mr. Cage has been free to develop the rhythmic element of composition, which is the weakest element in the Schönbergian style, to a point of sophistication unmatched in the technique of any other living composer.

His continuity devices are chiefly those of the Schönberg school. There are themes and sometimes melodies, even, though these are limited, when they have real pitch, to the range of a fourth, thus avoiding the tonal effect of dominant and tonic. All these appear in augmentation, diminution, inversion, fragmentation, and the various kinds of canon. That these procedures do not take over a piece and become its subject, or game, is due to Cage's genius as a musician. He writes music for expressive purposes; and the novelty of his timbres, the logic of his discourse, are used to intensify communication, not as ends in themselves. His work represents, in consequence, not only the most advanced methods now in use anywhere but original musical expression of the very highest poetic quality. And this has been proved now through all the classical occasions — theater, ballet, song, orchestral composition, and chamber music.

One of the works was played yesterday by the composer, the other two by Arthur Gold and Robert Fizdale, duo-pianists. The perfect execution of these young men, their rhythm, lightness, and absolute equality of scale and the singing sounds they derived from their instruments, in spite of the fact that the strings were all damped in various ways, made one wish to hear them operate on music less special, as well. The concert was a delight from every point of view.

January 22, 1945

Swiss Festival

NICOLAS DE FLUE, dramatic legend, French text by *Denis de Rougemont,* music by ARTHUR HONEGGER, American premiere last night at Carnegie Hall by the Dessoff Choirs, *Paul Boepple,* conductor, assisted by the Orchestra of the New Friends of Music and a chorus of children from the Fort George Presbyterian Church (*Mary Arabella Coale,* director), from St. Mary's in the Garden (*Grace Leeds,* director), and from Warren Foley's Choral Ensemble of the Church of the Blessed Sacrament, through the courtesy of *Mgr. Foley.* Narrator, *Fernand Auberjonois.*

DENIS DE ROUGEMONT'S text deals with politics. It is about how the Swiss Federation foolishly got itself into a war, surprisingly won, quarreled among itself about the peace terms almost to the point of civil war, and finally came to its senses at the exhortation of a hermit named Nicolas de Flue. It was intended, with music by Arthur Honegger, to be performed as an outdoor spectacle of the sort not uncommon in Switzerland, where a thousand or more executants sometimes participate in festival pageants celebrating local history or legend.

Last night's performance mobilized no such army of amateurs, but it did fill the stage of Carnegie Hall with three choirs, an orchestra, and three gentlemen "speakers," one of whom, as a matter of fact, never spoke. It filled the hall with good, loud musical noises, too, a fine specialty of Mr. Honegger's, and with bad, loud, and thoroughly unmusical noises during those moments, all too frequent, when music and a speaker, transmitted through a public-address system, were both going full blast. Speech with instrumental accompaniment ("melodrama" is the musical word for this) is, heaven knows, silly enough most of the time. Speech with choral accompaniment is not even silly; it is just unfortunate, since no listener can possibly follow one set of sung words and another set of spoken ones at the same time.

Aside from these moments, which one gathers were no part of the composer's intention (the original pageant and its subsequent abbreviation for concert purposes requiring no such makeshift as last night's amplified narrator), Honegger's score is pointed and dramatic. If it is musically not very original or intensely inspired, it is still a resonant and workmanlike job. It reminds one of his twenty-year-old *King David*, which it resembles without excelling. Indeed it is far less fresh and spontaneous. It is essentially the same piece rewritten twenty years later by a man who has learned from long practice in the films how to write minutes and minutes and minutes of adequate music in the shortest possible time. He has not written cheap music, at least not often; but he has repeated all his best formulas over and over, ever more confidently and more economically and ever less and less convincingly as to their original sincerity.

Honegger is really a curious case. Gifted and skillful like few. Industrious like almost none. More insistent than most at producing works that aim to storm Parnassus by sheer weight (the French call this kind of thing *le genre chef-d'oeuvre*). Constantly subjected to the public failure of these (*vide Rugby* and *Horace Victorieux*). Constantly signing movie scores, even writing many of them himself, I imagine. His musical texture is never below a respectable level in quality, rarely up to that of his early works.

He does two pieces admirably, a pastoral and a battle scene, puts them everywhere. I have never heard his opera *Judith*, said to be excellent. I have often heard and enjoyed *King David* and the famous *Pacific 231*, a mechanization of the battle piece. He can produce effective and dignified work when he is moved by the subject of it, which isn't always. He can make the most uninteresting and ineffective "machines" of any well-known living musical author when he isn't. I shall never forget *L'Impératrice aux Rochers* at the Paris Opéra, which fell as flat as anything could fall in spite of the presence on the stage at one and the same time of the Pope, the Emperor, the Virgin Mary, Madame Ida Rubinstein, and twenty live horses.

Nicolas de Flue did not fall flat last night, was a success with the public, in fact. Part of this I credit to the utter and rather charming Swissness of the whole thing, part of it to the admirable execution of the Dessoff Choirs and part of it to Honegger's neat and businesslike way of writing music. I cannot imagine any of it as due to Denis de Rougemont's poem, which is inflated, bromidic, in every way lacking in distinction.

May 9, 1941

Democracy and Style

PHILHARMONIC-SYMPHONY ORCHESTRA, *Artur Rodzinski*, conductor; concert last night at Carnegie Hall. Guest conductor, *Darius Milhaud*; soloist, *Yehudi Menuhin*, violinist.

OVERTURE, NOCTURNE, INTERMEZZO, and SCHERZO from A MID-
SUMMER NIGHT'S DREAM   MENDELSSOHN
SUITE FRANÇAISE   MILHAUD
       (First time by the Philharmonic, conducted by the composer)
LE BAL MARTINIQUAIS   MILHAUD
       (First performance, conducted by the composer)
VIOLIN CONCERTO IN D MAJOR   BEETHOVEN

GUSTO and poetry, tenderness and strength and no fear of anything or anybody, these are the elements that make the music of Darius Milhaud inspiring to composers and heartwarming to audiences. And they are the qualities that made his *Suite française* and *Bal martiniquais*, which the composer conducted at last night's concert of the Philharmonic in Carnegie Hall, a unanimous delight.

There is humanity in the very texture of Milhaud's writing. Tunes and countertunes and chords and percussive accents jostle one another with such friendliness, such tolerance, and such ease that the whole comes to represent what almost anybody might mean by a democratic way of life. Popular gaiety does not prevent the utterance of noble sentiments, and the presence of noble sentiments puts no damper at all on popular gaieties. The scenes have air in them and many different kinds of light, every brightness and every transparency, and no gloom or heaviness at all.

The *French Suite* is in five parts, all based on folk material. Normandy is represented by a cocky march, Brittany by an ethereal revery interrupted here and there by tiny gusts of discord, by little drafts, as it were, on the back of the neck. The Ile-de-France is a cancan, not a floor-show cancan, but a real one, such as young women might dance in a public square on the night of a victory celebration. Alsace-Lorraine is a sustained song with faith in it and a constancy half amorous, half religious. The finale, Provence, is a carnival of songs and dances from Mr. Milhaud's native region. The whole suite is a model of how to treat folk material, a little masterpiece of musical landscape-with-figures.

Le Bal martiniquais consists of a Creole song and a beguine. The treatment is similar to the French scenes, and the material is even gayer. This beguine is a sort of Calypso-style hoe-down of the most colorful orchestral texture imaginable. It should serve well as a dessert piece to end orchestral programs. I wish that Mr. Milhaud might always be available to conduct it, because he has a firmly delicate hand that knows how to make music sound loud but not rude.

His delightful executions were framed by performances of Mendelssohn and Beethoven that were in different ways not quite satisfactory. No sooner had the *Midsummer Night's Dream* got under way than your reporter was awakened by a drizzle of rain that continued to fall for some thirty or forty minutes in the region where he was seated and that somewhat disturbed, in consequence, his concentration on the music.

The Beethoven Violin Concerto, which ended the evening, took place in dry weather; but Mr. Menuhin, the soloist, seemed to be having atmospheric trouble with his instrument, for he played off pitch, mostly flat, in a way that is not his habit. Parts of the second movement were harmonious, but mostly the performance was a disaster.

December 7, 1945

Musical Gastronomy

THE MENU of Manuel Rosenthal's *Musique de table,* which the Philharmonic-Symphony Orchestra played at its second pair of subscription concerts, October 10 and 11, and on its broadcast concert of Sunday the 13th, is perhaps a trifle copious for American digestions. We have lost, since Victorian days, the ability to consume at one sitting an hors d'oeuvre, a fish, an entrée, a roast, a vegetable, game, salad, cheese, ice cream, coffee, and a liqueur and then go on joyfully to cigars and conversation. An American composer, designing for musical depiction his ideal dinner, would certainly either have left out half of this abundance or topped it off with a finale about bicarbonate. A Frenchman, writing before the war, would probably have extended it even further to include soup.

The program of Mr. Rosenthal's *Dinner in Music,* to render the title freely, contains another curious omission, that of wines. I understand his leaving out the soup. Even before the last war, diners among the Paris international set had shown a tendency to skip this traditional observance. Lady Mendl (an American by birth and consequently only a mild soup addict) invented in the 1930's the slogan, "You can't build a good meal on a lake." And during the Occupation, watery brews with very little nourishment in them were so nearly everybody's whole diet in France that today nobody there, preparing a feast for guests at home or ordering one in a public place, would think of including a *potage* in the menu. With all such greaseless nourishment the French are quite literally fed up.

Wine, on the other hand, which they have lacked since 1940 and which even now is neither overabundant nor cheap, is essential to the ingestion of any reasonably good French meal, not to mention the majestic menu dreamed up in 1942 by Mr. Rosenthal. Perhaps its omission from the program notes provided with his score is merely a device for circumventing the wine snobs, for no subject in gastronomy is so riddled with pretentiousness and vanity.

In any case, no wine is mentioned; but this listener was convinced that he heard in the luscious and delicious scoring of this memorable work plenty of appropriate grape. The characteristic blood flavor of roast beef and the darkly outdoor taste of venison, rendered in the scoring by trumpets and trombones in the one case and by hunting-horn sounds in the other, were so aptly set off by contrasting instrumental timbres that the richness of the whole effect could only have been conceived with something more on the imaginary palate than meat alone. The salad, on the other hand, with which one does not drink wine, because it tastes already of vinegar, had no such third dimension. It was all light and high and clear and clean and pale, fresh and quite without perspective to the taste.

It is unfortunate that the Philharmonic's program notes did not include a translation of the menu, that they did not even give it complete, as it appears in the musical score. Let us try our hand at it, though with all hesitation, since the rendering of cookery terms in English is beset with pitfalls. The meal begins with *salade russe,* a dish for which the term *Russian salad* is a far from precise description. Precisely, this is a mixture of diced vegetables in mayonnaise, somewhat meager, in fact, as an hors d'oeuvre unless accompanied by cold ham, which Mr. Rosenthal does not offer. (A musical prelude, entitled *Entrée des convives,* or "The Guests Enter the Dining Room," has previously introduced us to the party.) This slender hors d'oeuvre is followed by a *matelote d'anguilles,* eels in red wine. The entrée, untranslatable by this writer, is *quenelles lyonnaise. Quenelles* are a paste of chicken or of pike fish mixed with cream, a little flour, and the beaten whites of egg. Shaped like small sausages, they are poached and served with a sauce. As presented in the *lyonnaise,* or Lyons, manner, this is a fresh cream sauce with a chicken-broth base. In classical gastronomy, pike *quenelles* are served with a fish sauce, usually one made of fresh-water crayfish, and chicken *quenelles* with the chicken-stock-and-cream sauce.

The roast is a simple tenderloin of beef, followed (in the French manner, rather than accompanied) by a dish of mixed fresh vegetables. The game is *cuissot de chevreuil,* or loin of venison. *Salade de saison* is whatever the market offers. *Fromage de montagne* I take to mean goat cheese, admirable for the gustation of red wines. Ice cream, liqueurs, cigars, and conversation end the ceremony. Coffee is not mentioned in the text.

The musical rendering of all these delights is most suggestive, though the piece about *quenelles lyonnaise,* a bland dish and a luxurious one, contained an allusion to spicy street songs that I did not understand. As a piece of musical design the work is solid and skillful. As orchestration it is masterful in a manner not at present to be matched in the work of any other living composer. Its finale, representing animated general conversation, is one of the liveliest pieces I know. Its whole effect is a triumph of orchestral cuisine, as delicious as its stated subject. And if it represents, as so much of contemporary French music does — the works of Messiaen, of Jolivet, of Barraud, of Poulenc, and even of Honegger — a return to the Debussian, or Berlioz, esthetic, in which color is as important an element of composition as linear drawing, it carries the technique of coloristic design into realms of brightness, especially through the use of high, thin sounds, that the Impressionists, who worked most originally in the bass ranges, had left untouched. *Musique de table* is an utterly charming piece and an utterly French one. Like many other good things French, it combines skill of hand with the frank assumption that living is a pleasure. Thank you, Mr. Rosenthal, for a delightful party!

October 20, 1946

Children's Day

PHILHARMONIC-SYMPHONY ORCHESTRA, *Artur Rodzinski,* conductor; *Heitor Villa-Lobos,* guest conductor; concert in Carnegie Hall last night. Violin soloist, *Zino Francescatti.*

"Toy" Symphony   Haydn
Choros No. 8 for Large Orchestra with Two Piano Soli
                                                                Villa-Lobos
            Soloists *Raoul Spivak, Ignace Strasfogel*
Choros No. 9   Villa-Lobos
      (First Performance in North America; Composer conducting)
Violin Concerto in D major   Paganini
Mephisto Waltz   Liszt

Heitor Villa-Lobos, who conducted two of his Choros for orchestra, Numbers 8 and 9, last night with the Philharmonic in Carnegie Hall, is one of the world's most prolific composers. Also one of the most gifted. His works are innumerable and full of bright ideas. Their excellent tunes, their multicolored instrumentation, their abundance of fancy in general, and their easy but perfectly real modernity of thought have made them universally acceptable as valid musical creations of this century. For all the French influence on their harmonic texture (chiefly that of Milhaud), they are also valid musical creations of this hemisphere.

They sound, as is, indeed, their composer's intention, most convincingly like Brazil.

Choros Number 8, last heard here at the World's Fair, sounds to me like rural Brazil, like rivers and plains and mountains and Indian villages and jungles. The jungles seem to have lots of trees in them, big ones and small ones, also some snakes and wild animals. Certainly there are birds around of all sizes. And I thought I spotted, as the civilized note, a sturdy stock of European canned nourishment and a few reels of the best Hollywood sentiment.

Choros Number 9, which was a North American première, is more urban. It has dance music and crowds and general gaiety and some wit and quite a lot more of Hollywood sentiment. It is all very pleasant, and it is loosely enough constructed so that one doesn't have to pay attention all the time. The composer conducted one through both pieces with courtesy, making everything clear and keeping us interested at every moment. If one felt at the end like a tourist who has seen much but taken part in little, one was grateful for the trip, all the same. One could almost hear the voice of the travelogue saying, "Now we are leaving beau-u-u-tiful Brazil."

We left it for the comfortably suburban Violin Concerto of Paginini and some astonishingly accurate violin playing by Zino Francescatti. And thus safely returned to Europe and the nineteenth century, we paid ourselves an old-style treat in the form of Liszt's great orchestral Mephisto Waltz, which was certainly the original of Ravel's *La Valse*. A wonderfully beautiful piece this, and not a bit devilish, just sweet and romantic and full of an inward light. Our thanks to Artur Rodzinski, who thought of playing it, and who played it enchantingly.

Mr. Rodzinski's little treat for himself, which he shared, of course, with us all, was the playing, to start the evening off, of Haydn's charming and absurd "Toy" Symphony, a publicity tribute to his newborn son. Perhaps it was all this preparation — the toy trumpet and the cuckoo and the whistles and all, then the educational trip through picturesque Brazil, then the dressing-up-in-grandpa's-clothes effect of the Paginini concerto — that made the Mephisto Waltz sound like adult music. In any case it did. And it was most welcome.

February 9, 1945

Revueltas Evening

ANNA SOKOLOW and Dance Group, program dedicated to the Mexican composer, SILVESTRE REVUELTAS, last night at the Mansfield Theater. Orchestra conducted by *Alex Saron;* vocal soloists, *Estelle Hoffman,* soprano, and *Arno Tanney;* pianist, *Alex North.*

OPENING DANCE; Ballad in a Popular Style (*Mr. North* at the piano); SLAUGHTER OF THE INNOCENTS   Music by NORTH
VISIÓN FANTASTICA (after Goya): Children's Games (music by *Padre Antonio Soler*), Disasters of War (music by *Alex North*), Carnival (music by *Soler*)
HOMENAJE Á GARCÍA LORCA   Music by REVUELTAS
CANCIONES PARA NIÑAS: Five Hours, Little Horse, Foolish Song, Song of the Moon, Serenade, It Is True   Music by REVUELTAS
       Singer, *Miss Hoffman;* pianist, *Mr. North*
EXILE   Music by NORTH
       Singer, *Mr. Tanney*
EL RENACUAJO PASEADOR   Music by REVUELTAS

EUROPE has often produced composers like the late Silvestre Revueltas, the Americas rarely. Our music writers are most likely to do the light touch with a heavy hand. Revueltas's music reminds one of Erik Satie's and of Emmanuel Chabrier's. It is both racy and distinguished. Familiar in style and full of references to Hispanic musical formulas, it seeks not to impress folklorists nor to please audiences by salting up a work with nationalist material. Neither does it make any pretense of going native. He wrote Mexican music that sounds like Spanish Mexico, and he wrote it in the best Parisian syntax. No Indians around and no illiteracy.

The model is a familiar one of the nationalist composer whose compositional procedures are conservative and unoriginal but whose musical material consists of all the rarest and most beautiful melodies that grow in his land. Villa-Lobos is like that and Percy Grainger; so was Dvořák. The contraries of that model are Josef Haydn and Satie and a little bit Georges Auric, certainly Darius Milhaud. These writers use the vernacular for its expressivity. But their musical structure and syntax are of the most elegant. Their music, in consequence, has an international carrying power among all who love truly imaginative musical construction.

Revueltas's music could never be mistaken for French music. It is none the less made with French post-Impressionist technique, amplified and adapted to his own clime. It is static harmonically, generously flowing melodically, piquant and dainty in instrumentation, daring as to rhythm. He loves ostinato accompanying figures and carries them on longer than a more timid writer would. He orchestrates à la Satie, without doubling. He fears neither unexpected rhythmic contrasts nor familiar melodic turns. His music has grace, grandeur, delicacy, charm, and enormous distinction. It was a pleasing gesture on Miss Sokolow's part to give us three meaty works last night from a composer so excellent and so little played.

Of the three works the *Homage to García Lorca* was the richest musically, though the *Songs for Little Girls* (if I may correct the program's translation of *Canciones para Niñas*) are indeed worthy to rank beside the best child-inspired music we know, including that of Schumann and of Maurice Ravel. *The Fable of the Wandering Frog* sounded less convincing to me. Was it unexpectedly given us in pianoforte reduction, I wonder? The program mentioned a conductor, not a pianist.

The rest of Miss Sokolow's recital was consecrated to Mr. Alex North and to a ballet (after Goya) called *Visión Fantástica,* by Padre Antonio Soler, a capable and skillful eighteenth-century Spanish composer. Mr. North's best work of the evening, *Slaughter of the Innocents,* was of Spanish inspiration too. It sounded, in spite of good musical ideas, as if it had been written to fit a dance number already conceived. This is not good procedure. It invariably makes the music sound timid and the orchestra like a projection (by means of slave labor) of the chief dancer's will, instead of making the chief dancer seem like the personification of the collective imagination of the instrumentalists. Neither did it seem very good taste to insert in the middle of the Soler work a section written by Mr. North in another style, particularly since that section was not the equal in either elegance or expressive power of the Soler music that surrounded it.

March 4, 1941

A Master in Our Time

CONCERT IN MEMORY OF BÉLA BARTÓK last night at the New York Public Library, Room 213. Participants: *Curt Sachs*, lecturer; *Enid Szantho*, contralto; *Gyorgy Sandor* and *Paul Ulanowsky* pianists; and the Lener String Quartet (*Jeno Lener* and *Michael Kuttner*, violins; *Nicholas Harsanyi*, viola; and *Otto Deri*, cello).

A TRIBUTE   *Dr. Sachs*
From the Twenty Hungarian Folk Songs:
     SONGS OF GRIEG; IN PRISON; SONG OF THE EXILE
NEW SONGS: Oh My Dear Mother; Ripening Cherries; At Doboz; Yellow
     Corn-Stalk; Wheat, Wheat
             Miss Szantho; Mr. Ulanowsky at the piano
Five Pieces from MIKROKOSMOS: Jack in the Box; Harmonics;
     Wrestling; Melody; From the Diary of a Fly   arr. TIBOR SERLY
                 Lener Quartet

DANCE SUITE   *Mr. Sandor*

BÉLA BARTÓK, by virtually any criterion Hungary's top-ranking composer of our century, died in New York City on September 26 of last year. The New York Public Library's music division held a memorial concert to his memory last night in the Main Library, at which works of the late master were sung by Enid Szantho and played by Gyorgy Sandor, pianist, and the Lener String Quartet. Paul Ulanowsky accompanied Miss Szantho. The executions were admirable, and the occasion was wholly devotional and touching. It would have been more impressive musically than it was, however, if Bartók had been represented by at least one major work.

Dr. Curt Sachs, of New York University, in an opening tribute, remarked that Bartók had never used Hungarian folklore as an exotic element for spicing up his own musical language, in the manner of Brahms or of Liszt, but that he wrote it as the very substance of his musical thought. The idea, as expressed, sounded convincing. But when one remembers that Bartók treated the folk music of Rumania, Bulgaria, Yugoslavia, and French North Africa with equal aptness and by not dissimilar musical procedures, one wonders if it was altogether the Hungarian turns of folklore that constituted his musical mother tongue, if he did not envisage all the folklores of the Mediterranean regions as a sort of lingua franca.

Certainly Bartók's public for music of Hungarian (and points south) material was an international one. His musical procedures, no matter what kind of melodic material he used, were so widely imitated in the 1920's that they became the standard formula for producing, with no matter what melodic material, a piece of "modern music" that could be played on any modernistic program anywhere in the world. He thought of himself, I am sure, as always and predominantly a Hungarian; but he was in effect an internationalist and the inventor of one of the most widely practiced international styles of the period between the two wars.

Today that style seems as old-fashioned to us as the flatchested girls in Chanel dresses one fox trotted with in 1926. But let us not be hasty to condemn it, or them. The twenty-year armistice that lasted from 1918 to 1938, from Versailles to Munich, was a brilliant and a fecund period of musical creation. If few of its masterworks are current in repertory today, many are remembered and will be revived in a later decade. Bartók was one of the masters of that period, the third in stylistic carrying power, I should say, of all the musicians who represented to the rest of the world modernistic *Mittel Europa*. Schönberg and Hindemith have survived him. His influence on the young was even in his lifetime less than theirs.

Nevertheless, it was a wide influence. And any musician can see, from the mere skill of his musical textures, that he was a master. The prestige of the Bartók style is today less than the respect and admiration in which the man himself is held. His music will probably pass through a period of decline in currency and then be rediscovered. He never touched the musical masses of the world very deeply, but he wrote well. In another decade or so we shall be able to estimate his stylistic power and to understand his communication better, I think, than any of us can do just now. He has been a master in our time. That we can be sure about.

January 12, 1946

Going Contemporary

BOSTON SYMPHONY ORCHESTRA, *Serge Koussevitzky*, conductor, concert last night at Carnegie Hall.

OVERTURE TO CORIOLANUS	BEETHOVEN
SYMPHONY No. 6, IN F MAJOR ("Pastoral")	BEETHOVEN
SYMPHONY No. 5, OP. 100	PROKOFIEV

PROKOFIEV's Fifth Symphony, which the Boston Symphony Orchestra played here for the second time this season at last night's concert in Carnegie Hall, remains on second hearing chiefly interesting to his listener as a neo-Romantic work by a formerly neo-Classic-and-Impressionist composer. Its more picturesque sections, which are the second and fourth movements, present no novelty of any kind, though they are good Prokofiev, the first of these being a sort of Soviet-style blues, or Muscovite one-step, and the other standard finale in the composer's best calisthenic vein. Both are brightly, if a little weightily orchestrated. The last has even more reminders than mere coloration of Strauss's *Till Eulenspiegel*.

The first and third movements, which are less striking, deal with a more difficult problem, namely, making a piece of some length out of pliable material. The third movement, a lament, or elegy, is less successfully developed than the first. Slow movements have never been Prokofiev's forte, and of late years he has taken more and more to concealing their lack of expressivity (and of rhythmic variety) with an overlay of cinema sentiment.

The first movement, however, is as neat a piece of symphonic workmanship as has been exposed to us locally in many a day. The rounded, graceful theme of it is no theme at all in a classical sense. It is a motif that generates a flow of music. This is not made up of themes or of formal melodies; it is rather a constant outpouring, an oratorical discourse that never repeats itself but that springs always from the original motif, or source, and that returns constantly to it for refreshment.

The movement is a neo-Romantic work because it faces the central problem of neo-Romanticism, which is the making of sustained music out of non-angular material. This is a technical statement of the neo-Romantic meaning-problem, which is that of sustained personal lyricism. But the two problems are one. The neo-Classicists of the 1920's used angular or motionless material. Any neo-Classicist who, knowingly or unawares, has got involved with rounded or flowing material has found himself up to his neck in personal lyricism, the most treacherous of contemporary esthetic currents. That Prokofiev has not, in this work, found himself out beyond his depth either technically or emotionally is proof that he is not an old man yet. That he has walked out after one movement on all the serious difficulties presented proves also that he is not quite at home in contemporary waters.

The concert began with Beethoven's *Coriolanus* Overture and "Pastoral" Symphony. Both sounded to perfection instrumentally; but as meaning, they were poor and thin. The first was over-dramatized till it resembled Dargomizhsky. The second was over-corseted rhythmically till all the jollity went out of it. The slow movement, scored in twelve-eight time, was conducted in six-eight. And quantitative meter was consistently mistaken for accentual. As a result, two hundred years' evolution of the German pastoral style, of which this work is the apex and flower, came to nothing but beautiful tone.

February 14, 1946

Brilliant Farewell

NEW YORK CITY SYMPHONY, *Leonard Bernstein,* conductor, assisted by men's chorus directed by *Robert Shaw; Norman Corwin,* speaker, and five soloists; concert of music by *Igor Stravinsky* last night at the New York City Center.

OEDIPUS REX, opera-oratorio with text by *Jean Cocteau.* (Jocasta, *Nell Tangeman;* Oedipus, *Hans Heinz;* Creon, *Ralph Telasco;* Shephard, *Nathaniel Sprinzena;* Tiresias, *James Pease;* Speaker, *Norman Corwin*)
PASTORALE for five instruments
RAGTIME for piano (*Leo Smit*)
ELEGY for two violas (*Beatrice Brown* and *Walter Trampler*)
ROYAL MARCH from L'HISTOIRE D'UN SOLDAT
SUITE from THE FIRE BIRD

THE FINAL concert of our City Symphony's all too brief season took place last night at the City Center of Music and Drama. The program, devoted to Stravinsky, was anything but a stale one, the *Firebird* suite being the only number on it that is current in repertory. Leonard Bernstein, the conductor, made a pretty speech. Divers soloists from the orchestra played expertly chamber works by the White Russian master. And Mr. Bernstein led a handsome and (for once) thoroughly prepared performance of the rarely heard dramatic oratorio, *Oedipus Rex*.

The latter, which your scribe had not encountered since its first performance in Paris nearly twenty years ago, is the same troublesome work it was then. It has not aged becomingly, as *L'Histoire d'un soldat*, from 1917, has, nor lost its savor altogether, like the *Ragtime*, of 1919, both of which were represented on the program. It is a great big lump of wonderful music, some of which never did come off right and still doesn't.

It is noble, grandiose, complex, massive, stony. Only a master could have written it; and only a master with purely instrumental turn of thought, like Stravinsky or Sebastian Bach, could have written it so ungratefully for the human voice. A linguistic problem is somewhat responsible for the vocal ineptitudes; but so is the composer's imperfect acquaintance with vocal ranges; and so is a certain stylistic willfulness on his part that he hoped, I presume, would conceal the faults of the original literary conception.

The text, believe it or not, is a translation into modern Sorbonne Latin of a French adaptation of an English literal translation of Sophocles. It is no wonder that all literary quality got lost in the process. There was not much Stravinsky could do with such a text but what he did is to make it sound as much as possible like Russian. Last night Mr. Norman Corwin went further and, using a public address system, recited between the numbers a sort of explanation, translated, I imagine, from Jean Cocteau's French, which is quite elegant, into radio American, a far from distinguished literary idiom.

For all its final ineffectualness, and forgetting Mr. Corwin, the work has considerable expressive power and a musical seriousness of the grandest kind. It is full of real invention, also of outmoded stylistic affectations. The latter, imitated mostly from Verdi and from Handel, just barely, in some cases, escape the comical. The former, plus its strong dramatic plan, saves the work from silliness.

Neither saves the singers from giving an effect of swimming in molasses, because their solos are all conceived as if the human wind instrument were a trumpet or a keyed trombone. Linear shape and ornament are expected to produce all the expressivity, verbal color and vocal sweetness being omitted wholly from the requirements. Even the male chorus, save for a few really terrifying percussive moments, did not sound as if the music they were singing was their music, though Robert Shaw had obviously prepared them thoroughly. The work is not well written vocally, simply that. But it is nobly conceived.

Hearing it occasionally is a privilege, and Mr. Bernstein is to be thanked for giving it to us. Also for so thoroughly efficient a rendering. He knew the score, and so did his executants. The final *Firebird,* though far more familiar to all, was less clearly read.

Mr. Bernstein, along with tantrums and occasionally immodesty, has given us lots of good music, especially in the domain of modern revivals otherwise not available. One will miss the concerts of his orchestra. Their programs have been more distinguished intellectually than those of any similar group, in spite of the brilliant season the Philharmonic has lately been offering. And the relation of all this to the City Center audience has been of a vivacity unique in the orchestral world. Also, Bernstein conducts like a master when he knows and really likes a score.

November 26, 1946

The Poetry of Precision

PHILHARMONIC-SYMPHONY ORCHESTRA, guest conductor, *Igor Stravinsky,* concert in Carnegie Hall last night. Assisting pianist, *Beveridge Webster.*

OVERTURE TO RUSSLAN AND LUDMILLA   GLINKA
SYMPHONY NO. 2, IN C MINOR   TCHAIKOVSKY
ODE, in three parts, for Orchestra (first time by the orchestra);
   CONCERTO FOR PIANO AND WIND ORCHESTRA; FOUR NOR-
   WEGIAN MOODS (first time by the orchestra); CIRCUS POLKA
   (first time by the orchestra)   STRAVINSKY

IGOR STRAVINSKY, who conducted the Philharmonic-Symphony Orchestra last night in Carnegie Hall, prefaced a delightful little concert of his own works with a spirited reading of Glinka's *Russlan and Ludmilla* overture and a correct but on the whole pedestrian excursion through Tchaikovsky's rarely explored Second Symphony. Whether this work is worthy of the respect that the greatest living Russian composer has long borne it is not a matter on which this reviewer has any opinion. It is obviously a well-written work, full of original fancy and clearly expressed. Whatever feelings anybody may have about it (and feelings are all most people have about Tchaikovsky) are his own business. Myself, I was not enthralled; but I am not a Tchaikovsky fan.

Having long been a Stravinsky fan and long an admirer of the Piano Concerto that Beveridge Webster played so brilliantly last night, your reviewer spent one of the pleasanter moments of the season rehearing it under the composer's direction. Noble of thematic invention, ingenious of texture, and eloquently, grandiloquently sustained, this brilliant evocation of Baroque musical sentiments and attitudes has too long been left on the shelf. It was last played here, if the files in my office are correct, exactly twenty years ago. If patrons walked out on it in scores then, as they did last night, one can understand the hesitancy of conductors to revive it. But if the ovation it received last night from those who stayed (and they were a vast majority) means anything prophetically, the concerto will one day be as popular as Tchaikovsky's in B flat.

The *Ode* retains its elegance on rehearing and gains in intellectual interest, but it remains for this observer a little distant in sentiment. The *Norwegian Moods* are not distant at all. They are warm and picturesque and cheerful, wonderfully melodious and impeccably tailored. At present a sort of *Peer Gynt* suite for the musically sophisticated, they will shortly, I am sure, find themselves at home in the "pop" concerts. The *Circus Polka* has already done so. And indeed a lively picture it is of the sawdust ring. Apparently, the only music lovers who haven't enjoyed it are the elephants for whose dancing it was written. I am told that they scented satire in it, a bit of joking about their proportions (which they are extremely sensitive about) and didn't like working to it. They did not, however, walk out on it.

Mr. Stravinsky's conducting of his own works was, as always, a delight to those who take his works seriously. His rhythm was precise, his tonal texture dry, the expressivity complete. It was complete because only through the most precise rhythm and the driest tonal textures can the Stravinskian pathos be made to vibrate or the Stravinskian tenderness to glow. His is a poetry of exactitude, a theater of delicate adjustments and relentless march. Conductors who sweep through his works as if they were personal oratory of some kind inevitably find these going weak on them. Stravinsky admires Tchaikovsky but he doesn't write or feel like Tchaikovsky. How much added juiciness the latter can stand is an unsettled problem of interpretation. Stravinsky can bear none. It is all written in. His scores are correctly indited, and the composer's reading of them is the way they go. It is also the way they go best.

February 2, 1945

Viennese Lament

N. B. C. SYMPHONY ORCHESTRA, *Dimitri Mitropoulos* conducting; concert yesterday afternoon in Studio 8-H, Radio City. Soloist, *Joseph Szigeti,* violinist.

OVERTURE AND ALLEGRO from LA SULTANE	COUPERIN-MILHAUD
CONCERTO for Violin and Orchestra	BERG
OVERTURE TO KING LEAR	BERLIOZ

DIMITRI MITROPOULOS, who conducted, and Joseph Szigeti, who played the violin solo, lent an unaccustomed distinction to yesterday afternoon's program of the N. B. C. Symphony Orchestra at Studio 8-H, Radio City, by giving us Alban Berg's Concerto for Violin and Orchestra. They lent to the work itself their inimitable comprehension and care of execution, as well. One may understand or not, "like" or not Berg's music; but one can scarcely fail to be grateful for the rare occasions when one is allowed to hear it.

This music is largely atonal in texture; and this particular piece of it is elegiac in character, introspective and deeply sentimental. It is concentrated Vienna, the Vienna of this century, between the two wars. It could not have been conceived, expressively or technically, at any other place or in any other time. It is as Viennese as the music of Erik Satie is Parisian. For the initiates, therefore, it is full of a heart-rending nostalgia. For the profane it is inevitably something of a bore. Either one melts before its especial expressivity or one stiffens at the seeming exaggeration of both its content and its texture. But whatever way one takes it, it is sincere and skillful music.

Myself, I do not care for it with passion, but I enjoy hearing it. It is full of lovely moments. I am not sure, however, that its beauty is entirely transparent. I suspect that its technical procedures are not wholly at the service of this work's generative emotion, that part of the time they limit the free flow of the expressed feeling and part of the time give it a lachrymose and lugubrious tone that overstates it. I may be wrong; I have only heard the piece once. Clearly it is a work of more than ordinary intensity and, if you respond to it, charm.

Mr. Mitropoulos had framed it between Darius Milhaud's arrangement of selections from Couperin and the Berlioz *King Lear* overture, both of them works that are rarely played here and both of them brilliant theatrical evocations. Milhaud has not forgotten in orchestrating Couperin that the latter was an organist. He has imitated organ registration with many octave doublings and with marked contrasts in volume and color. The Allegro, in which orchestral brasses play rapidly, like the bright and brilliant reed stops of Couperin's own instrument (which is in excellent condition at the Church of St. Gervais in Paris), has a dazzling alacrity.

The orchestra's rendering of the Berlioz overture had been elegantly drilled; but the sound of it suffered somewhat from the dark and weighty character of American trombone and double-bass tone, which was no part of its composer's calculation.

December 31, 1945

Schönberg's Music

On September 13 Arnold Schönberg, the dean of the modernists, will be seventy years old. And yet his music for all its author's love of traditional sonorous materials and all the charm of late nineteenth-century Vienna that envelops its expression, is still the modernest modern music that exists. No other Western music sounds so strange, so consistently different from the music of the immediately preceding centuries. And none, save that of Erik Satie, has proved so tough a nut for the public to crack. Only the early *Verklärte Nacht* has attained to currency in our concerts. The rest remains to this day musicians' music.

Musicians do not always know what they think of Schönberg's music, but they often like to listen to it. And they invariably respect it. Whether one likes it or not is, indeed, rather a foolish question to raise in face of its monumental logic. To share or to reject the sentiments that it expresses seems, somehow, a minor consideration compared with following the amplitude of the reasoning that underlies their exposition. As in much of modern philosophical writing, the conclusions reached are not the meat of the matter; it is the methods by which these are arrived at.

This preponderance of methodology over objective is what gives to Schönberg's work, in fact, its irreducible modernity. It is the orientation that permits us to qualify it as, also, in the good sense of the word, academic. For it is a model of procedure. And if the consistency of the procedure seems often closer to the composer's mind than the expressive aim, that fact allows us further to describe the work as academic in an unfavorable sense. It means that the emotional nourishment in the music is not quite worth the trouble required to extract it. This is a legitimate and not uncommon layman's opinion. But if one admits, as I think one is obliged to do with regard to Schönberg, that the vigor and thoroughness of the procedure are, in very fact, the music's chief objective, then no musician can deny that it presents a very high degree of musical interest.

This is not to say that Schönberg's music is without feeling expressed. Quite to the contrary, it positively drips with emotivity. But still the approach is, in both senses of the word, academic. Emotions are examined rather than declared. As in the workings of his distinguished fellow citizen Dr. Sigmund Freud, though the subject matter is touching, even lurid, the author's detachment about it is complete. Sentiments are considered as case histories rather than as pretexts for personal poetry or subjects for showmanship. *Die glückliche Hand, Gurre-Lieder,* and *Pierrot Lunaire,* as well as the string sextet, *Verklärte Nacht,* have deeply sentimental subjects; but their treatment is always by detailed exposition, never by sermonizing. Pierrot's little feelings, therefore, though they seem enormous and are unquestionably fascinating when studied through the Schönberg microscope for forty-five minutes of concert time, often appear in retrospect as less interesting than the mechanism through which they have been viewed.

The designing and perfecting of this mechanism, rather than the creation of unique works, would seem to have been the guiding preoccupation of Schönberg's career; certainly it is the chief source of his enormous prestige among musicians. The works themselves, charming as they are and frequently impressive, are never quite as fascinating when considered separately as they are when viewed as comments on a method of composition or as illustrations of its expressive possibilities. They are all secondary to a theory; they do not lead independent lives. The theory, however, leads an independent life. It is taught and practiced all over the world. It is the lingua franca of contemporary modernism. It is even used expertly by composers who have never heard any of the works by Schönberg, by Webern, and by Alban Berg that constitute its major literature.

If that major literature is wholly Viennese by birth and its sentimental preoccupations largely Germanic, the syntax of its expression embodies also both the strongest and the weakest elements of the German musical tradition. Its strong element is its simplification of tonal relations; its weak element is its chaotic rhythm. The apparent complexity of the whole literature and the certain obscurity of much of it are due, in the present writer's opinion, to the lack of a rhythmic organization comparable in comprehensiveness and in simplicity to the tonal one.

It is probably the insufficiencies of Schönberg's own rhythmic theory that prevent his music from crystallizing into great, hard, beautiful, indissoluble works. Instrumentally they are delicious. Tonally they are the most exciting, the most original, the most modern-sounding music there is. What limits their intelligibility, hamstrings their expressive power, makes them often literally halt in their tracks, is the naïve organization of their pulses, taps, and quantities. Until a rhythmic syntax comparable in sophistication to Schönberg's tonal one shall have been added to this, his whole method of composition, for all the high intellection and sheer musical genius that have gone into its making, will probably remain a fecund but insupportable heresy, a strict counterpoint valuable to pedagogy but stiff, opaque, unmalleable, and inexpressive for free composition.

There is no satisfactory name for the thing Schönberg has made. The twelve-tone technique, though its commonest denomination, does not cover all of it. But he has made a thing, a new thing, a thing to be used and to be improved. Its novelty in 1944 is still fresh; and that means it has strength, not merely charm. Its usage by composers of all nations means that it is no instrument of local or limited applicability. Such limitations as it has are due, I believe, to the fact that it is not yet a complete system. So far as it goes it is admirable; and it can go far, as the operas of Alban Berg show. It is to the highest credit of Schönberg as a creator that his method of creation should be so valuable a thing as to merit still, even to require, the collaboration of those who shall come after him.

September 10, 1944

FROM OUT OF TOWN

Overtrained

BOSTON SYMPHONY ORCHESTRA, *Serge Koussevitzky*, conductor, first concert of the season in Carnegie Hall last night.

SYMPHONY NO. 3, IN E FLAT MAJOR, "Eroica," OP. 56
HAROLD IN ITALY, symphony in four movements   BERLIOZ
                    (*William Primrose*, viola solo)

THE BOSTON SYMPHONY ORCHESTRA'S first concert of the season, which took place last night in Carnegie Hall, consisted of two works and lasted two hours. They were beautiful works and handsomely executed. With the exception of the impossible horn passage in the trio of Beethoven's "Eroica" scherzo, your commentator could find no fault in the playing. And yet he was aware of the passage of time.

Serge Koussevitzky's tempos were not slow. In the Beethoven symphony they were, in fact, most gratefully animated. And the mechanism of orchestral articulation was, as always with this group, delightful to observe. Everything was right, including William Primrose, who played the viola solo of Berlioz's *Harold in Italy*. It was the old story, I am afraid, of familiar pieces so elegantly turned out that one scarcely recognized them. They were not deformed. Their clear spirit was not violated. They were simply so completely groomed that one was not aware of any spirit present. The slickness of their surfacing made them seem hollow and laborious underneath, which they are not.

The truth of the matter, in my opinion, is simply that the Boston Symphony Orchestra is overtrained and has been for several years. Its form is perfect, but it does not communicate. The music it plays never seems to be about anything, except how beautifully the Boston Symphony Orchestra can play. Perfection of execution that oversteps its purpose is a familiar phenomenon in art. That way lies superficiality and monotony. And music has no business sounding monotonous, since no two pieces of it are alike. Whenever a series of pieces or of programs starts sounding that way you may be sure that the execution is at fault, is obtruding itself.

One longs, in listening to this orchestra's work, for a little ease. It is of no use for all the sonorous elements to be so neatly in place unless some illusion is present that their being so is spontaneous. Music is not the result of rehearsal. It is an auditory miracle that can take place anywhere. When it occurs among disciplined musicians its miraculous quality is merely heightened. When the frequency of its occurrence in any given group starts diminishing, there are only two possible remedies. Either the members must play together more often, or they must get some new pieces.

Obviously, this group does not need more rehearsing. And it knows now all the pieces there are in standard repertory; it even knows all the kinds of pieces there are for large orchestra. There is nothing to be done about it. It has passed the peak of useful executional skill, and executional hypertrophy has set in. The pattern is a familiar one, and regrettable. But there is no use trying to deceive one's self about it.

November 16, 1944.

Chicago's Orchestra

AMONG America's symphony orchestras that of Chicago stands third in seniority (only Boston and the New York Philharmonic being older) and among the first four in quality (its standards of execution being comparable to those of New York, Boston, and Philadelphia). For fifty-one years it had only two permanent conductors, Theodore Thomas and Frederick Stock, though Eric Delamarter took it over for two seasons during the other World War, when Dr. Stock, at that time a German citizen, was in retirement from public life. On Dr. Stock's death, two years ago, the post fell vacant, his assistant Hans Lange being asked to carry on for the rest of the season.

From an artistic point of view the post is a plum, since the orchestra is first-class, the Chicago musical public both large and enlightened, and the tradition of long tenure for conductors one inspiring of any man's best efforts. Among many distinguished applicants, the appointment fell a year ago to the Belgian conductor Désiré Defauw previously known on this continent chiefly through his work with the Montreal Symphony Orchestra and from a few guest appearances in Boston. Chicago has been a battle ground ever since.

The front of the opposition has been Claudia Cassidy, music critic of the *Chicago Tribune,* who has carried on a press campaign of no small vigor to expose what she considers to be Mr. Defauw's musical unworthiness for a post so rich in tradition and so high in responsibility. Being curious to taste the qualities of a workman who has been the object of so sustained a discussion, your reviewer took occasion last week to attend the opening concert of the Tuesday afternoon series in Orchestra Hall. With no wish in the world to insert himself into a Chicago dispute and one which shows signs of quieting down this season, anyway, he offers here no reflected opinion of Mr. Defauw's work (nor could he from one hearing) but simply a review of a musical occasion that he happened to attend.

The program was one well designed to show off any conductor's gifts and weaknesses; it might have been set as an examination. There was a Berlioz overture (the *Benvenuto Cellini*), a Brahms symphony (No. 2), Prokofiev's *Scythian Suite* and (of all things) the Scriabin *Poème d'Extase.* The Berlioz is an easy piece, though few play it well; they mostly let it go rackety. The Scriabin is not at all an easy piece either for the players or for the conductor. Its rhythm has a tendency to go spineless and its instrumentation to get blurred. It requires eight horns, moreover, an outlay of brasses difficult to produce in wartime. Their presence is required also for the *Scythian Suite.* As for Brahms and Prokofiev, the conductor does not live who can interpret both writers equally well, so utterly opposed are they in their understanding of rhythm.

Brahms, as you may well imagine, came off least well among the composers represented. I say you may well imagine, because

Mr. Defauw is a musician of French rather than of German training and because, as a youngish man (turned fifty, I should guess), he is a child of the twentieth century rather than of the nineteenth. His Brahms was handsomely phrased and cleanly articulated, but it didn't seem to be about anything. It was not careless or mushy or overweening. It was just too neatly sculptured to make any of the kind of sense Brahms's music must make if it is to avoid being pompous. Certainly it had none of the dreamy quality that made Stock's playing of this same music so lovely and so enveloping.

The Gallicism of Mr. Defauw's musical mind was exemplified constantly in the clarity of his orchestral textures. Loud or soft, you could always hear what was being played. That orchestra in that hall can make the most resonant fortissimo in America. Terribly, wonderfully loud, these were always beautiful and always clean. The modernity of his rhythmic understanding was exemplified in the Prokofiev and Scriabin works, where quantitative scansion and tonic stresses must be kept separate. Defauw is a clear-minded musician, a master of equilibrium, of rhythm, and of phraseology; and he has a taste for brightness of sound. For these qualities I can forgive him much. He makes good programs, too, if the four or five printed in the program book are typical, mixing the nineteenth century constantly with our own and not forgetting the eighteenth.

It is not for what musicians play badly that we remember them but for what they play well. And this listener will long remember the performance he heard in Chicago of Prokofiev's *Scythian Suite* and of Scriabin's melodically outmoded but orchestrally still sumptuous *Poem of Ecstasy*. He has heard many pretentious and vain renderings of both. Neither is it the first time he has slept through somebody's Brahms. He has never heard the two Russian works rendered with so high a degree of luminosity. That luminosity was the result of precise orchestral balances and correct rhythmic scansion. One is grateful for these qualities in a world where overworked orchestras and overadvertised conductors are becoming increasingly careless about both.

October 29, 1944

Orchestrally News

DETROIT SYMPHONY ORCHESTRA, *Karl Krueger,* conductor, concert in Carnegie Hall last night. Soprano soloist, *Marjorie Lawrence.*

SYMPHONY NO. 2	RACHMANINOFF
DIDO'S LAMENT, from DIDO AND AENEAS	PURCELL
BATUQUE	FERNANDEZ
THE WHITE PEACOCK	GRIFFES
DANCE OF THE SEVEN VEILS; Final Scene from SALOMÉ	STRAUSS

EVEN through the mud and sugar of Rachmaninoff's Second Symphony, it was clear in Carnegie Hall last night that Karl Krueger is a virtuoso conductor and that the Detroit Symphony Orchestra is one of our top professional outfits. The string work in particular is the sort of thing one hears only from first-class workmen, trained by a musician who knows about workmanship and cares. Deep, rich, and suave, or light as transparent silk, the tone of it has that sumptuous sound that Leopold Stokowski used to produce from the Philadelphia strings twenty years ago. Whether this opulence might cloy under sustained acquaintance, as that of the old Philadelphia group was likely to do, remains to be learned from experience. One evening of it was luxurious and one would like more.

Mr. Krueger's program would have been better suited to an outdoor "pop" concert than it was to a New York winter occasion. Excepting for the short air from Purcell's *Dido and Aeneas,* which Marjorie Lawrence sang (I think in English) without any stylistic restraint, there was not one piece on it that could be considered classical symphonic music, ancient or modern. The final scene from Strauss's *Salomé,* which Miss Lawrence sang with a fine dramatic gusto, and which Mr. Krueger conducted with full exploitation of all its grand theatrical violence, was the only piece that had even any serious entertainment value for this listener. The rest of the time he observed the sound orchestral work and admired the courtly elegance of the conductor's deportment.

For the record, let it be put down that Mr. Krueger was born in Atchison, Kansas, that he learned his art in Vienna, and that he perfected it during a decade's tenure at the Kansas City Philharmonic. He has been in Detroit for two years now. I have heard him work in both cities and found him excellent, if a little heavy-spirited, perhaps, by temperament. He is a virtuoso performer, however, and, for all his Viennese dignity, a born showman. His repertory has been notable for breadth and for its high percentage of novelty.

Just why so skillful an operator should have offered us the program he did last night escapes me. It was successful enough in terms of a full house and massive acclaim. I put the latter down to the sad fact that a New York audience will applaud with abandon anything that is handsomely enough executed, which last night's program certainly was. It may be, of course, that I overestimate our musical needs. More likely I am underestimating Mr. Krueger's sagacity. In any case, and giving him and his men full credit for a show pulled off, the calculation behind it all may well have been the advertising maxim: "Tell it to Sweeney; the Stuyvesants will understand."

January 31, 1945

From Hollywood via Indianapolis

INDIANAPOLIS SYMPHONY ORCHESTRA, *Fabien Sevitzky*, conductor, first New York concert in Carnegie Hall last night.

OVERTURE, ROMAN CARNIVAL	BERLIOZ
SYMPHONY IN D MAJOR, "LA CHASSE"	HAYDN
PRAELUDIUM AND FUGUE	BARRYMORE
(First New York Performance)	
SYMPHONY No. 5	SHOSTAKOVICH

THE INDIANAPOLIS SYMPHONY ORCHESTRA, of which Fabien Sevitzky is the conductor, made its first appearance in New York last night at Carnegie Hall before a large and warmer than warm audience. Though scarcely ten years old as a major orchestra ("major" means that the annual budget exceeds $200,000), it has already made itself known in the Middle West for high standards of execution and throughout the country for advanced program making. Only Boston tops Indianapolis in the proportion of annual playing time consecrated to the works of either living composers or American composers.

Last night's bouquet of works, I must say, was far from novel, its one fresh flower being a work by, of all people, Lionel Barrymore. For the rest, there were a Berlioz overture, a Haydn symphony and one of those interminable Shostakovich numbers. The orchestral execution and the conducting throughout were excellent. Mr. Sevitzky is a sound musician, a leader of force and refinement. It seems a shame to waste him and his men on a program that might have been heard at almost any time during the last five years at the Stadium or other "pop" concerts.

Mr. Barrymore's *Praeludium and Fugue* (sic) is an eclectic work of not much interior tension; but it is painstakingly, rather elaborately, indeed, composed. Orchestrated, though the program did not say so, by a Hollywood expert, its surface overlay contains just about everything, including a storm, some "Chinese" effects and, of course, chimes at the end. It evokes Ronald Colman getting out of an airplane in a snowstorm or Miss Lana Turner in trouble or about anything one might care to select along that line, simply because it has been dressed up to sound that way. A pianoforte reduction of the piece would show, I am certain, a very different expressive content.

The prelude is a wandering improvisation such as any church organist might make who had been brought up on Bach but who admired Richard Strauss more. The fugue has a Straussian subject derived from *Also Sprach Zarathustra*. This is treated successively in ironic, atmospheric, pathetic, and oratorical vein. Put through such a workout, it ceases, long before the end, to mean anything at all. Mr. Barrymore's good will in all this seems impeccable; but his instructors should have told him that the purpose of fugal device is to magnify the subject's characteristic expression, not to obliterate it.

The curiosity interest of this little work and the excellent playing of the orchestra were not, unfortunately, quite enough to hold the interest of the concert up to where one felt all the time it should be. Perhaps Mr. Sevitzky's tempos are a shade slow, too. In any case, this listener found the music all evening, though clear and in every way shipshape, not completely absorbing.

December 7, 1944

Music in Pittsburgh

FRITZ REINER's excellence as a conductor, though we do not hear him here as often as lovers of fine musical workmanship could wish, is well known to New Yorkers. And the Pittsburgh (Pennsylvania) Symphony Orchestra, his regular charge, has of late become more and more agreeably familiar to collectors of gramophone records. Hearing the two together and *in situ* was the privilege of your reporter on a recent week end spent in the city of smoke and steel, birthplace of Stephen Foster and of Oscar Levant.

The orchestra's habitat, a building in the arabesque taste called Syria Mosque, is not ideal acoustically. Its auditorium, which is at least twice as wide as it is deep, has no proper focus of sound. All the same, the orchestra makes good music in it, Mr. Reiner's impeccable clarity of texture replacing most effectively auditory advantages that the architect's proportions fail to provide. His program was a pretty one, lively, modernistic, and not banal. It contained, in reversed chronological order of their composition: Milhaud's *Suite française*, a novelty of this season; Stravinsky's suite from *Pulcinella*, a masterpiece of twenty-six years ago that is more familiar to audiences as a violin or a cello solo piece than in its orchestral version, and Debussy's *Ibéria*, now in its thirty-ninth year. There was also a conservative work, Wieniawski's Violin Concerto, No. 2, the chief attraction it presented being the more than merely beautiful violin playing of Isaac Stern.

To a New Yorker the evening was a delight. We do not often hear in Carnegie Hall a program so fresh, so light of texture, so still alive. The Milhaud piece we have heard just once. We almost never hear *Pulcinella*. And we are not overaccustomed to *Ibéria*. I don't think I have ever heard, even from Pierre Monteux, so eloquent, so absorbing a performance of this beautiful and troublesome work, so difficult to project because of its evanescent continuity. In Reiner's hands it made both music and sense; and the rhythm, for once, as Debussy must have intended, sustained its supple strength like a spinal column.

On another evening there was a concert of modern sonatas, presented at the Carnegie Institute of Technology by the newly formed local chapter of the International Society for Contemporary Music. The program included piano sonatas by Aaron Copland, by Stravinsky, and by the present writer; a sonata for cello alone by Jerzy Fitelberg, a world première; and one for violin and piano by Hindemith. The executant artists were Webster Aitken, pianist; Stefan Auber, first cellist of the symphony orchestra; Isaac Stern, violinist; and his admirable accompanist, Alexander Zakin. It is not often that one hears modern works, either standard or new, performed with such technical brilliance and such conviction. Their stimulating effect on the audience present was proved by the vigor of the discussion that took place for over an hour in the forum that followed. The composer Nikolai Lopatnikoff, professor of composition at the Carnegie Institute, presided over this, the other composers present, as well as the evening's executant artists, participating from the platform. It was a lively evening.

A performance by the local opera company of Puccini's *La Bohème* proved less rewarding. Musical *verismo* is not for amateurs, because dramatic continuity, rather than musical, is its sustaining element. With this missing (and it is normally missing from amateur operatic performance) Puccini's music, which has little sustained rhetoric, however great its moment-to-moment expressivity, tends to fall apart, to lack concentration and trajectory. Even the presence of experienced soloists (mostly imported) like Dorothy Kirsten, Hugh Thompson, and Giulio Gari (a soundly resonant Rodolfo) and of an unusually well-prepared local artist, Mary Martha Briney, who sang Musetta, could not keep the evening alert.

The week end, as a whole, however, was more than satisfactory to one who, in spite of season's-end saturation, can still take musical nourishment. And spring in Pittsburgh, with trees and grass picked out in baby-leaf green against the blackened violet that is the city's tone, is not without a certain poetry.

April 14, 1946

A Touching Occasion

BALTIMORE SYMPHONY ORCHESTRA, *Reginald Stewart*, conductor, first New York concert last night at Carnegie Hall. Soloist: *Georges Enesco*, violinist.

FUGUE IN C MAJOR	BACH-WEINER
CHORAL PRELUDE: "Komm süsser Tod"	BACH-STEWART
SYMPHONY NO. 3, IN F MAJOR	BRAHMS
PANTOMIME FOR ORCHESTRA	LUKAS FOSS
(First New York Performance)	
CONCERTO FOR VIOLIN AND ORCHESTRA IN D MAJOR, OP. 77	BRAHMS

THE BALTIMORE SYMPHONY ORCHESTRA played last night in Carnegie Hall under the leadership of Reginald Stewart its first New York concert. The program was conservative, the execution clean but not very communicative. The evening would have been, on the whole, uneventful had not Georges Enesco, as soloist in the Brahms Violin Concerto, brought fire to the program and tears to all our eyes.

The great Rumanian composer, conductor, and violinist has not previously appeared in downtown Manhattan since before the war. Wartime privation and suffering, which have left their mark of arthritic distortion on a once noble figure, seem to have affected hardly at all Enesco's mastery of his instrument. His tone is full and sweet, his pitch impeccable, his style in every way serious and grand. Not only was his playing a musical pleasure, but his return to Carnegie Hall physically bowed but spiritually indomitable was the occasion for cheers and solid applause. I think all hearts were deeply touched.

Lukas Foss's *Pantomime for Orchestra*, which received its first New York hearing last night, is a spotty and discontinuous composition, not at all lacking in fancy but insufficiently sequential for concert listening. It sounded as if it had been composed to accompany an acrobatic comedy number and as if the composer had followed in his score, step by step, the stage routine. Lacking program notes, I cannot be sure that I am right about the work's origins. With or without notes the piece lacks continuity. One has faith in Mr. Foss's very real talent as a composer, in his skill, his fancy, his dedication. But he does mature more slowly than most. Perhaps that is a favorable sign.

Mr. Stewart's orchestra is not one of America's finest, but it is a reasonably efficient machine for making music. Its sound lacks cohesion, as Mr. Stewart's conducting lacks the ultimate in urgency. All is sane and civilized but not, to surfeited New York ears, completely absorbing. The readings are clean, but they are only readings. They are not in any sense interpretations. That is why, especially in the familiar works, last night's concert was somewhat short of compelling. In music making it is always better to be wrong than reserved.

February 6, 1947

Landscape Music

DALLAS SYMPHONY ORCHESTRA, *Antal Dorati*, conductor, broadcast yesterday afternoon in the National Broadcasting Company's "Orchestras of the Nation" series.

SYMPHONY No. 27, IN G MAJOR	MOZART
SYMPHONIA SERENA	HINDEMITH
(First Performance)	
THREE DANCE EPISODES from RODEO	COPLAND

THE DALLAS SYMPHONY ORCHESTRA, Antal Dorati, conductor, gave yesterday afternoon in a program broadcast by NBC the first performance of a work in four movements by Paul Hindemith entitled, *Symphonia Serena*. At today's concert of the same orchestra in Fair Park Auditorium, Dallas, Texas, the first public performance will take place. Yesterday's broadcast was one of a series called "The Orchestras of the Nation," which occupy the three o'clock hour, locally speaking, on Saturday afternoons over WNBC. The work in question, a commission of the Dallas Symphony Orchestra, was composed during November and December 1946. On yesterday's program it was preceded by Mozart's jolly G-major Symphony, No. 27, and followed by Three Dance Episodes from Aaron Copland's ballet, *Rodeo*, a concert suite not yet heard in New York. (One of these dances was conducted by Leonard Bernstein at a Stadium concert on July 8, 1945.)

The Hindemith symphony, this composer's second, is a large essay in pastoral vein. Eschewing voluntarily the pathetic style, the composer has aimed, I think, at a direct rendering of landscape. No land or seascape so specific as that of Debussy's *Ibéria* or *La Mer* is invoked; but the piece is a pastoral symphony all the same, a formal communion with nature not dissimilar in approach to Mendelssohn's "Italian" and "Scottish" symphonies. Whether the landscape is one with or without figures is hard to say, though there is certainly an echo present in the slow movement. All the same, there is no such broad humanity included as that which joins in the village dancing of Beethoven's Sixth Symphony.

The first movement seems to be about the countryside, perhaps a walk through this in spring or summer; at one point water, possibly a rivulet or cascade, is suggested. The second, a scherzo for wind instruments based on a quickstep theme by Beethoven, is light in texture and extremely animated. Possibly insect life may be its subject. The third is a dialogue for two string orchestras, two solo strings (a violin and a viola), and two more of the same playing off-stage right and left. Its sentiment is tender, sweet, and not without a deliberate nobility. Echo effects evoke a décor with some distance in it. A certain pathos of expression indicates a spectator. The last movement, which is one of considerable thematic complexity, is certainly dominated by the sound of birds.

The entire piece is contrapuntally complex in the sense that almost no theme is ever stated without a countertheme in contrasting rhythmic values being present. This procedure gives objectivity to the expression, impersonality and reserve. The work is distinguished of texture and most agreeable in sound (the dissonant diatonic is its syntax). It will take its place in the repertory of evocation rather than in that of symphonic sermonizing. Exactly what that place will be is difficult to predict; but if manliness of spirit and sound workmanship have any carrying power in our land and century, that place will be one of honor. Hindemith's *Symphonia Serena* is a solid, conservative work from the studio of one of the solidest and most conservative workmen alive.

Copland's *Rodeo* dances are outdoor music, too, and with lots of humanity in them. They are gay and sweet, jolly and heart-breakingly sentimental. Their reading by Mr. Dorati and the Dallas orchestra was vivid, clear, animated. So was that of the Hindemith symphony. The Mozart reading was admirable for clarity and cleanliness, but its rhythmic layout was perhaps a shade foursquare.

February 2, 1947

Modernistic Piety

SAN FRANCISCO SYMPHONY ORCHESTRA, concert last night at Carnegie Hall, *Pierre Monteux* conducting.

PASSACAGLIA AND FUGUE IN C MINOR	BACH-RESPIGHI
L'ASCENSION — Four Symphonic Meditations	MESSIAEN
(First New York Performance)	
DEATH AND TRANSFIGURATION	STRAUSS
SYMPHONY NO. 1, IN C MINOR, OP. 68	BRAHMS

PIERRE MONTEUX, who conducted his own orchestra, the San Francisco Symphony, last night in Carnegie Hall, is one of the greatest among living conductors. His orchestra, unfortunately, on account of budgetary limitations, is not so perfect an instrument as he is a musician. Its imperfections were somewhat exaggerated, moreover, last night by the unfamiliarity of the players with Carnegie Hall's rather special acoustics. It is hard for any group to strike a balance on a stage which projects sound so fully that not enough resonance is left on that stage to enable the men to hear one another. Also, it is very easy, with the present soundboard, for any conductor to overencourage the brasses.

Both the brasses and the woodwinds of this orchestra are of good quality. It is the strings that are weak. Not weak in sound, because they do make quite a racket, but not entirely transparent, because of incomplete unanimity both of pitch and of rhythm. Their tone is live but scratchy. In fast passages or under heavy bow-arm pressures it explodes, goes brittle and overbrilliant, loses tonal focus. All the animated passages sounded last night, in consequence, in spite of Mr. Monteux's admirable tempos and careful phrasing, a little rowdy.

The novelty of the evening was Olivier Messiaen's four "symphonic meditations," entitled *The Ascension*. This work, though not by any means its author's masterpiece, is pleasant music, easy to listen to and, with or without footnotes, easy to understand. I shall not use up my space today repeating its footnotes and subtitles. Suffice it to remark that Messiaen alone among the composers of our day has achieved a convincing synthesis of musical modernism with devotional piety. He has thus enlarged not only his art's technique but also its expressive range. His music is vibrant and fresh in sound, deeply affecting also as emotion communicated. Its faults of both technique and taste, and it has many, are as nothing compared to its originality and its force. It is new, powerful, and good.

So, I presume, was Richard Strauss's *Death and Transfiguration* fifty years ago. Today it seems labored and obvious, but it still has a kind of life in it. The juxtaposition of this work to Messiaen's piece on a similar subject was a happy thought on Mr. Monteux's part. It brought out more similarities, indeed, than basic differences. Strauss pulls at the heartstrings with a violin solo accompanied by harp, a procedure no doubt infallible in the nineties. Messiaen uses a trumpet solo accompanied by other brass to achieve a similar result. Once the contemporary charm of the latter procedure has worn off, the effect may be about that of Strauss's violin solo today.

Neither composer's reputation rests or is going to rest on one work. Both are abundant and masterful writers, and I should hazard the guess that Messiaen presents right now the spectacle of a musical genius in almost full-blown flower not dissimilar in either contemporary appeal or prospects of permanent value to that offered fifty years ago by Richard Strauss. Though neither composer, as I said before, was represented last night by his best piece, their treatments of a certain subject (the shaking off of mortality) at almost the same age (when in their thirties) give a basis for comparison. Both pieces played last night came off well in that comparison. One, perhaps, is overglamorous with up-to-dateness, but thrilling nevertheless, the other more than a little faded, but still good for jerking a tear.

April 12, 1947

University Festival

FISK UNIVERSITY in Nashville, Tennessee, is one of America's major institutions of learning. Its high academic standards and elevated cultural tone, as well as its seniority, have long justified its familiar appelation, "the Negro Harvard." Not the least of its titles to distinction is its possession of one of the largest and best music departments to be found in our whole Southern region. During the course of a recent visit to the campus it was your reporter's privilege to be present at the annual Festival of Music and Art, a three-day series of concerts and similar ceremonies, and at the formal inauguration of an important addition to the musical resources of the Fisk Library, namely the George Gershwin Memorial Collection of Music and Musical Literature.

The latter, a gift to the university from Carl Van Vechten, is housed in a special room that the library authorities have provided and for which the heirs of the late Lee J. Loventhal, long a benefactor of the university, have provided the furnishings. Mr. Van Vechten, one of our best-documented writers on both musical and Negro subjects, has here disposed of his large musical collection in a manner well designed to enhance its usefulness. He had already founded at Yale a collection of material by and about Negroes which bears the name of a former professor of Fisk University, the poet James Weldon Johnson. His musical offering bears the equally appropriate name of America's most celebrated composer, George Gershwin, and is deposited at the library of an institution where music is a major subject of study. The fact that this library is situated in a region only too scantily supplied with music libraries makes the choice of the depository all the more a happy one.

The collection, which is large, contains the vocal and piano scores of "almost every opera in the world," to use Mr. Van Vechten's words, an unusual number of composers' manuscripts and of letters from both composers and executants, and several thousand photographs of well-known musicians. There are, in addition, standard historical works and copies of practically all the books on musical subjects that have appeared in the United States in recent years. A great many composers and other musicians have already given priceless items to the collection, and Mr. Van Vechten himself has undertaken to continue supplying contemporary books about music for the period of his lifetime. The present collection is thus not only a valuable library but also a nucleus about which an even larger and more valuable one has begun already to grow. And Fisk University, long a pioneer in the South both for musical studies and for sound race relations in matters scholarly, is the perfect location for such a library.

The festival ceremonies of which the Gershwin Collection's inauguration was a part consisted of an opera performance, a piano recital, and two concerts of contemporary music. The opera produced was Puccini's *Madama Butterfly.* I missed the performance itself; but I saw photographs of the production, which was visually most stylish; and I heard sing on another occasion the leading soprano, Lenora Lafayette, an artist of unusual vocal gifts and professional qualifications. I missed also the final concert of choral music sung by the Fisk University Choir (a student organization not to be confused with the Fisk Jubilee Singers, who are a professional group having no connection with the Music Department). On this occasion the program consisted of Gustav Holst's celebrated but seldom performed *Hymn of Jesus,* William Schuman's *Requiescat,* Aaron Copland's *Lark* and Igor Stravinsky's *Symphony of Psalms,* the latter helped out by members of the Nashville Symphony Orchestra.

The two musical occasions that I did attend were a concert of contemporary American music and a piano recital played by Philippa Duke Schuyler. This talented young artist has long been popular as a child prodigy. At the age of fifteen she is no longer a child, but her musical performance is no less prodigious. It is prodigious not from a technical point of view, since technical mastery among young musicians of that age, though far from common, is a musical phenomenon less rare than among children. What remains prodigious about Miss Schuyler's work is the sincerity of her musical approach and the infallibility of her musical instincts. Though thoroughly accustomed to platform appearance, and with every other circumstance lending itself to personal exploitation, she makes no personal play whatsoever. She plays music, not Philippa Schuyler, even when she performs her own compositions. And she gets inside any piece with conviction. Her emotional understanding of longer works is about what one would expect from a young person of considerable musical experience. That is to say that it is immature. But her understanding of music as a language and the confidence with which she speaks it are complete. Her work has a straightforwardness comparable to that of the great interpreters; and the clarity of her execution, no less than the absorption of her musical thought, is proof that Miss Schuyler is a musical personality of the first water.

The contemporary concert began with my own *Medea* choruses and ended with a goodly chunk of Marc Blitzstein's *The Airborne*. Between these choral works came a violin sonata by Piston, songs by Diamond, Ames, Naginsky, Strickland, and Still, an organ piece by Sowerby, and divers piano versions. Among the latter, only Copland's *Danzon Cubano*, for two pianos, is originally a piano work. Excerpts from Miss Schuyler's *Fairy Tale Symphony* were played by the composer in pianoforte transcription; and two movements of John W. Work's *Yenvalou* suite (originally for strings) were played in a two-piano arrangement that might well have passed for an original, so idiomatic was the piano writing.

Miss Schuyler's symphony, composed several years ago, is the work of a gifted child. It is harmonically plain, melodically broad, brilliant but not original as figuration. Like her piano playing, it shows a thoroughly musical nature and a real gift for expression, for saying things with music. It is in every way as interesting as the symphonies Mozart wrote at the same age, thirteen. Mr. Work's suite is the finest piece on a Haitian subject I have yet heard. If it sounds as well for string orchestra as it does on two pianos, it is one of the finest pieces of contemporary music in the whole American repertory. First performed at Saratoga in 1946, it has not yet been played elsewhere. One looks forward to its introduction into symphonic repertory with eagerness and with confidence about its success. It is a charming work and thoroughly interesting to listen to. The high points of the festival in this reporter's experience of it came from making the acquaintance of

Mr. Work's composition, of Miss Schuyler's piano playing and general musicianship, and also that of one of the university's non-Negro instructors, Elmer Schoettle, a pianist of the highest attainments both technical and musical.

May 4, 1947

FROM OVERSEAS

Paris Items: Oratorios and Organs

THE NEWS of things musical in Paris, as that reaches me from military correspondents and from press clippings, indicates that concert repertory there has virtually settled down to normal, normal meaning, in that enlightened capital, the constant performance of new works, as well as the revival of old.

The recent winter season has offered repeatedly homage to Gabriel Fauré, 1945 being the centenary of his birth. Festivals devoted to the works of other standard modern composers have honored Ravel, Stravinsky, and Milhaud. Hindemith and Schönberg have reappeared in repertory, too, the latter calling forth the usual French opinion about it that although one may not like it much, it is remarkable music, all the same. Come to think of it, that is about the standard opinion of it everywhere among persons who have been brought up to respect contemporary creative effort. Some English music has been played, too, and a teensy weensy bit of American, William Grant Still's "Afro-American" Symphony, when played at the Concerts Pasdeloup, provoking the comment from a press critic that "it was not disagreeable to hear, *certes;* but we would rather have had Louis Armstrong."

Among the new French works in large form, Manuel Rosenthal's oratorio, *Saint Francis of Assisi,* seems to have been liked by almost everyone. A Requiem of Tomasi, the Fifty-sixth Psalm (or Fifty-fifth by our count) of Jean Rivier, and the *Benedictiones* of Roland-Manuel were also given for the first time. These works, all for large chorus with orchestra, are significant of two trends in present-day French music. One is the revival of choral singing that dates back to the time of the Popular Front of the mid-1930's. The other is the funeral note, the memorializing of those killed in military action and of those who have lost their lives as hostages or as active resisters to tyranny. All the non-collaborating dead are considered martyrs to the cause of freedom. And artists who have survived trying times seem eager to honor those whose personal sacrifice and courage have re-created, at least temporarily, the dignity of man.

The high position that Olivier Messiaen holds among the young in France, and even among his elders, is an expression of the same spirit. Leader of *La Jeune France,* a group formed in the 1930's of young composers who admitted openly to a religious orientation of thought, professor at the Paris Conservatory and organist at the Church of the Holy Trinity, this brilliant executant and abundant composer has become, in Darius Milhaud's absence, the chief rallying point of the younger creative spirits in French music. His recent emergence as a national figure corresponds to that preoccupation with spiritual grandeurs that has seemed more appropriate to many, during the last decade's visible decline of France's temporal power, than the cultivation of sensual delicacies and poetic refinements that was characteristic of French music in the preceding epoch.

He represents thus the serious-minded intellectual tradition of the Church and of the universities rather than the more witty and worldly one of the literary salons, the poet-and-picture-dealers' conspiracy, and the luxury trades. He is not even involved with Marxism. He is a sort of cultural fundamentalist. And whether this position represents in the France of today a reactionary influence remains to be seen. In any case, it is the position of the Conservatory and of the universities. The Marxists, who run the radio, are frankly demagogic, the operatic establishments and the orchestras maintaining a respectable, if not very exciting, policy of detached bourgeois liberalism.

Two brochures sent me by Pvt. Lincoln Kirstein deal with one of the noblest of all French musical traditions, namely, that of organ building. *Les Cliquot, facteurs d'orgues du Roy,* by Norbert Dufourcq (Librarie Floury, 1942), is the history of a family of organ builders that, from around 1670 to 1785, designed, executed, and curated some of the finest organs in France. Several of these are still in use, those of Saint-Nicholas-des-

Champs and of Saint-Merry in Paris having been restored in our time from the original specifications, those of the Abbey of Souvigny and of the Cathedral of Poitiers having survived intact. Others, like that of the Palace chapel at Versailles, have been reconstructed. All form part of that unique heritage that has enabled the organ to survive into our time as a major musical instrument in the one country where the tradition of its design as a serious musical instrument was never really lost.

The other brochure, also by Dufourcq, deals with the most recently built of France's great instruments, the organ at the Palais de Chaillot. This largest and newest of the Paris concert halls was completed in 1937, replacing the unlamented Trocadéro of 1878 in a new architectural layout of the whole hill that dominates from the Right Bank of the Seine the Eiffel Tower and the Champ de Mars. The new organ, an eighty-stop instrument, employs many pipes from the one that Aristide Cavaillé-Coll had installed in the original Trocadéro. Completed in 1938 and fully adjusted only in the following year, it was not till after the armistice of 1940 that it began the brilliant career as a solo instrument that has revealed to French music lovers in a time of national mourning a vast repertory of great music and that has drawn to an instrument formerly considered to be the prize among musical bores the enthusiasm of a whole youthful generation.

The most novel element of this instrument's design consists in the placement of the whole organ, which weighs seventy tons, in a metal cage that can be closed away from public view at the back of the stage by a metal curtain or moved forward on tracks a distance of some forty feet. The work of Cavaillé-Coll, soundest of the nineteenth-century organ builders, and of V. and F. Gonzalez, expert among modern restorers of ancient instruments, this organ represents, like the new organ at the Church of Saint Mary the Virgin in New York, the maximum available today of classical scholarship and of modern convenience. And just as the cases and façades of the historic organs of France are more often than not examples of the finest decorative art from their respective periods, this one presents to the eye, with its row upon row of exposed pipes in functional geometric arrangement, a matchless piece of contemporary design.

April 1, 1945

Olivier Messiaen

"ATOMIC bomb of contemporary music" is the current epithet for Olivier Messiaen. Whether France's thirty-seven-year-old boy wonder is capable of quite so vast a work of destruction as that unhappy engine I could not say. But certainly he has made a big noise in the world. And the particular kind of noise that his music makes does, I must say, make that of his chief contemporaries sound a bit old-fashioned.

What strikes one right off on hearing almost any of his pieces is the power these have of commanding attention. They do not sound familiar; their textures — rhythmic, harmonic, and instrumental — are fresh and strong. And though a certain melodic banality may put one off no less than the pretentious mysticism of his titles may offend, it is not possible to come in contact with any of his major productions without being aware that one is in the presence of a major musical talent. Liking it or not is of no matter; Messiaen's music has a vibrancy that anybody can be aware of, that the French music world is completely aware of, that has been accepted in France, indeed, for the postwar period as, take it or leave it, one of the facts of life.

Messiaen's pieces are mostly quite long; and their textures, rhythmic and harmonic, are complex. In spite of their length and their complexity their sounds are perfectly clear. They are nowhere muddy in color but always sonorous. Their shining brightness takes one back to Berlioz. So also does their subject matter. "Dance of Fury for the Seven Trumpets," "The Rainbow of Innocence," "Angel with Perfumes," "The Crystal Liturgy," "Subtlety of the Body in Glory," "Strength and Agility of the Body in Glory," "God with Us," and "Vocal Exercise for the Angel Who Announces the End of Time" are some of the simpler subtitles. And the renderings of these are no less picturesque than Berlioz's description of doomsday (in the Dies Iræ of his Requiem Mass) for chorus and full orchestra plus twenty-eight trumpets and trombones and fourteen kettledrums.

Messiaen is a full-fledged romantic. Form is nothing to him, content everything. And the kind of content that he likes is the convulsive, the ecstatic, the cataclysmic, the terrifying, the unreal. That the imagery of this should be derived almost exclusively from religion is not surprising in a church organist and the son of a mystical poetess, Cécile Sauvage. What is a little surprising in so scholarly a modernist (he is organist at the cultivated parish of La Trinité and a professor of harmony at the Paris Conservatory) is the literalness of his religious imagination. But there is no possibility of suspecting insincerity. His pictorial concept of religion, though a rare one among educated men, is too intense to be anything but real. Messiaen is simply a theologian with a taste for the theatrical. And he dramatizes theological events with all the *sang-froid* and all the elaborateness of a man who is completely at home in the backstage of religious establishments.

The elaborateness of Messiaen's procedures is exposed in detail in a two-volume treatise by him called *The Technique of My Musical Language*, (*Technique de mon langage musical*; Alphonse Leduc, Paris, 1944). The rhythmic devices employed, many of them derived from Hindu practice, are most sophisticated. The harmonic language is massively dissonant but not especially novel. It resembles rather the piling of Ossa on Pelion that formerly characterized the work of Florent Schmitt. There are layer cakes of rhythms and of harmonies but there is little linear counterpoint. The instrumentation is admirably designed to contrast these simultaneities and to pick them out. Derived from organ registration, it exploits the higher brilliancies (as of mixture stops) to great advantage. The weaker elements of Messiaen's style are his continuity, which, like that of many another organist-composer, is improvisational rather than structural, and his melodic material, which is low in expressivity. The themes are lacking in the tensile strength necessary to sustain long developments because of his predilection for weak intervals, especially the major sixth and the augmented fourth, and for contradictory chromatics.

Among the works which one hopes will soon be heard in New York are *Forgotten Offerings* (*Les Offrandes oubliées*) for orchestra, by which Messiaen became known way back in 1935, I think it was, as a major talent, and *The Nativity of Our Lord*, nine meditations for organ, published in 1936. These pieces have charm and youth in them and a striking virtuosity of texture.

Among the more recent works of some length are *Seven Visions of the Amen*, for two pianos; *Twenty Admirations of the Infant Jesus* (unless I mistranslate *Vingt Regards sur l'enfant Jésus*), for solo piano; *Three Short Liturgies of the Divine Presence* (they last a good half-hour, all the same), for women's voices and orchestra; and a *Quartet for the End of Time*, which was composed during his German captivity.

The most satisfactory of these works to me is the two-piano work. The most impressive to the general public, however, is the orchestral one, which was first presented last April at a concert of *La Pléiade* in the Salle du Conservatoire. I have heard a recording of these liturgies, made from a subsequent broadcast under the direction of Roger Désormière; and though certainly they have a spasmodic flow (and no little monotony) they do make a wonderful noise.

The instrumentation, though top-heavy, is utterly glittering. It consists of vibraphone, celesta, maracas, gong, tam-tam, nine sopranos singing in unison, piano, *les ondes Martenot* (a form of theremin), and strings. The three sections are entitled: "Antiphon of Interior Conversation (God present in us . . .)," "Sequence of The Word, Divine Canticle (God present in Himself . . .)," and "Psalm of the Ubiquity of Love (God present in all things . . .)." The text employed by the singers is of Messiaen's composition, as were also program notes printed on the occasion of the first performance. Of the "Antiphon" he writes:

"Dedicated to God present within us through Grace and the Holy Communion. After a most tender beginning ('My Jesus, My Silence, Abide with Me'), accompanied by the songs of distant birds (on the piano), there follows a contrapuntal middle section of great polyrhythmic and polymodal refinement. ('The Yes which sings like an echo of light.' 'Red and lavender melody in praise of The Father.' 'Your hand is out of the picture by one kiss.' 'Divine landscape, reverse your image in water.')"

All these are clearly a believing organist's ideas. César Franck and Anton Bruckner, though neither had Messiaen's humor, worked from just such preoccupations. I once described this religio-musical style as the determination to produce somewhere in every piece an apotheosis destined at once to open up the heavens and to bring down the house. Certainly the latter action is easier to accomplish in modern life than the first. And certainly

Messiaen has accomplished it several times in the *Liturgies*. The success of his accomplishment is due to a natural instinct for making music plus the simplicity and sincerity of his feelings. These are expressed, moreover, through a musical technique of great complexity and considerable originality. The faults of his taste are obvious; and the traps of mystical program music, though less so, are well known to musicians, possibly even to himself. Nevertheless the man is a great composer. One has only to hear his music beside that of any of the standard eclectic modernists to know that. Because his really vibrates and theirs doesn't.

September 23, 1945

Lively St. Francis

MANUEL ROSENTHAL'S oratorio *Saint Francis of Assisi*, which I have been listening to of late through gramophone recordings of its original broadcast by the orchestra of France's National Radio under the composer's direction, is one of the most striking and picturesque musical works of our time. Composed in 1937, 1938, and 1939, it was first performed in November of last year; and though its repercussion in musical circles, both lay and professional, has been considerable, the slowness of publication procedures and the difficulties of international traffic in general have retarded the propagation of a work that in more normal times would certainly have begun already to be heard around the world. Indeed, since Arthur Honegger's piece of twenty-five years back about a type of railway locomotive, *Pacific 231*, I have not encountered a musical *grande machine* so obviously built to travel.

The biography of the Saint is recounted in speech and through choral recitative. His major moments are described by orchestral set pieces. The program of these runs as follows: "Prayer," "Youth," "The Kiss to the Leper," "Saint Clara," "Sermon to the Birds," "Hymn to the Sun," "The Angelic Kithara," "The Grand Miracle" (of the stigmata), "Death," and "The Choiring Angels" (or "Chorus Angelicus"). Certain of these numbers are more vividly picturesque than others, but all are displays of orchestral workmanship of the highest virtuosity and of the most ingenious fancy. And though Mr. Rosenthal's use of the vibraphone and of an electronic instrument somewhat like our theremin known as "*les ondes Martenot*" (rather a favorite with the contemporary French) is not without a certain vulgarity of effect, his musical textures are notable for the purity of their design.

By purity I mean honesty and straightforwardness. Basing his pictorial descriptions on orchestral device alone, he has chosen at all times melodic material, harmonic filling, and contrapuntal device of the plainest nature, formed his musical phrases, as Berlioz did, for what he wishes the whole to imitate or evoke rather than for the expression of personal lyricism or for the striking of any classic poetical attitude. The sounds he uses, like the colors of an impressionist's palette, determine the nature of his drawing, which in itself on the score page is about as neutral, as subservient to the coloristic effect as could be imagined.

The piece that depicts the Saint in his roistering youth is a serenade of plucked instruments constantly interrupted by street fighting and by dancing. "The Kiss to the Leper" imitates the sound of ancient church organs, with all the strings divided into four, five, and six parts to recall composite organ stops, and woodwinds playing in hollow double octaves, while three trumpets, played very softly with the Ball mute, give a lifelike effect of the higher mixtures. "Saint Clara" is a bell piece, with big bells, little bells, loud bells, every kind of bell in the world, all sounding at once by means of musical suggestion and acoustic imitation.

The "Sermon to the Birds" is perhaps the most astonishing auditory evocation of all. Certainly the twittering of our feathered neighbors is not a new subject in music any more than bells are. But no such deafening bird noise as Rosenthal's have I ever heard outside a zoo. The "Hymn to the Sun," which I take for a representation of sunlight, is less striking than the auditory evocations. But the sound of the angelic popular music that Saint Francis once heard in a dream (after Brother Pacificus had refused to play the kithara for him out of scruples about light-mindedness) is a delicious concert of mandolins and lutes. "The Miracle of the Stigmata" and the 'Saint's Death," sober pieces not unlike the opening "Prayer," lead up to a final "Chorus Angelicus," which represents a jostling of hallelujahs rather like what one hears when several military bands are parading all within hearing distance.

The work should not be difficult to give in New York, because the purely orchestral sections, though requiring exact rehearsal, are not beyond the powers of a good American orchestra; and the choral parts, partly in Latin and partly in French, are not difficult at all, save in the "Chorus Angelicus," which lies a bit high. The French choral recitatives could even be translated with little alteration of their rhythm patterns; and I think on the whole such a procedure would be of advantage to the full understanding of a work that seems destined to enjoy a season or two, at least, of real popularity. Make no mistake about it; Rosenthal's *Saint Francis* has not one drop of mystical content. It is a realistic picture, both touching and vivid, of real events. At least they seem real as one listens. And though the work lasts in performance some fifty minutes, at no point did your hardened reporter find his interest in it less than complete.

September 16, 1945

The Vacant Chair

Viewing the French musical scene in close-up, one is impressed with the cardinal importance to it of him who is absent; of the central position in the picture that is being reserved for the return of Darius Milhaud. Just as Ravel before him, and Debussy before that, was in the eyes of all beholders clearly the first composer of his country, Milhaud's primacy is no less obvious than theirs in a landscape that is no less copiously adorned by figures of considerable brilliance.

These figures are of three functions — the academic, the impressive, and the poetical. The academics, the standard masters of the borrowing procedure, are Jacques Ibert and Jean Rivier. The work of such men is never very commanding and rarely wholly offensive. It usually passes for well written, and indeed its presence is a mark of the higher musical civilizations. It has to be there if only as an example to the young of the ultimate futility of knowledge as a point of departure toward style.

The composers whose chief aim is impressiveness, the hit-'em-between-the-eyes-and-knock-'em-over boys, are in descending order of seniority Arthur Honegger, Manuel Rosenthal, and Olivier Messaien. Masters of the picturesque and of the obviously striking, these authors are at their best in the sort of oratoriolike number for complex musical forces that was Berlioz's invention and that has always been dear to the heart of the Paris (as also of the London) musical public.

Jeanne au bucher (*Joan at the Stake*) and *La Danse des morts* (*The Dance of the Dead*), both written to texts by Paul Claudel, are Honegger's latest creations in the genre. We heard another in New York a few years back called *Nicolas de Flue,* on a nationalistic Swiss poem by Denis de Rougemont. *Jeanne au bûcher,* first given in Brussels and in Paris before the war, with Ida Rubinstein speaking the lead, is still a successful work. And *La Danse des morts,* of more recent composition, has been recorded commercially.

Rosenthal's *St. Francis of Assisi* and Messaien's *Three Short Liturgies of the Divine Presence* have been described recently in this column. Rosenthal's equally sensational *Musique de table,* which describes such succulent dishes as stewed eels and venison, I have not yet had occasion to hear. All these works are examples of program music pushed to its, for the present at least, ultimate assertion. Their authors are specialists of the objectively grandiose and of the striking. None of them has ever shown himself apt at personal lyricism.

The poetical writers in France are still Francis Poulenc, whose songs and choral pieces are tops in our time; Georges Auric, whose film music is the most apt in the world (he is doing Shaw's *Caesar and Cleopatra,* for England at the moment); and Henri Sauguet, whose short opera *La Gageure imprévue* (after an eighteenth-century comedy by Sedaine) and ballet *Les Forains,* both produced last season, are his latest and most impeccable gifts to the theater of delicacy. His string quartet and piano concerto, both begun before the war, have since been completed. The latter is recorded, I believe. Sauguet's full length opera *La Chartreuse de Parme,* which was produced during the season of 1938–9 and removed from the repertory during the German occupation because of its librettist's religion, has not yet been restored to production.

Among the newer composers in a lyrical and poetic vein the most skillful is Henry Barraud, whose chamber music is delightfully embroidered and who seems from the ballet I have heard, *Le Diable à la kermesse* (*The Devil at the Fair*), to have considerable theatrical force. Of grander pathos (and indeed rather wonderfully lugubrious) are the works of André Jolivet, a member of Messaien's original *La Jeune France* group. His *Trois Complaintes du soldat* for baritone, text by himself, are deeply touching as expression and original. There is also an evocative and ghostly work after Poe's *Eleonora* for four woodwinds, trumpets, harp, *les ondes Martenot* and strings, by Yves Baudrier, another member of *La Jeune France*. The fourth of these gifted and highly serious young men is Daniel-Lesur, whose *Pastorale variée* (from 1937) for a similar though not identical combination of instruments, is delicately conceived but a little jerkily paced and whose *Suite française* for piano is a lovely piece.

Darius Milhaud fits into this picture as the great man who dominates all the categories. His is no limited palette; he works in all the styles save that which is forbidden to genius, the eclectic one. His *grandes machines, Les Choréophores* (after Æschylus), *Maximilien,* and *Christophe Colomb* (both after Claudel) are no less impressive than Honegger's and far more humane. His ballets are both bright and sensitive. His religious works are deeply serious. His light operas are completely gay. His orchestral works are comparable with the noblest of our century. His twelve string quartets are models of the intimate poetic style. And his opera *Bolivar* (on a play by Jules Supervielle), as yet unproduced, will probably, if my acquaintance with its score entitles me to place a bet, constitute the crowning glory of a great career.

Milhaud has written music in all the kinds and for all the occasions. Some of it, as is inevitable with so fecund a workman, is inferior in quality. But the amount of it in all the kinds that is of the first quality is sufficient alone to denominate him as a master. And the variety alone of the occasions for which he has produced work of the first quality places him as the most ample among living masters. No amount of professional intrigue can conceal a matter of patent fact. That is why, in spite of all the brilliant figures now occupying the musical scene in France, there is a vacancy in the center of the stage. Neither Honegger nor Rosenthal nor Messaien, for all their spectacular qualities, can fill it. Nor can Sauguet, for all his delicacy and tenderness, be quite sufficient for the place. And so everybody is working busily and beautifully at writing music for the repertory adorning, to change the metaphor, France's musical house — already and by far the richest of our century — in view of what all musical France hopes will not be too long delayed, the return of its master — Darius Milhaud.

September 30, 1945

Pelléas and Pénélope

ON Election Day in the afternoon, October 21, the Opéra-Comique gave a perfect performance of what all musical France esteems its most perfect operatic monument, Debussy's *Pelléas et Mélisande*. On the following day it was my pleasure to hear at the Opéra an excellent performance of a far from perfect work, but one that is nevertheless inspired by such a deep instinct for rectitude of expression that it nobly merits honor as a lost cause, Fauré's *Pénélope*.

The latter is all wrong from a theatrical point of view, but it is musically beautiful. Its poem, by René Fauchois, nowadays an experienced and successful playwright (New York admired ten years ago his *Prenez garde à la Peinture* under the title of *The Late Christopher Bean*), is not striking as either literature or drama. Its music, moreover, by a master of the recital song, is intimately expressive but without breadth of line. It creates no ambiance, no atmosphere, no excitement, delineates no character, paints no scene. It is recital music orchestrated, and not by its own composer at that. For Fauré, who was not a master of orchestration, customarily farmed out this privilege to friends and commercial hacks.

Its timing is all wrong, too. The action, thin enough at best, is stretched out for musical purposes to such lengths, though the opera itself is not a long one, that the actors are left for most of the time standing around with nothing to do but sing. Or worse, waiting for it to be their turn to sing. Moreover, in all three acts a chorus is almost constantly present on the stage without singing at all. It murmurs here and there a chord, but it never plays any musical role commensurate with its dramatic function. The vocalized conversation that makes up the opera is impeccably prosodied and of the utmost musical beauty. But the whole is essentially a *pasticcio* of Fauré songs, without contrast or dramatic progression. And the orchestral accompaniment, though far from ugly, fails wholly to support or to create a dramatic line.

The performance I heard was conducted with real sensitivity by François Ruhlmann. Suzanne Juyol, in the title role, displayed a dramatic soprano voice of rich color. Her musical artistry might well have appeared as equally striking if it had not been overshadowed by the literally perfect style and emission of the tenor Georges Jouatte, who sang Ulysses. Such beauty of voice, of diction, and of phraseology, such refinement of musical utterance at all the levels of pitch and of power, is unique, to my knowledge, on the contemporary musical stage. One wishes that all vocalists, all musicians, all music lovers could know this impeccable workmanship and cherish in their memories forever the proof that singing in public is an art and not a stunt.

Debussy's *Pelléas et Mélisande* has, as music, every beauty that *Pénélope* has, with none of its faults. It has atmosphere, continuity, shape, style, and progress. It delineates character and tells a story. That story, moreover, the play itself, by Maurice Maeterlinck, is literature. It, too, has atmosphere, continuity, shape, style, and progress. The marriage of the literary and musical elements in Debussy's opera is one of the miracles of the modern world. There has been nothing like it since Mozart. And it is indeed touching that a state theater should celebrate France's first national election day in more than nine years and the anticipated birth of her Fourth Republic by the perfect performance of a work that may well go down in history as the chief artistic monument of her Third.

The perfection of that performance was due to the precise and loving care of the conductor, Roger Désormière. The vocal rendering under his direction was no less notable than the instrumental for its respect toward both the letter and the spirit of the work and for its observance of the musical amenities in general. The cast consisted of, on this occasion: Janine Micheau, as Mélisande; Renée Gilly, as Geneviève; Christiane Gaudel, as Yniold; Willy Clément, as Pelléas; Etcheverry, as Golaud, and Henry

Médus, as Arkel, with Jean Vieuille and Maurane singing the minor roles of the Doctor and of the Shepherd. Both the leading singers were appearing in this work for the first time.

Miss Micheau was impeccable both vocally and stylistically, though a little more statuesque in action than one might have wished. Mr. Clément, a very young man, revealed a warm tenor voice of great beauty and sound schooling. Miss Gilly and Miss Gaudel, Messrs. Etcheverry and Médus were all that one could wish for musically; and certainly in this work one wishes for a great deal. As dramatic action the performance had little warmth; it was almost oratoriolike, in fact, by its dignity and by its employment of minimum gesture. I suppose this is what happens to works that become national monuments. The concept is a legitimate one of a *Pelléas* all stylized and medieval and far away. But the *Pelléas* of Garden and Dufranne and certain tenors who really acted, including our own Edward Johnson, was warmer and more vigorously dramatic.

As for the auditory performance, I have never heard a lovelier one. I have never heard the work read with such clear rhythm and such sure progress and at the same time such complete orchestral transparency. The string sounds were like nothing in this world that has substance. Even the wind harmonies floated in the air like veils, the simplest phrase of bassoon or clarinet like an almost imperceptible sigh. Nothing was muffled. The instrumental timbres, in fact, as they should be in a proper Debussy rendering, even when the composer's coloration is somber, were light and clean. What gave them their ideal consistency is the fact that under Désormière's firmly delicate stick they were without weight, as without obscurity. To have achieved so luminous a texture without any softening up of Debussy's rapier-steel rhythm or any clouding of the vocal enunciation places Roger Désormière, long known as a precision workman, among the very great musicians of our time and among the great French conductors of all time.

He recorded three years ago, during the German occupation (but with no political collaboration involved), the entire opera. When shipping becomes available for cultural exchanges, American collectors will no doubt be acquiring these albums, though they are already hard to get here. I have not heard the disks myself; but if they approach in quality his rendering of the opera in the pit, they must long provide a model to musicians of what *Pelléas* should and can be made to sound like, namely, the most beautiful and the most monumental work for the musical theater in all the modern world.

November 4, 1945

Méhul's *Joseph*

ETIENNE-HENRI MÉHUL's *Joseph,* which was revived at the Opéra on Friday, June 7, is one of the most famous stage works in the world and one of the least familiar to present-day audiences. Composed in 1806 and first presented to the Parisian public in February 1807, it enjoyed a wide popularity in Germany for several years before the French discovered that they had a classic on their hands. Its last Paris revival in dramatic form took place in 1896. There were two concert performances in 1935 at the Salle du Conservatoire. It was for these last that Henri Rabaud composed the recitatives used in the present production. The work in its original form was not a grand opera at all, but an *opéra-comique,* with spoken dialogue.

Alexandre Duval's poem is not, however, at any point comic. Nor does it tell a love story. It simply narrates, in somewhat pastoral vein, the story of Joseph and his brethren. The music of Méhul's score is straightforward in style, quite without displays of local color, noble but not pompous, varied in expression, and remarkably touching. The characters, when they sing, have life in them; and they express themselves with an astonishing simplicity. There is not a vocal high note or arpeggio in the whole opera. But its musical composition is not, for all that, unsophisticated. There is, indeed, in Méhul's music a contrapuntal life that is lacking in that of Gluck, his master, and that gives to his simplest hymn or romanza an intrinsic musical interest that supports the expressivity of the whole without thickening the texture.

The unobtrusiveness of Méhul's musical mastery is particularly advantageous to the ensemble pieces, where the individuality of the different characters is preserved at no sacrifice to apparent simplicity. The chorus of Joseph's brothers, for example, is a notable piece of contrapuntal writing without any of the baroque or rococo ornateness that we are used to associate with the contrapuntal style. The whole opera, in fact, like many another triumph of fine French workmanship, is deceptively plain. And it achieves by a masterful but abstemious use of the more elaborate musical procedures a humanity of expression that is as sweet today as it was nearly a century and a half ago.

Méhul's career as a composer, which covered the years 1787 to 1817, comprised the Revolution, the Directory, the First Empire, and Napoleon's fall. His style, which was formed in the Revolutionary years, is comparable to the neoclassic manner in architecture and decoration that was practiced contemporaneously in France and that we call in America the "Federal style." A republican simplicity was its ideal; clean, light colors were its taste; the Rights of Man was its Bible. Méhul, Gossec, and Cherubini perfected the style together. Though they all left handsome works behind them, the style itself did not survive the Bourbon Restoration. The dynamism of Beethoven and the violence of Berlioz made it seem, by comparison, picayune to the Romantic age. It is a noble style, all the same, and one that has left its ideals of personal modesty and of professional perfection on the tradition of the Paris Conservatory, where all three masters worked, and where they left their perhaps most lasting mark on music.

Méhul's *Joseph* is not passionate and grand, like Beethoven's *Fidelio,* nor fun, like Rossini's *Barber of Seville,* though as a professional job it is probably superior to either. It is a quiet piece and a well-nigh perfect one. It remains after a hundred and forty years one of the sweetest in all dramatic literature. Its revival just now, in a period of musical, as well as of political, unrest, was a more than merely bright idea on the part of the Opéra's directors. It seems to point a moral to the effect that art, at least, can be efficient without having recourse to sensational measures. The appropriateness of its subject matter, too, which treats of displaced persons and Jewish resettlement, is inescapable.

The performance is a sweet one. Reynaldo Hahn conducts it in that restrained manner, virtually without dynamic accent, that the French call the "classical style." Édouard Rambaud, replacing on the opening night the indisposed Georges Jouatte, sang the tenor role of Joseph with the utmost of vocal grace and musical dignity. Charles Cambon, baritone, as the confidant Utobal, sang, as always, like a master. And the American Endrèze, though lacking nowadays ideal vocal resources, was a model of both vocal and dramatic elegance. Hélène St. Arnaud, who sang Benjamin, was a delight to eye and ear. And the decorations of Pierre Chéreau, though not unusual or striking, were pleasant to look at.

The opera was paired on the opening night with a ballet divertissement called *Suite in White* (*Suite en Blanc*), danced to music from Edouard Lalo's *Namouna*. The execution of the girls, particularly that of Miss Bardin and of Miss Vaussard, was pretty high-class, that of the men disappointing. Lalo's music is utterly delightful; and its musical performance, directed by Roger Désormière, was the finest piece of musical work, bar none, that I have heard this trip. Indeed, to match it for precision, clarity, inner animation, and beauty of tone, all the qualities that make the difference between conducting and mere reading, I am obliged to go back to a performance heard at the Opéra-Comique last fall of Debussy's *Pelléas et Mélisande*, also led by Désormière. No other opera company with which I am acquainted has conducting to offer that is comparable in either beauty or efficiency to Désormière's. As for what most ballet troupes give us nowadays as orchestral accompaniment, especially in America, the best that can be said is that it seems to presuppose a public wholly visual-minded.

June 23, 1946

Thaïs with Geori-Boué

GEORI-BOUÉ's return to the Paris Opera in Massenet's *Thaïs* on Monday evening, June 3, after eight months' absence, was greeted by an impressive audience demonstration. Indeed, few French lyric artists have Miss Boué's natural gift for provoking displays of audience gratitude. She is young, well under thirty, beautiful, and a great actress; and although her vocal resources are by no means under control, these are enormous and in their ensemble most striking.

Trained in the provinces, without benefit of the Paris Conservatory or of the great private studios, this remarkable Miss made her operatic debut less than five years ago at Toulouse, from which city she came directly to the capital. As wife of the tenor Roger Bourdin, with whom she frequently appears in recital, she has had access to the subtleties of French vocal style. Actually, save for the lack of that assured vocal perfection that almost nobody ever achieves nowadays under forty, she is a more absorbing operatic performer both to watch and to listen to than almost any other now appearing before the public.

Her voice is a strong lyric one with the range and agility of a coloratura. Its timbre is bright, in loud passages almost trumpet-like. Loud passages are not, however, what Miss Boué does best. It is in these that she sings off pitch occasionally and is often unpleasantly brilliant. She does not force; she does not need to do that with a voice that is naturally penetrating and that attains without effort heights that for another might be precarious. She simply is not yet firmly schooled in the classical, the proper way to sing both high and loud.

In all the kinds of singing that lie below the ultimate of loudness she is most skillful. Her mezza voce in all ranges is sweet and quite without the banality that characterizes the middle intensities of most operatic singing. And her pianissimo is unique. It has been many years since one has heard anyone sing so softly, so clearly, and withal so easily. The sound is objective, no crooning involved; and her words are heard in every part of the house. Indeed, Miss Boué's diction is of the kind one dreams about but hasn't heard in a theater practically since Mary Garden.

There is, in fact, a great deal about the work of this pint-size redhead that recalls that of Garden, as the Scottish beauty must have looked and sounded in the earliest years of her career. Whether Garden ever had such a natural glory of voice, I do not know; certainly she did not have it in 1911, when I first heard her. And whether she ever sang so badly in public as Miss Boué, on any evening, is likely to do, I doubt. But the two artists are of a type, musically gifted, physically beautiful, and with an instinct for the musical stage that is not only infallible as taste but in every way sensational in its effect upon the public.

So far Boué's chief roles have been Thaïs, Juliette (in Gounod's *Roméo et Juliette*) and the name part in Gounod's *Mireille*, all of them roles requiring dramatic skill, high notes, and a luminous personality. On the one occasion when I heard her it was the high notes that came off least well. Not because she doesn't possess them, but simply because she is young and courageous and sings a little wild.

All that is easily enough corrected by experience and a good trainer. Miss Boué shocks the devotees of sheer vocal opulence, just as Garden always did. She has a lovely voice, just as Garden did, too, perhaps a bigger and better one than Garden ever had, though it is less thoroughly schooled than Garden's. She uses it, moreover, to the same end, as an instrument of dramatic projection, not, for all its extraordinary qualities, as the subject of the evening's entertainment. One cannot avoid the conclusion, observing her work, that her faults are of no gravity at all beside the splendor of her qualities and that one is in the presence of a real star.

Paul Cabanel, who sang the baritone role of Athanael to Miss Boué's Thaïs, has a fine, big voice, perfect diction, a noble singing style, and distinguished qualities as an actor. He will be heard, I understand, in America next season. The rest of the cast was most agreeable and the scenery excellent. As pacing, the musical direction was a shade pedestrian. The conductor, François Ruhlmann, observed tempos as close as is humanly possible to those prescribed in 1894 by the composer and carefully preserved since in the establishment. But in spite of the fervor of the two chief singers and all their ingenuity, the music never quite got going. And it is not stupid music, either. For all its thinness of texture, it is cleanly composed, melodically charming, and expressive.

The house itself has, of course, an architectural disadvantage in the great breadth of its orchestral pit that tends to slow up the effective speed of any musical execution. The singers are removed not only from the audience by a chasm too wide to bridge with personal warmth but from the conductor, as well, by a distance that diminishes his visibility to a point where the prompter is obliged to replace him for effective vocal leadership in delicate passages. This double direction tends to stiffen any performance, and long waits between scenes add nothing to dramatic animation.

Strict observance of traditional tempos, too, though preferable to our Metropolitan's irresponsibility in this matter, gives nowadays to all performances at the Paris Opéra a pedagogical flavor, as of classics read rather than played. There is considerable misunderstanding these days on both sides of the ocean about the nature and value of musical traditions. The Paris Opéra has a whole library of recorded traditions; our Metropolitan has no library at all, even of scores. The advantages are probably in favor of Paris, in the long run, though not for the reason obvious. Because what is important about traditions and their preservation is not only that a given conductor should observe such of the recorded ones as please his fancy, since he cannot observe them all, but also that his deviations should be recorded, as evidence of his contribution to the history of the work. Mr. Ruhlmann seemed the other night to be making little contribution to such a record.

June 16, 1946

Purging the "Collabos"

WHO collaborated with the enemy and what sanctions are being meted out to those who did are the subject of constant queries to reporters working in those European countries that were occupied during the war by German troops. A full answer is impossible, because no complete documentation exists or can exist till the purgings shall have been completed. These are being operated differently in each country and differently by various trades, professions, and social groups. They are being applied in France to the musical confraternity in the following manner:

Let us distinguish, to begin with, collaboration from treason. Any citizen who betrayed state secrets to the enemy, who denounced Communists, Jews, Allied agents, or members of local resistance movements or who by maladministration allowed works of art or other national wealth to fall into enemy hands is a traitor to his country and must be punished. Collaboration is more difficult to define and consequently to judge. It is doubtful, indeed, whether there is any basis in law for judging it at all. Certainly the facts are so confusing — because everybody has at some point or other made some compromise, and because even the most cynical among the "collabos" have all concealed Jews in their houses or helped French young people to avoid deportation—that no clear division is possible of sheep from goats.

Nevertheless, every social group and professional body feels the need of expressing its disapproval of those members whose conduct toward the enemy has been lacking in moral dignity, and of imposing some kind of punishment for this. Consequently, in those cases where the law does not apply (which means in the majority of cases), sanctions have been left to the social groups and professional bodies whose moral prestige has been lowered by such conduct. At the beginning a good deal of spontaneous direct action by the Resistance troops took place; but most of that has ceased now, and purging is orderly. It is not, however, a state action except in treason cases. The French have avoided, as far as possible, defining collaboration as a political crime, because that would have involved them in the very abuse of power that they hated most in the German and Vichy administrations, namely, political arrest.

There is today no legal hindrance to the public appearance of musicians who collaborated, excepting of those who are under provisional arrest. They can accept any engagement offered and they can organize any concert they wish, short of hiring for it state-owned premises, like the Théatre de l'Opéra. Even here the hindrance is one of administrative discretion, not of legality. There are certain things that are hard to do, however, such as to work for the state radio or for the state theaters. All the state theaters were purged a year ago by committees of their own members. Singers and instrumentalists formerly working at the Opéra, for instance, whose conduct has been judged unpatriotic by their own Musicians' Resistance Committee are not being allowed to work in that house for the present. The committee has not been oversevere. Every group, in fact, has tended toward tolerance in the judgment of its own members.

Every group has tended equally toward intolerance in judging the conduct of others. It is not the musicians and dancers, for instance, who are preventing the return to the Opéra ballet of Solange Schwartz and Jean Peretti and Serge Lifar. It is the stagehands' union, which threatens to strike every time the subject is broached. Since nobody wants a public controversy with so powerful a union on any subject (and particularly not on that one), the stagehands remain masters in fact of the situation, though purging musicians is properly no right of theirs, any more than purging the backstage is any right of the orchestra. The Soviet Embassy is at the moment, for reasons unknown, being kind to Lifar (a White Russian); and it seems likely that pressure from that source on the Communist cell within the stagehands' union may eventually bring about his return to the Opéra, for which there is considerable public demand. The orchestra of the Opéra-Comique has recently refused to perform a work by Marcel Delannoy which the management had planned to revive this fall, though the composer is under no formal ban of any kind, official or unofficial.

The musical profession and the musical public, at least in Paris, are eager to forget the whole collaboration story, if not to forgive, and to get back the use of music's full effectives, throwing just a few of its more outrageous sinners to the wolves of superpatriotic opinion. Already the cultural department of the Foreign Office is sending to England as propagandists for French music many artists it does not dare yet to bless at home. And the composer Henry Barraud, musical director of the state radio, has on several occasions used artists who are on the radio's black list. He has used them because he needed them and because he considers the present procedure of radio black-listing to be unjust.

The radio purges have been the strictest of all, because they have been made not by musicians but by Resistance politicians, and because they follow a logical method. Playing publicly in the symphony orchestras involved no trading (technically) with the enemy, because these are co-operative associations. Neither did working at the state opera houses, because there one was employed by one's own government. (The stagehands are forgetting, however, in their present moralistic fervor that they accepted tips from Germans at the German-organized gala performances.) Performing at Radio-Paris, however, which was German-run, entailed open acceptance of money from the enemy, of working directly for him.

Now it happens that the bookkeeping of Radio-Paris is intact. So, instead of allowing the musicians' union or some similar professional body to make up the black lists, the government office in charge of the radio (I think it is the Ministry of Information) simply black-listed everybody who had ever received a check from Radio-Paris. The time an artist has to remain in Coventry is two weeks for each broadcast he made under the Germans. In some cases the period is brief; in others it mounts as high as seven years. In the case of choirs, quartets, dance bands, and other name groups only the leader is black-listed, because he is the one who received the money. There is no way of punishing the associates who broadcast with him, because their names are not on the Radio-Paris books.

The system, as you can see, is both logical and completely unfair. It is unfair because judgment has been imposed on artists by nonartists in a matter where no crime, but only professional misconduct, is charged. It is unfair also because it has chosen its scapegoats from lists that are not complete. And it is unfair because it has condemned, on a mere technicality, a very large part of the profession with a severity that neither the profession itself nor public opinion condones. The poor musician or entertainer who, in order to eat, occasionally performed French music (he was not allowed to perform German) at Radio-Paris may not be the noblest form of man. But to penalize him financially and morally, while not punishing at all the workers at state theaters who performed occasionally, under orders, German music that the French state paid for is one of the injustices that is bringing the whole operation of purging musician collaborators into disrepute. If the discussions of it that I have heard (and during my recent two months in Paris I heard many) indicate a general trend in French public opinion, I think that the purging of the artistic professions is likely to be dropped within another year and that practically everybody will be glad.

November 18, 1945

Orchestral Standards

AMERICAN symphony orchestras differ from those of Europe chiefly by the high finish of their execution. Whether they offer many deeper perfections has long been a disputed question. Renewed contact with our Big Three of the Eastern seaboard, after a recent visit abroad during which I had occasion to work with several of the Paris associations, has brought to my mind certain further comparisons that are not wholly to our advantage.

Notable as a characteristic of contemporary American orchestral style is the systematic employment of forced tone, of overbowing and overblowing. Alone among our Eastern orchestras, that of Philadelphia has resisted this heresy. Western Europe, excepting, a little bit, Italy, has never subscribed to it. Paris, London, Vienna, and Berlin have always operated on the assumption that auditory beauty (and, indeed, expression) diminishes where forced tone begins. Brilliance rather than mere weight of sound has always been their ideal for loud passages, exaggerated dynamic impact being considered as a sort of bluff, a playing to the audience's grosser nervous and emotional reactions in lieu of making specific sense — what the theatrical world calls *ham.*

The French orchestras do not have our power of crescendo, even within the range of legitimate tone. At its best and still unforced, our loud playing is louder than theirs. This added power is due partly to the instruments employed. The fine Cremona fiddles that our players are able to afford are capable of a wider dynamic range, both loud and soft, than mediocre instruments can give. The B-flat trumpet, which we commonly employ, is also more powerful than the C and D trumpets beloved of the French. Another source of power is our indifference about exact balances of sound. We allow our first flute, first oboe, first trumpet, horn, or trombone to dominate his colleagues simply because he is usually a more accomplished player and able to produce by legitimate means a larger tone. All this adds to the decibel count, though not necessarily to richness of effect.

Our habit of constantly showing off the wind instrument soloists makes for an impoverishment of sound that is peculiarly American. A passage for three clarinets, oboes, or bassoons, for instance, always sounds here like a solo for the first desk, the other parts constituting merely his more or less harmonious shadow. And we almost never achieve the equilibrium in trumpet, horn, or trombone chords that is characteristic of even the most routine French playing. Identical training is partly responsible for the French superiority in this regard. Because musicians who produce the same kind of tone are able to blend, and consequently to harmonize, far more effectively than players who, however excellent individually, have been trained in different schools.

Thus it is that the French orchestras, like the singers of the French opera, make a more in-tune, a more harmonious music than ours do. In spite of the inferior conditions under which they work, their equilibration of complexities is more subtle, more clear, and more varied of texture. The finished product they present to the public is, however, not nearly so expensive sounding as ours. There are likely to be bad spots in any rendering, places where the whole thing goes higglety-pigglety for a moment, because low standards of living, undernourishment, and fatigue are unquestionably productive of inattention.

Many American soldiers have spoken to me about what they consider the low general standard of execution at the French orchestral concerts. Accustomed to a high polish in performance, they are shocked at its absence. The younger ones, of course, don't know that French taste has never considered a high polish essential to first-class workmanship. The French work from another premise. They work from the inside out, believing that correct phraseology, appropriately varied coloration, and exact balances, particularly among instruments of the same family, will produce live music and that live music needs no make-up. Its natural bloom is considered to be sufficient.

Europe should hear our Philadelphia Orchestra. Our still admirable Boston and our improved Philharmonic have also many delights to offer. And I do hope that the Paris Conservatory and London Philharmonic orchestras will come over and play for us. Europe has much to learn from us now, particularly the advantages to music of high economic standards. But we need to be reminded again about the relative importance of interior equilibrium in music as against luxury surfacing. Also of the increased expressivity that comes from eschewal of all passional camouflage, particularly that of forced tone. Indeed, a multiplicity of cultural visits, of which orchestral exchanges would be only one, seems to me the correct basis for rebuilding international artistic standards, which have suffered everywhere during the war far more, I think, than we like to admit.

November 25, 1945

Atonality in France

FRENCH music today presents a novel, and to many surprising, development, namely, the successful implantation on Gallic soil of Schönbergian atonality. By successful I do not mean that the public likes it. This kind of music is genuinely popular nowhere. I merely mean that it is being written in France by French composers, written skillfully and, within the composing fraternity, taken seriously.

Twelve-tone row atonality, invented in Austria during the first decade of this century and perfected there during the succeeding two, has since spread all over the world. A sort of musical Esperanto, it is current practically everywhere now except in Russia, where state policy discourages the recondite. In our hemisphere from Iceland to the Tierra del Fuego and in the western European enclave from Norway to Jerusalem and to Gibraltar, no country, no musical region now lacks its twelve-tone school. And if the cult seems to be dying out in the Austro-German regions that nurtured its beginnings, its adoption by France and Italy, following on earlier successes in South America, means that this new language of Germanic origin has conquered the most unfriendly of all possible terrains, has taken root, indeed, at the very center and stronghold of the Latin tradition.

Schönberg's music has long been known in Paris to a few initiates, of course; and his *Pierrot Lunaire,* which Darius Milhaud gave there as early as 1922, has several times produced a striking effect at public concerts. So has Alban Berg's *Lyrische Suite,* for string quartet. But the other music of these masters has made slow progress in general acceptance by musical Paris. Its sincerity has long been acknowledged, but its acquaintance and real understanding have been postponed for some eventual rainy day.

That day seems now to have arrived, and the brighter young, reacting against an outmoded nationalism, are passionately involved with the new international style. Some embrace it, and some resist with vehemence. But all are having to deal with it, and many are practicing it with assiduity. It has ceased to be a curiosity and become a cause. And the principal persons available who actually learned its technical procedures in Vienna —

Max Deutsch, a pupil of Schönberg, and the young René Leibo-
witz, who once had some lessons from Anton Webern — are enjoying a prestige as mentors that their somewhat literal and stiff
adherence to the system's rules of composition would probably
not have gained for them as composers.

The most pretentious of the young atonalists is Serge Nigg, a
former pupil of Messiaen. He has written in the strict technique
of the twelve-tone row a piano concerto that is far from easy to
listen to but that is also a work of far from negligible ponderous-
ness. No less ingenious and learned but more digestible as a musical dish is a Sonata for Flute and Piano by Pierre Boulez. This
young man is the most brilliant, in my opinion, of all the Parisian under-twenty-fives. Whether he remains attached forever to
"la musique sérielle et dodécaphonique," as the French term precise adherence to the twelve-tone-row syntax, he is bound to
write interesting and lively music, because he has a talent for
that. And the practice during formative years of the strictest
counterpoint available to the modern world cannot fail to liberate by discipline the creative faculties of any genuinely gifted
musician.

The attractions of the system are, I think, two. Its first delight
is its seriousness. No composer primarily occupied with merely
pleasing or with getting on in the world ever takes it up. It is not
easy to listen to; no public likes it. Its adoption is proof that one
wishes to write music for music's own sake and that one is willing to sacrifice money and quick fame to that end. One can accuse the twelve-toners of scholasticism, but no one can say they
are not consecrated. Its practice has literally no meretricious success to offer anybody.

Its second fascination is its dangerousness. It presents all the
charms and all the perils of logic, of complete consistency. Consistency can lead artists to high triumphs of style, but it can also
lead them into sterility of expression. Nobody knows yet whether
consistent atonality is a new road to expressivity or an impasse of
noncommunication. With the Austrians it has been a fair medium
for the communication of limited sentiments. Outside of Austria
it has so far remained pretty closely involved with the sort of
psychoanalytic depiction of intimate sentiments that was its chief
expressive achievement in Vienna. If any nation in the world can
enlarge this music's scope, that is the French. They should be

able to give it sweetness, lightness, charm, ease, and to adapt it even more successfully to the theater than Alban Berg has done in *Lulu*. (His *Wozzek*, though highly chromatic, is not a twelve-tone work.)

The discipline should have a good effect on French music, too, which is in danger right now of falling into eclecticism of style. French music needs tightening up both in thought and in technique. And the international atonal style needs loosening up. Its expressivity is too tenuous, too introspective, too hopelessly standardized; and its technical practice lacks freedom. The French are good about freedom and good about objectivity. The Italian atonalists are already adding to standard practice that gracious and soaring lyric line that has long been the joy of Italian music. If the French can add to the new idiom precision of thought, taste, drama, and the power of evocation, the twelve-tone world will seem less oppressive to music lovers than it does just now.

Atonality is the last of the modernisms remaining unacceptable to the general public. Straussian expressionismus, Debussyan impressionism, the dissonant neoclassic style, and the neoromantic rounded contours are all a part of standard musical language. Even the symphony-orchestra public, the last bastion of lay conservatism, takes them as normal. If the French can't make an airplane that will fly with the twelve-tone syntax, nobody can. But if they succeed in doing so, then the last battle of modernism will have been won; and our century can enter on its second half with no regrets. A modern classic period will no doubt then ensue, with everybody writing in an amalgamated modern style. A very few years more should suffice to determine whether the twelve-tone manner is to be part of this style or not.

October 27, 1946

State and Private Radio

RADIO-LUXEMBOURG is the only major broadcasting station in Europe that is privately owned. Before the war, there were a number of such stations, the most successful in western Europe, besides Luxembourg, being one in Athlone, Eire, and Radio-Normandie at Fécamp.

The chief *raison d'être* of these stations was the broadcasting of advertising matter in English, though accounts involving German and French were not refused. Today there is a certain amount of advertising, largely local, to be heard over the European air; but it comes from government-owned stations reduced to this expedient in order to keep alive. There is advertising with the programs of the largely French-government-owned stations in Monaco and in Andorra and with a few of those that come from Toulouse. Italian state broadcasting is supported almost wholly by this means.

Outside these exceptions, however, all radio in Europe is state radio, whether operated directly by a government, as in France and Belgium, where it is a function of the Information Ministry; by a special agency virtually indistinguishable from the government, like the British Broadcasting Corporation; or by a private corporation working under government directives, as in Sweden.

Before the war, France permitted the existence of commercial stations, along with government-owned ones, and granted them wave lengths; but nowadays in that country broadcasting is a state monopoly, exactly as it is in Britain, Ireland, Spain, Portugal, the Low Countries, Finland, Czechoslovakia, Poland, the Balkan states, and the Soviet Union. In occupied regions it is run by the occupying power. The British and the American armies also operate continental networks that serve their troops.

Luxembourg remains unique. Here a private company, chiefly owned in France, runs the station as a concession, annually paying the Duchy a part of its profits from advertising. At the moment the profits are not large, the most impressive account being Coca-Cola, which offers during the winter a weekly program by the Luxembourg Radio Symphony Orchestra; the concert is performed publicly at the same time. The station has been running for the last year chiefly on money paid during the previous year for its loan to the United States Army.

Nevertheless, the station is considered in business circles to be a good investment; and an Anglo-American group is thought to be trying to buy the plant and its broadcasting concession from the French owners. Winston Churchill's visit to the Duchy in July was explained to your reporter as having to do with this attempt.

But regardless whether the ownership changes in the next few years, there is supposed to be money for somebody in Europe's one station that is devoted to the art of making friends for commercial products and influencing people to buy them. And this in spite of the fact that the station, formerly known as "the pirate of the air," has never had an official wave length assigned it by the international commission that regulates such matters.

Operating for the present on a limited budget, the musical director, Henri Pensis, back from the United States to his prewar post, has assembled a symphony orchestra that is surprisingly efficient and that plays programs of musical distinction equal to any in Europe. The city of Luxembourg offers, too, a string quartet that is usable for chamber-music broadcasts. Otherwise the programs are much like those of any other commercial station. There are news reports, light opera, dance music, and folklore of the Stephen Foster school arranged after the manner of André Kostelanetz or of Morton Gould. It is hoped soon to introduce a European version of the soap opera. Through polling procedures similar to those employed in America, the management keeps itself informed of the approximate number of listeners in France, Britain, and elsewhere.

State broadcasting operates on a quite different premise. Its purpose is not the mass sale of inexpensive products but the spreading of information and education. At its worst, state radio goes in for mendacious political propaganda. The German stations were notorious sinners in this regard, and the Yugoslav station in Belgrade, the radio world in Trieste tells me, is becoming one. At its best, however, state radio is a cultural arm of great power and complete responsibility. In all cases it is a form of public instruction, an autonomous enterprise responsible only to the intellectual world and to its representatives in the government. Henry Barraud, musical director of the French radio, says he is not interested in the number of his listeners or overfearful of diminishing this by the performance of recondite music. The duty of a state radio is, in his opinion, to produce everything, at every level of intellectual difficulty, that is in itself excellent, offering a sufficient variety of programs simultaneously so that every listener will have always a choice among several kinds of fare.

These include, as music, on any well-run station, opera, orchestral music, classic and modern chamber music, operetta, musical comedy, folklore, popular songs, dance music, and jazz. All together these make up a balanced musical diet; and it has seemed to me that the French, the Belgian, and the British broadcasts are admirably designed in this regard. Holland and the Swiss lean unduly, perhaps, toward the serious side; Spain, Hungary, and Ireland go in for nationalistic sentimentalities somewhat too stereotyped to be convincing. All provide a more varied musical fare than does Luxembourg or any single American station. One of the happiest virtues of state broadcasting is its abstention from song plugging, as well as from all those procedures by which the listener's mind is subjected to a third degree, preliminary to extracting from him a vow to change, or not to change, his habitual brand of something or other.

All the Big Three state radios (France, Belgium, and the BBC) give lots of modern music. So much, in fact, that those radio systems have largely replaced private subsidy and the mobilizing of chic society for the launching of new works. Nowadays these are given directly to the whole public, and the time lag of their general acceptance has been thus considerably speeded up. The most extreme in its modernism among Europe musical programs is the Belgian Flemish radio. Its director, Paul Collaer, searches the world over for novelties of the most unaccustomed kinds. Nothing delights him so much as to feed his faithful Flemings atonality, harmonic complexity, and the newer percussive schools. Schönberg, Ives, and John Cage are his oyster. Varèse, Webern, and Henry Cowell jostle one another on his programs, which remind one of the heroic days of the BBC, before the political purges of 1934, when British radio was musically afraid of nothing.

Beside the abundance that European radio offers in music of every kind, every period, every style, our American programs seem falsely weighted. We overdo the plugging of both standard symphonies and commercial songs. Our preoccupation with large numbers of listeners makes us unfair toward modern music and toward all those members of our public who are capable of taking part in its evolution. There is no government agency in America now that is prepared to assume any part of the responsibility of supplying information and culture to our people, and it is far from proved that such an undertaking would be desirable.

Certainly it would be fought. Nevertheless, the cultural broadcasts that the better state radios put out in Europe make a reflective visitor wonder whether there isn't some way, with all our financial and intellectual resources, of achieving programs comparably unhackneyed and broad.

September 8, 1946

Musical Belgium

THE MUSICAL life of Belgium, as this reporter has observed it recently, is marked by dependable standards of execution and by an efficiency of organization rarely to be met with in Europe during these postwar days. Indeed, save for the visible ravages of bombing, which in Antwerp alone amount to the gutting of every third house or building, the whole country is nearer like its prewar self than almost any other in Europe. There is an abundance of food and clothing; and the gap between price levels and wages is not the abysm that one encounters in Italy, say, or even in metropolitan France. In Brussels, moreover, there are taxis; and the restaurants and cafés for which that rich and cultivated city has long been justly celebrated are full of decently dressed people eating a large variety of foods, drinking good beer, and even ordering French or Rhenish wines.

Richest of all the Belgian musical institutions, the National Radio, which receives from the government 250,000,000 francs a year (nearly eight million dollars at official rates), enjoys in addition the convenience of a modern plant, built just before the war, and achieves the kind of efficiency that only special concentration can offer. All the Belgian programs, including those in Flemish, originate within its walls and are broadcast from its studios. (In Paris the National Radio works in thirty-eight converted houses and office buildings scattered all over town.) These studios represent the last word in acoustical luxury; and the establishment's three concert halls are, if not acoustically ideal, admirably laid out for the comfort of executant musicians and no end handsome to the eye.

The station possesses a symphony orchestra of first quality, also chamber-music resources that are seemingly inexhaustible, and a chorus. The conductor, Franz André, leans in his programs toward a modernism and a receptivity to foreign works similar to the practice, in these regards, of the French radio. Paul Collaer, who directs the music of the Flemish broadcasts, is even more devoted to the rare and the advanced. His programs represent an extreme of modernism that is without parallel in contemporary broadcasting. They read like a festival of the International Society for Contemporary Music.

The Belgian radio emits two simultaneous broadcasts, one known as the French program and the other as the Flemish. All programs are announced in both languages, since the country is officially, as well as really, bilingual. But the Flemings, who make up some sixty per cent of the population, are proud of their language and disdainful of the Walloons with their Frenchified ways. The Flemish programs are designed, consequently, by Flemings for Flemish tastes. And since Flemish taste has long been more courageous and more catholic than that of the Gallic contingent, the Flemish radio programs, like those of the National Flemish Opera in Antwerp, express a policy of giving to the dissident majority (for the ruling group is still Walloon), if not the separate administration that it demands, at least the kind of art it likes.

In Antwerp, the Flemish metropolis, the Opera has already produced in the Flemish tongue Benjamin Britten's *Peter Grimes,* which the Théatre de la Monnaie in Brussels, though an advanced establishment by our standards, or even by Parisian, has not yet got round to. Your correspondent witnessed at the Antwerp Opera an off-season performance in Flemish of Offenbach's *Tales from Hoffmann* that was remarkable for musical solidity and general satisfactoriness, in spite of the absence of star casting and other costly production circumstances. La Monnaie, in Brussels, which is one of the great opera houses of Europe by anybody's standards, leans, regarding repertory, toward the conservatism of its kind. But Antwerp gives everything. And the more new horizons music opens to the mind the more the Flemings enjoy it and take pride in it.

As characteristically Belgian as is the Flemish love of musical advance are the country's famous "singing towers," carillons, or musical chimes. Your correspondent, visiting one Sunday those of the cathedral at Malines, was surprised at the delicacy of their sound. This resembles far less the genteel oratundity of the chimes at New York's Riverside Church or at St. Thomas's in Fifth Avenue than it does the tinkling of a trayful of glasses. Indeed, its climactic moments are not unlike the sound of that same tray dropped.

As readers of Dorothy Sayers's *The Nine Tailors* all know, English chime playing is numerological and nonexpressive. To "ring the changes" is simply to toll the bells in all the sequences arithmetically possible. The Belgian school, on the other hand, plays tunes and even harmonies; and Belgian chimes are designed with this end in view. The carillon of Malines contains a full chromatic scale in three sizes or pitches of sound. There is a range of high tinkling bells, another of medium-pitched bells and a third of lowish ones. The booming bass range is omitted, probably because it might overpower and would certainly confuse the lighter sounds in *tutti* passages.

The prettiest music these keyed, hand-played instruments offer is a kind of three-part counterpoint, abstract in design and lacy in effect. The least effective is music of personal expressivity. Hymn tunes and carols make excellent matter for bell composition if appropriately treated. Transcriptions of well-known vocal airs, however great their sentimental appeal, risk being found comic. Delightfully so, indeed, your reporter found an execution, complete with *tempo rubato* and *tremolando* effects, of Saint-Saëns's "My heart at thy sweet voice," from *Samson and Delilah*. The musical chimes in general he found to be a limited but not wholly ineffective instrument. What they seem to him to need is music by John Cage, especially composed to bring out their percussive character.

The present musical travelogue would not be complete without reference to an admirable Belgian institution known as the Palace of Fine Arts. This is a building in Brussels, paid for by the government and free of taxes, in which some fifteen or twenty diversified cultural activities, all self-supporting, present themselves to the public. There are a symphony orchestra, a chamber-music series, lectures galore, recitals, a film library with public showings, an auction room for works of art, a theater, a restaurant, the handsomest modern concert hall your announcer has ever seen, and about a mile of gallery for loan exhibits. Whatever needs doing in culture, whatever is not being done by business or government initiative, gets done by the Palais des Beaux Arts.

Its latest success is a combined music-appreciation and youth movement known as Musical Youth, or *Les Jeunesses Musicales*. This international society, formed in 1940, has at present 15,000 members in Belgium alone and some 300,000 in France. It holds meetings, conventions, classes, competitions, and concerts. And the young people choose their own programs. This writer is notoriously suspicious of all such movements, both on musical grounds and on political. But he is also aware that laymen with musical predilections profit by access to what we call "good" music and that in most of western Europe guidance toward the understanding of this has hitherto been denied to all but professional students. *Les Jeunesses Musicales* is but one of many projects aimed to remedy this state of affair. The French school system plans a systematic alteration of it as soon as the necessary army of teachers can be trained in the conservatories. Meanwhile, French-speaking young people have sort of taken the matter in hand themselves; and the Palais des Beaux Arts has encouraged them.

September 1, 1946

Trieste's Music and Radio Setup

TRIESTE is a clean, modern seaport of some 300,000 inhabitants with little of the picturesque about it save for the mountains at its back and the vast blue bay in front. Like any other Italian city of its size, it has two lyric theaters, one for winter and one for summer.

The Allied Military Government, as sole administrative authority in the province of Julian Venetia, has taken on, along with the other municipal services, the direction of these, as well as of the local radio station and of the Trieste Philharmonic Orchestra. Virtually the entire musical life of the city is thus in the hands of British and American army officers who, if they lack in most cases experience of the routines involved, are equally without the cynicism of the professional impresario.

Summer music takes place in the square courtyard of the Castello San Giusto, a medieval hilltop fortification entered by a drawbridge. Arranged in 1938 for outdoor opera and concerts but ruined for this purpose by bombings during the war, the theater has been restored and put to use under the direction of the British officer in charge, Major the Hon. J. H. St. Clair-Erskine. The stage is in one corner of the square, with dressing rooms and wardrobe space below it. The seats, accommodating 6,000 spectators comfortably or 10,000 in a pinch, are aligned diagonally across the square. Scenery is stored behind a false stone parapet at stage left that matches the real one at stage right. There are lighting towers but no flies and no curtain, bright projectors turned toward the audience replacing the more usual velvet or canvas. Décors are painted on the spot, costumes hired from rental houses in Milan. Similarly, the orchestra and chorus employed are local, soloists being imported for the season.

The present season, which runs through July and part of August, has a repertory of four operas — Boïto's *Mefistofele*, Ponchielli's *La Gioconda*, Bizet's *Carmen*, and Verdi's *La Forza del Destino*. Each of these works receives three or four performances, operatic evenings being interspersed with symphony concerts and with cinema.

The concerts employ guest conductors and visiting soloists. Lawrence Tibbett and Robert Lawrence appeared earlier this summer. George Chavchavadze, playing with orchestra a program of piano concertos, is billed for later. The Austrian conductor Herbert von Karajan seems to have impressed all with his dynamism and clarity. He had led four concerts last winter before the purging commission decided that he was not yet acceptable politically.

The performance of *La Gioconda* that your correspondent attended would have done honor to any operatic establishment in the world. The cast, excellent all through, contained three artists of such outstanding quality that they seem worth writing to New York about. The first of these, in rising order of impressiveness, is a young tenor, Nino Scattolini. Powerful of voice, skilled in its use, and handsome of figure in a way not common among tenors of any age, this modest youth (somewhat too modest, indeed, to be a really good actor) held the stage without effort beside two of the most accomplished divas in Italy, Maria Grandi and Cloe Elmo.

Miss Grandi, Irish by birth, has sung in all the best Italian opera houses. A dramatic soprano of wide range and perfect mastery, she gave the other evening a vocal performance impeccable for style and beauty. Unfortunately she is not a young woman. The decline of her vocal powers, though as yet barely evident, cannot fail to appear as grave before many years. At present she is a distinguished dramatic soprano.

Cloe Elmo, mezzo-soprano or contralto, as you will (for she sings both kinds of role), is the most brilliant bravura singer that the writer knows of anywhere. He first heard her in 1940 as Azucena in *Il Trovatore,* in a performance broadcast from La Scala at Milan. It seemed to him at the time that he had never heard a vocal display at once so brilliant pyrotechnically and so terrifying dramatically. Seen on the stage, as Laura in *La Gioconda,* she turns out to have a personal projection of the first magnitude in addition to her unique vocal strength. In her middle thirties, she is now at the height of her powers, with a possible twenty years of great work ahead of her. I cannot imagine her not being engaged for American appearance; and once engaged, I cannot imagine her not having a durable success. Her trumpetlike alto voice is both strong and agile; her personality is warm; and she is mistress of her art.

The Allied Information Service has two radio stations in the region, one in Trieste, at the very center of the present political storm, and another near Udine, which is some forty miles away, in the undisputed Italian province of Friuli. Both stations operate musically on records and on what live music the city of Trieste provides, chiefly opera and the symphony concerts, though there is also a first-class chamber-music organization known as the Trio di Trieste. Announcements are made in both Italian and Slovene, sometimes in Serbo-Croat as well. But the Trieste station is aimed at an Italian-speaking audience. It is the station at Udine, safely installed in Italian territory, that broadcasts to Yugoslavia.

This is a field station, complete in nine trucks, that was captured from the Germans. Compact, efficient, powerful, it projects a signal twenty kilowatts strong, twice that of the permanent installation in Trieste. It is an extremely complex mechanism, however, and one that the Allied engineers have proved unable, without plans, to make function. It was got into operation by German prisoner-of-war technicians who had worked with it before its capture; and these are the men at present in charge of its technical maintenance. The German major in command of their detail was actually one of the original designers, I believe, of the equipment, or at least connected with its manufacture.

He and some eight or nine assistants live in tents on a hilltop five miles from Udine, commanded by a British officer and guarded by American soldiers. Programs in Slovene and Serbo-Croat are received by wire from Trieste and broadcast directionally to Yugoslavia. The German prisoner-engineers work twelve hours a day, and their life is not gay. But they are proud of their complex and powerful machine and of their ability to make it work. A more responsible or dependable team of technicians could scarcely be imagined; and they are not anti-Nazis, either. Either they or their chief, a strong pro-Nazi, could sabotage the machinery at any moment without our knowing what had gone wrong. It is from sheer pride of workmanship that these men do for the Allied Information Service a job that they may or may not favor politically.

In addition to the radio's nine trucks and the men's living tents, the barbed-wire hilltop enclosure contains a tar-paper shack arranged as a broadcasting studio. This is not in use now, all programs being received by underground cable from the Trieste studios. But the day that the "Jugs" (as U.S. soldiers call our Yugoslavian allies) attempt, if they do, to capture Trieste, the news will be broadcast to the world from Italian territory over German equipment operated by German technicians for an Anglo-American joint operation known as Allied Information Service.

August 18, 1946

Venice Unvanquished

VISIBLE Venice has not been touched by the war. Its historic stones are all in place, their meringue textures and ice-cream colorings intact. Walking among them and looking in the shops, calculating one's expenditures in dollars, one might easily imagine that the city's life, like its aspect, were little altered, save for the temporary general inconvenience of a strike among waiters and hotel help. For the citizenry, of course, monetary inflation, run-away prices, and rising tuberculosis rate make a life picture not wholly composed in appetizing tints. An increased tourist trade, moreover, sovereign remedy for most of the city's monetary ills, cannot be expected till state railways and civil aviation shall have been got into a running order capable of transporting foreign gold bearers.

Auditory Venice, on the other hand, bears on its surface the signs of poverty, while the inner structure of the musical life is scarcely damaged at all. The city's chief summer holiday, the Feast of the Holy Redeemer (or Redentore), which your correspondent witnessed on July 20th, was notable for the absence of brass bands and of other paid musical ensembles on the decorated floats and barges that crowded the lagoon. There is no music nowadays at any time in the Piazza San Marco save that of occasional itinerant singers or accordion players. Even gondola parties seem less vocal than formerly, probably because there are fewer Venetians on any evening just riding around, at the present price of water taxis.

There are excellent concerts, however, of a Sunday, in the sculptured courtyard of the Doge's Palace or, in case of rain, in the color-of-peaches-and-roses-and-ivory opera house, La Fenice. Sometimes these are symphonic, executed under visiting conductors by the opera's own orchestra, which is a quite good one. (It enjoys an especially fine first horn player and the best oboe soloist, by general admission, in all Italy.) On other evenings the concerts are choral or mixed. A singing society from Vicenza performed, on one evening of your reporter's stay, madrigals and sacred set pieces by Monteverdi, ending up with Carissimi's oratorio, *Jephtha's Daughter.*

The local conservatory, the Liceo Benedetto Marcello, long one of the most highly reputed in Italy, has been directed since 1938 by Italy's number-one composer (estimating him by both his national influence and his foreign prestige), Gian Francesco Malipiero. Surrounding him is a group of his maturing pupils who might almost be said to constitute a Venetian school. Esthetically these writers do not represent either of the chief trends now dominant in Italian composition, namely, the neo-Classic and the atonal. They follow rather the neo-Romantic humanism of their master, an esthetic that seems to offer more freedom to the Italian mind than does direct adherence to the tenets of either Paris or Vienna.

These last are represented elsewhere in Italy by Petrassi, who derives from the later works of Stravinsky, and by Dallapiccola, a former Malipiero pupil lately turned Schönbergian, or dodecaphonic, as the Italians term the twelve-tone syntax. That Italian composers should practice to some extent the major modes of international thought is to be expected. Indeed no country today, not even France, is without its twelve-tone school. But that beside such observances there should exist music making based on an indigenous intellectual tradition, itself one of no mean prestige, is a sign of vigor most agreeable to encounter in a time of general international conformism.

It was a privilege to inspect the scores of certain young Venetians and to hear them performed, if only under studio conditions. The most impressive of these in expressive content, as well as in technical complexity, is a Requiem Mass for double chorus, soloists, strings, three pianos, and thirteen brasses, by Bruno Maderno. A short concerto for eleven instruments, by the same author, scheduled for performance at the September Festival of Contemporary Music, is gay and ingenious, but less handsomely planned than the Requiem. This last, for all its attachment to contrapuntal textures, achieves an intensity of expression that places its young author in the high company of Berlioz and Verdi. It is not every day that one encounters religious music at once so noble of tone and so striking in effect. One wonders if this boy of twenty-six might not perhaps be destined to make that rejuvenating contribution to the Italian opera that his master has long essayed and never quite pulled off.

Even more notable for instrumental effectiveness, though thinner as expression, is a quintet for piano and strings by Gino Gorini which recalls by its instrumental aptness the string quartets of Malipiero himself, which are among the most individual contributions of our century to string repertory. Previews of the master's own recent work included a choral *"sinfonia eroica,"* entitled *Vergilii Aeneis,* and the purely instrumental Third Symphony. Both will be heard next season in the United States.

The Festival of Contemporary Music, formerly held every autumn at the Lido, is being resumed this year during the week of September 15–22. Guest conductors include Hermann Scherchen, Gregor Fitelberg, Fernando Previtali, Ildebrando Pizzetti, and several younger, less famous musicians. There will be six concerts, four of them orchestral. American composition is represented by George Antheil's Fourth Symphony and Leonard Bernstein's *Jeremiah,* France by Milhaud's *Death of a Tyrant* and songs of Messiaen. Heard for the first time in Italy will be Schönberg's second Chamber Symphony, Bartók's Third Piano Concerto, and Stravinsky's Sonata for Two Pianos. The twelve-tone faith is represented by Schönberg, Webern, Dallapiccola, and Nielsen, who is Italian in spite of his name; up-to-dateness in general by England's Benjamin Britten, Belgium's Chevreuille, Italy's own Petrassi, and some half-dozen of her genuinely young. Nor are the indispensable festival modernists — Martinů, Malipiero, Szymanowski, and Pizzetti — omitted. The programs are not designed this year to attract foreign novelty fanciers so much as to inform the Italian public. The several festivals of this kind held in Rome, Florence, and elsewhere since the liberation of the peninsula have all received high public favor and the most considered critical attention.

Among the young Venetian executants whom this writer had occasion to hear during his recent visit, the most notable are the composer Gino Gorini, an excellent pianist, and the Nuovo Quartetto Italiano. The latter is one of the most charming string quartets I have ever heard. Their work is not always traditional, but it is invariably beautiful. They play without notes, as is the contemporary Italian fashion, and with a lyrical warmth that is juvenile, poetic, inspired. Like the equally juvenile Trio di Trieste, they combine technical precision with musical freshness in the most touching way imaginable. Indeed, financial circumstances permitting, they may well, and in very few years, become one of the great quartets of Europe. They are already one of the lovely ones. Their present quality, I may add, like so much else that is valuable in the music life of Italy, is largely the result of Gian Francesco Malipiero's encouragement and counsel.

August 25, 1946

Salzburg Festival

THE SALZBURG FESTIVAL of last year, according to the reports of those present, was but a shadow of its prewar self. That of 1946, which this reporter attended, was a first-rate show, both socially and musically. To be sure, there was no Toscanini, no Walter to conduct, no Flagstad on the stage; and few of the old international smart set were out front. But there was the Vienna Philharmonic Orchestra; there was Charles Muench from Paris, conducting; there was some definitely first-class singing; there was the best-prepared performance of Mozart's *Figaro* I have ever heard; and the audience was starred liberally with dignitaries from our military and civil administrations. Indeed, the neighboring estates, occupied in many cases by high-ranking American officers, offer nowadays week-end parties at which visiting generals, judges from Nürnberg, ambassadors, handsome aides-de-camp, well-dressed wives and daughters, and cavalcades of Packard cars present a spectacle of no mean brilliance. In the city itself there are Austrian music lovers and the French from Innsbruck. Every seat is always full at every festival performance. And the Oesterreichische Hof is still a hotbed of political and musical, if no longer of amorous, intrigue.

The opera repertory consists this year of Mozart's *Don Giovanni* and *Marriage of Figaro* and Strauss's *Rosenkavalier*. The spoken plays are Goldoni's *Servant of Two Masters* and the old morality, *Everyman*, both in their prewar Reinhardt staging. The conductors of the Vienna Philharmonic concerts have been Alceo Galliera, Karl Schuricht (an excellent classical musician whom I heard earlier this summer in Venice), Bernhard Paumgartner, John Barbirolli, Ernest Ansermet, and Charles Muench, the latter paired with the only orchestral soloist of the festival, the excellent French pianist, Nicole Henriot. There were four serenade concerts, recitals by Grace Moore, by Yehudi Menuhin, and by the Swiss pianist Edwin Fischer, and quartet evenings by the Philharmonia, Winterthur, and Calvet Quartets. Religious music was furnished by the Vienna Choir Boys and by performances with the Cathedral Choir and the Mozarteum Orchestra of Masses by Schubert, Bruckner, and Mozart.

Rosenkavalier and *Figaro*, a Philharmonic concert with Muench and Miss Henriot, the Philharmonia Quartet, and a performance of the Mozart Requiem were the fare during your correspondent's three-day visit. The Strauss opera, ill cast and sloppily played, was the performance among these least worthy by Salzburg standards, though Hilde Konetzni, who sang the Feldmarschallin, is both a singer and an actress of quality. The Requiem was no better given than choral works are anywhere, which means it was pretty rough. It did have, however, the kind of ease that comes from devotion and familiarity, the quality that the Bach Mass has in Bethlehem, Pennsylvania, as if performing it and listening to it were a perfectly natural thing for everybody to be doing. Equally easy and natural, but more refined, were executions by the Philharmonia Quartet, from Vienna, of works by Haydn and Dvořák and Schubert. At the head of the writer's memories of the whole will long remain a reading by Muench of Berlioz's *Fantastic Symphony*, unique for its lyric grace and for its fiery white light, and a performance of Mozart's *Figaro* that was not only well sung in the solo numbers but wholly delicate and precise in the concerted work.

Maria Cebotari, who sang the Countess, has a beautiful voice and grace of phraseology. Though eight months with child, she sang the difficult-to-breathe *"Dove Sono"* with a sustained line and a nobility of expression rarely to be met with in these days of the vocal art's decline. Irmgard Seefried, the Susanna, has a fine voice, too, and is clearly a good musician. Both artists are worth watching. The conductor who prepared the performance, Herbert von Karajan, is Austria's coming man, an original and a powerful musician. Temporarily under political ban (his is a "mild," or borderline case), he did not conduct the performance. But through a connivance between the Festival directors and the American political authorities, he was enabled to rehearse for another conductor a production that everyone present, I think, will long be happy to have heard. Delicate without being bloodless, exact without being mechanical, quiet in the ensemble passages almost to the point of being conversational, this interpretation is nevertheless one of high dramatic intensity and wide dynamic range. It is also, as expression, humane and sweet. There may be here the model for a new approach to the musical execution of Mozart's operas.

The Austrian style of playing Mozart, as prewar visitors to Salzburg knew it, is no ancient tradition. It was invented in Vienna about fifty years ago by Gustav Mahler and transmitted to our own time by Bruno Walter. Noble in proportion but careless of detail, at least in the Walter version, it resembles more the whipped-cream-in-stone aspect of Austrian baroque architecture than it does the firm workmanship of Mozart's music. As a reaction against the outmoded romantic style of playing Mozart, it was more than welcome after the last war; and it brought to a great master new public favor. But there is nothing eternal about it. A new kind of Mozart would not now be unwelcome to musicians. It could, as well, if properly exploited, bring much-needed money into Austria's coffers.

September 15, 1946

Germany's Music Life

OUR control officers in Germany for theater and music, virtually all of whom this reporter has talked with and observed in action, are devoted men and miracle workers. All four military governments, moreover, favor the reconstruction of Germany's artistic and intellectual life. The framework of this reconstruction, thanks to everybody's indefatigable effort, is already well above ground. There is music, for instance, lots of it, all over the land, some of it quite first-class. What differs from zone to zone is chiefly the flexibility with which the different high commands implement an identical policy. The Russians and the French are politically quite lenient toward artists. The British are more interested in getting on with their job than in hamstringing themselves on categorical regulations. The American generals seem to consider that the progress of intellectual reconstruction is less important than the preservation of the "hard peace" attitude that public opinion at home has so far favored.

In the American jurisdiction, which includes the provinces of Bavaria, of Württemburg-Baden, and of Greater Hesse, the Bremen Enclave, and our Berlin sector, there were on August 28 of this year 412 licensed theaters, theater troupes, and concert halls. This in addition to 705 film houses. The number of musical and dramatic artists cleared of Nazi party membership and permitted to work before the public amounted to 24,494. Among these the dramatic artists represent a much larger number than the musicians do. Thanks to the particular organization of the German spoken theater, which consisted chiefly of repertory troupes closely bound together and animated by a strong *esprit de corps*, the pressure toward Nazi party membership had made fewer inroads on Germany's dramatic personnel than on the musical profession, where many a free-lance singer or instrumentalist had found himself obliged to join up in order to earn a living. As a result, about half the actors in our zone have been cleared and can work, whereas less than one per cent of the musicians, according to an estimate of the American Control Officer for Music and Theater, are available for engagement.

Nevertheless, both music and drama flourish vigorously in all the zones; and the German population, with not much to do of an evening but sit around in its overcoat, if it owns one, is assiduous in attendance at musical and dramatic entertainment. The citizens of Munich can choose among fifteen legitimate theaters, ten variety halls, a political cabaret, a circus, a puppet show, and twenty-nine movies. In addition to these events there are nightly opera at the Prinzregenten Theater and an average of ten to twelve concerts a week, including three or four by the local Philharmonic Orchestra, plus innumerable occasions for indulgence in choral singing. If no other city in our zone offers quite such bounty, that is because no other German city in any zone is at present quite so well equipped with halls. It is housing, not money, that is scarce. There is lots of money in circulation; and subsidies, both state and municipal, are generous.

But, somehow, though Munich looks like a complete wreck, like a construction in pink sugar that has been rained on, more of it is usable than one might imagine. The opera house, the assembly halls of the University and of the Deutsches Museum are in good shape. The Bavarian State Theater, or *Staats-schauspielhaus*, has been rebuilt. The Philharmonic is building itself a new hall; so are various theatrical groups. The other usable locales employed are chiefly beer halls and converted gymnasiums. Nymphenburg Palace, untouched by bombing, provided in July a perfect Baroque setting for a three-weeks' festival of eighteenth-century music, including an opera by the little known von Seckendorff on a text of Goethe, *Lila, oder Phantasie und Wirklichkeit*. There is a municipal conservatory with seven hundred students, too; and the state conservatory, or *Bayerische Akademie der Tonkunst*, will open this fall under the direction of Josef Haas with two hundred pupils.

Stuttgart, though less bombed out than Munich, has fewer halls and theaters available for use. The opera house, which is intact, has been requisitioned by the Army for movies, USO shows, and a Red Cross club, complete with barber shop and shoe shines. It can be used for opera only at those moments that do not inconvenience our military. The situation in Nuremberg and Wiesbaden, where opera houses are also still usable, is even graver, because the military will not even lend them to the local opera company. In the latter city our Air Force continues to give movies in the opera house, while the opera company performs in a movie theater. The Army movies are not well attended anywhere. I counted in Stuttgart's opera house about one hundred people, though the place seats 1,400. Our military is fearful of releasing all such properties, lest the G. I. newspapers editorialize unfavorably. The pampering of our soldiers is considered everywhere to take precedence over the reconstruction of German cultural life, even when this has been thoroughly denazified.

All programs for re-educating the German people count heavily on the rebuilding of their intellectual life. As I mentioned in a previous article, overdenazification and undernourishment are a hindrance to the carrying out of the United States program. But these policies follow formal decisions of our military government and can be altered. Indeed, our severity toward minor collaborators is being relaxed already. Our general disdain, however, for honest German citizens (and a German had to be either pretty honest or *non compos mentis* to avoid Nazi party membership) is in every way deplorable. We treat them very much as we do Negroes in the United States. We expect them to work hard and to be very grateful to us. But we refer to them as "krauts" and do not eat with them in public.

Hard as it has been to liberate and to reconstruct the theaters and concert halls in the Württemberg-Baden area, it has been even more difficult to house German entertainment in Greater Hesse. Frankfurt's opera and state spoken theater are in ruins. All utilizable large halls are used for the necessary purposes of our central military administration, USFET. A year ago Frankfurt's first postwar musical event took place on the floor of the Stock Exchange, which still had three walls standing and half a roof. Today this same space has been remodeled and a small stage added. That is where the opera company plays. A gymnasium, or *Turnhalle,* in the suburbs is used for spoken plays. Recitals take place in the assembly hall of the university. There are in divers basements and beer halls a cabaret, a variety show, and a circus. The former stock exchange now offers almost any week two grand operas, two recitals, and four plays. The conservatory has about a hundred students. The Cæcilian Verein, a famous choral organization, gives two concerts a year.

Wiesbaden, a smaller city, has about the same number of halls available and a similar number of musical events per week. Both the opera house and the thermal casino, or *Kurhaus,* where a small theater is still in good shape, are used to entertain American soldiers. Darmstadt offers the public a reduced symphony orchestra that plays once a week at the Polytechnic Institute, a few musical lectures at the Palace and about two operetta or opera performances. That is all there is room for. Kassel, which is flat, has virtually no music at all. Neither Wiesbaden nor Darmstadt nor Kassel has a working conservatory.

The Bremen Enclave has eight theaters, 1025 licensed musical and dramatic artists. Our Berlin sector has fourteen licensed theaters and concert halls, 6870 artists registered and cleared of Nazi taint. The most important musical organization in this jurisdiction is the Berlin Philharmonic Orchestra. This distinguished musical body, which lives, except for the first-desk men, on No. 2 ration, is suffering from hunger. It has been a great orchestra; it has a place in the history of music. With a little more food and a little loosening of the denazification rules, it could take up its merited place again. Both the Russians and the British are more careful of the opera companies that work in their zones than we are of the Philharmonic.

Our denazification policy is slowly being altered, but our feeding policy is not. An American orchestra, or some related organization that has at heart the interests of music and of its faithful servants, could render both no more valuable service than to send food packages regularly to this orchestra. There are no Nazis in it; many of its members have done time in concentration camps. All of them are hungry and tired and discouraged. If our government will not pamper them a little, perhaps American musicians will. Last spring they played for a party given by an American Army officer, himself a professional musician in private life. Whether they were paid for their evening's work or not I do not know; but I do know that they were allowed to pass through a supper room in which buffet tables groaned with food, without being offered so much as a sandwich. It is illegal, I believe, to give away commissary merchandise to citizens of an enemy country.

September 29, 1946

Music in Berlin

BERLIN still enjoys two opera companies and one symphony orchestra. The State Opera Company (or *Staatsoper*) plays in the Russian sector. The municipal troupe (or *Städtische Oper*) plays in the British sector. The Philharmonic Orchestra is seated in the American sector and mostly plays there, though once a fortnight it gives a concert in the British sector for Allied troops. It also plays from time to time for the powerful Berlin radio station, which, though located in the British sector, is controlled by the Russian Military Government. All radio in Germany comes under the direction of the occupying armies. Music, theater, and film showings, excepting such entertainments as are provided for the troops themselves, are produced by Germans for the general public. In every case, the hall, the management, and the executant artists are licensed by the occupying military power. The strictness of the screening varies in Berlin, as it does in the whole German territory, according to the divers policies of the Big Four governments about previous relations of individual Germans with the Nazi party.

The Russians, the most liberal toward artists in their denazification policy, were the first to get their major Berlin musical enterprise, the State Opera, into successful operation. The British opened the Municipal Opera somewhat later. The Americans, who are so strict that more than ninety-nine per cent of the German musicians in their zone and sector are still black-listed, have not yet been able to bring the Berlin Philharmonic Orchestra back to anything like its former musical efficiency. It has given concerts from the beginning of the occupation, but its work bears little relation to the standards for which it was famous before the war.

Its present conductor, Sergiu Celibidache, a Rumanian by birth, is a musician of broad culture but not as sound a technician of the baton as one might wish. The program that your correspondent heard in the Titania-Palast, a former film house, consisted of Berlioz's *Benvenuto Cellini* overture, the second suite from Prokofiev's *Romeo and Juliet,* and Brahms's First Symphony. All were read clearly, but the sound of them had little charm. Neither the woodwind, the brass, nor the percussion of the orchestra is quite first-class. The strings are still those of a major symphonic ensemble, and the discipline in general still bears a resemblance to that for which this group has long been famous. But the ensemble is not invariably harmonious. The orchestra is a victim, in fact, of two American administrative tendencies, indifference about the fate of artists and overdenazification. Musicians cannot work properly on No. 2 ration, which represents barely a thousand calories. It is hoped that our recently adopted policy of handing over denazification to German tribunals, which have so far shown considerable leniency toward minor political peccadilloes while maintaining severity toward major fascist action, will permit the re-engagement of certain valuable musicians. Whether Furtwängler, the former conductor, is to be allowed to return to his post will probably be decided in the near future.[1]

The State Opera, which falls under Russian jurisdiction, is in better shape. The orchestra is excellent, the stage direction first-

[1] He was allowed to conduct slightly less than a year later.

class, the singing favorably comparable with that offered by any other house in the world. All the artists, moreover, receive special food packages from the Soviet government and a workers' ration of 1,350 calories, which enables them to rehearse and to perform with a minimum of fatigue and to conserve thus a reasonable artistic efficiency. A performance heard at the Admiralspalast, a former operetta theater, was, by anybody's present-day standards, first-class. And the public was entitled to consume food and drink during the intermission without ration points. There were available at the bar open sandwiches, thin soup, beer, vodka, and German cognac.

The musical offerings that your reporter heard were Puccini's *Il Tabarro* (*The Cloak*) and Busoni's *Arlecchino*. The Puccini work was presented in a charming set that really looked like Paris and that was architecturally interesting to play in. It is about the prettiest and most satisfactory realistic stage setting this reviewer has encountered in some years. Like that of *Arlecchino* (and the costuming of both operas), it was the work of the well-known painter Paul Strecker. The direction of the piece, both musically and visually, was a pleasure. The cast contained no celebrated stars; but the voices were warm, and the vocalism was schooled. Sigrid Ekkehard, Karola Goerlich, Jaro Prohaska, and Erich Witte sang the major roles with beauty and no little distinction. Both production and performance were superior in every way to those of *Il Tabarro* offered in New York last season at the Metropolitan Opera House.

Ferruccio Busoni's *Arlecchino,* based on a libretto by himself and subtitled "a theatrical capriccio," is cast in the mold of the *commedia dell'arte*. Which is to say that it tells its tale through the standardized masquerades of Harlequin, Pantaloon, and Columbine, with a few more characters added. Its full significance escaped your reviewer, though he was aware of both satirical and philosophical overtones. There was clearly a literary take-off on Goethe's *Faust,* and the music made open references to Mozart, to Richard Strauss, and to Wagner's *Lohengrin*. He gathered that the whole was supposed to be both witty and profound and greatly regrets his inability to find the work funny, even, not to speak of deep or moving.

Its musical texture, however, is, like all of this composer's work, utterly distinguished. Busoni's music is always skillful and civilized, even, by moments, original. It contains no bluff, no stupidity, no whiff of insincerity; and it evolves on the highest plain of competence, both esthetic and technical. What it lacks is plain feeling. Its manner is grand and thoroughly elegant, but its emotional content is weak. One is always glad to hear it, which happens seldom enough; but one tends to prefer for steady consumption the meatier simplicities of a Verdi or of a Puccini, on the one hand, the more incisive modernities in both thought and texture, on the other, of a Debussy, a Stravinsky, a Schönberg.

The production was a stylish one and carefully rehearsed. Mr. Strecker's set and costumes, like the choreography (for the work was played in strictly regulated pantomime), were well designed to situate the work in the period of its composition. Black-and-white post-World-War-I Expressionismus was the style, one long since outmoded, even in Germany, the land where it flourished most abundantly. What model its arrogance and ugliness can offer to today's postwar Berlin I cannot imagine, where Germans are, for once, being really humble and where the city itself, more than ever monumental in its ruined state, is for the first time really beautiful.

It is possible that the German mind, scraping history for whatever might possibly serve as lamp or guide in German culture's present state of anarchy and desolation, has seized on Germany's last original theater style that anybody had liked at all and revived it just to see if it still meant anything.

The Soviet cultural officers do not appear very enthusiastic about the work or about its production. The German public seems to like the show. For your reporter it represented an effort at artistic presentation unparalleled today in the musical repertory theaters of Paris or Milan or New York, but one scarcely justified, even if it were stylistically more congenial, by the slender content, literary and musical, of Busoni's opera.

September 23, 1946

German Composers

MUSICAL composition in Germany and Austria, relieved from Nazi censorship by the Allied invasion, has gone back to where it left off when Hitler came in. This is not to say that nobody in those countries wrote any good music during the Nazi years. I mean rather that the newer music now available there by print or performance bears a closer relation to that current in pre-Nazi times than most of the music honored by the Third Reich did. In other words, the break with the modernist tradition that accompanied the triumph of National Socialism is being repaired under the esthetically less dictatorial Allied Military Occupation.

The mending job will not, however, be complete, with no seams visible, because certain powerful influences on central Europe's music life that were exiled in the mid-1930's will never, can never return. The principal of these is that of the twelve-tone trinity — Schönberg, Berg, and Webern. The first of these masters, now resident in California, is seventy-two years old and not in perfect health; the other two are dead. And though their influence might be expected to go on through their published works and through the teaching of their pupils, the curious fact is that in Germany it does not. There is a little of it left in Austria, where the pre-Schönbergian atonalist, Josef Matthias Hauer, survives, along with two or three Webern pupils. The younger Austrians mostly follow other leaders, other styles. In Germany this reporter inquired diligently without encountering one twelve-tone writer or finding any German musician who knew of the existence of one in the land.

The influences of Paul Hindemith and of Kurt Weill, on the other hand, both resident in the United States, are considerable. That of the former is less notable on musical composition, curiously, than on pedagogy. Musicians who write like Hindemith are not so plentiful as those who teach his theory. In the process of getting the conservatories started again, a revision of German music teaching seems to be desired. And since personnel is lacking for the teaching of atonal theory, this school of composition is not represented on the faculties. But the Hindemith textbooks are held in high respect and seem likely to form the basis of the most advanced pedagogy. Hindemith's works are held in honor, too, but rather as proof of their author's personal gift than as models being followed. In any case, though Hindemith is a burning subject of discussion in music circles, it is his undeniable influence on music teaching that is chiefly defended and attacked rather than his direct influence on musical composition. Evidences of the latter are, though not wholly lacking, more rare. In Germany, as here, he has formed more good teachers than he has successful composers.

Kurt Weill, though not a theorist at all, seems to have left a strong mark on German music. At least, there is an influence around that is not easily explainable through any of the existing pedagogical traditions and that this detective strongly suspects to come out of *Mahagonny and Der Dreigroschenoper*. The academic German styles today are two, the Hindemith style and the Reger style, both contrapuntal. Like all contrapuntal styles, these are more entertaining to write in than to listen to; they lack expressivity. The rival style, which leans more on melodic and rhythmic device, is lighter of texture, more varied in expression, less pompous, and more easily digestible.

The most successful writer in this vein is Hans Orff, who lives near Munich. His works are chiefly dramatic oratorios, which is to say, choral works with orchestral accompaniment that require (or at least are enhanced by) staging. Their texts are elaborately cultural, their musical textures almost willfully plain. One, called *Carmine Catulli*, consists of odes by Catullus, in Latin, interspersed with modern recitatives, also in Latin, by the composer. Another, *Carmine Burana*, uses student songs in medieval Latin mixed with Old German. An opera entitled *Die Klüge* has a rhymed text by the composer. Another now nearing completion, *Die Bernauerin*, is in Bavarian dialect. The direct musical model of all these works is Stravinsky's *Les Noces*. They employ lots of rhythmic chanting, and the orchestral accompaniment is percussive. The music is simplified, however, to a point where the basic musical elements — melody, harmony, and counterpoint — are almost nonexistent. The rhythm itself, even, has not much intrinsic interest. What holds these works together is first-class handling of words and their excellent orchestration. Otherwise they are monotonous. Surprisingly enough, they have considerable success in performance, even on the radio, where stage spectacle is not there to help out.

More interesting musically, though also an example of the simplification for expressive purposes that I credit to Kurt Weill (radio work is also, no doubt, an influence), is the music of Boris Blacher and of his pupils. Blacher is Russian by birth, a child refugee of the Revolutionary years. He is musical director at present of the Russian-run Berlin radio station. His music, though aware of both Stravinsky and Satie, is gayer than that of either. At its simplest it is full of musical interest; at its most complex it is still full of life, clear and expressive. His suite, *Concertante Musik* (Bote and Bock, Berlin, 1938), would be an ornament to anybody's orchestral program. His pupil Gottfried von Einem, an Austrian, writes operas in which rumba rhythms turn up at the most tragic moments, unexpectedly but not always inappropriately. Blacher's work and von Einem's have a touch of wit that is welcome in German music. Blacher himself is the most vigorous single musical influence now present in the country.

Another composer that we shall all be hearing from is Kurt Hessenberg, of Frankfurt. This young man in his early thirties is the author of neo-Romantic songs, cantatas, and piano pieces that evoke directly and without detours the spirit of Schumann. His Symphony No. 2 is melodious and completely successful. Unfortunately it received a Nazi prize award in 1942, an honor that makes it something of a hot potato anywhere just now. It is a beautiful work, all the same, and will no doubt come later into its own. Everybody, literally everybody, I am sure, will love it. It is quite without the turgidity of the German contrapuntalists and equally void of those vulgarities in sentiment and in style that make the works of the more official Third Reich composers (Werner von Egk, for instance) not worth worrying about at present. Hessenberg is a schooled workman and a composer of very real, if somewhat obvious, poetic feeling.

Blacher and Orff are the most original composers whose work this reporter encountered in Germany. Whether Orff can remain long acceptable to musicians I cannot say, though I doubt that he will. Blacher is growing in interest and influence, but I do not believe he will remain long in Germany. After twenty-five years, he seems to have had enough. Hindemith, whether he ever returns or not to the land of his birth and major successes, will certainly continue to occupy there for many years the central musical position.

October 13, 1946

Visit to Dresden

THE SOVIET UNION'S control over cultural activities in the Russian zone of Germany is organized in imitation of ours. Ours, like the British, is an offspring of the Anglo-American Psychological Warfare Branch, the overseas equivalent of OWI. Our head information control officer, Brigadier General Robert McClure, was previously in charge of PWB. The French setup is slightly different, education and the fine arts being directed, as in France itself, by other persons than those controlling cinema, press, and similar media of direct information. In all zones the specialized field workers, whose job it is to help the Germans get theaters, opera houses, art schools, newspapers, the whole intellectual machinery, into operation, depend from central offices in Berlin. Their labors are necessarily somewhat decentralized, however, since the subsidies that support German cultural activities must come out of German taxes, which are at present collected only by the separate German state administrations and by municipalities, since no central German government exists.

The degree to which Allied control officers use Germany as an outlet for their divers national art products varies partly with the amounts of such art available. Theaters in our zone, for example, give a great many American plays, but the concert programs include only such American works as happen to be in the music library of the Quadripartite Control Commission in Berlin. These are chiefly photographed scores and parts inherited from PWB. The British and Russian shelves are somewhat fuller than ours; there is no French music there at all. So far, American publishers have not been willing to ship additional material, though the War Department has offered facilities. Performing rights fees are collected by STAGMA, the German equivalent of ASCAP, and held for the present in blocked marks.

In spite, however, of the large repertory of Russian works available (there is a Soviet book and music shop open to all in the ruined Unter den Linden), the Russian control officers do not overly encourage their performance. Major Sergei Barsky, music control officer for the Soviet military government in Germany, explained to your reporter in the following terms his government's present cultural policy as regards Germany. The concept of Russia as an exotic land with special ways of life and a morality of its own, a fairy-tale Russia, colorful, grand, and cruel, is to be slowly eradicated, if possible, from the Western mind. The Soviet Union hopes eventually to be considered as a part of the world, which is one world, rather than as a special case among countries, which people feel obliged to love or to hate. The choice of Russian operas and plays to be performed in German theaters, therefore, is encouraged in the direction of their classical-humanities content. The too picturesque and the violent are tactfully avoided, as are historical subjects showing the Russian nation as unfriendly to the German people.

Re-educating Germany through music, according to Major Barsky, who is a grandnephew of Anton Rubinstein, is less a matter of censoring repertory, however, than of building up a new style of execution. The works played, unless openly anti-Russian, are of less import than the manner in which they are played. Militarism, for two centuries, has been ground into the German mind and ground so deep that it has come to permeate every detail of living, every German way of doing anything. It must be removed because Russia's peace and prosperity are at stake. And the removal will be a long and tedious operation, "like picking out splinters one by one from a hand or foot." The Soviet military government would like, or at least Major Barsky would like, to reform German musical education with a view to inculcating eventually in German musicians a less narrow and vainglorious attitude toward music and a set of working methods that will oppose a deeper resistance to military tyranny than the existing German musical tradition has, in our century, proved capable of doing.

During the course of a recent visit to the Russian zone, your correspondent received similar declarations on this subject from Major Auslander, Soviet culture control chief for the State of Saxony. This officer also brought to a vodka-and-champagne breakfast in Dresden *Ministerialdirektor* Pappe, German Communist organizer of Union No. 17, the union of free-lance artists and intellectuals in the Russian zone, which was holding that day its first birthday celebration and annual congress.

This is an industrial union comprising musical soloists and stage artists, film and radio workers, vaudeville and circus performers, orchestral musicians, theater technicians, authors, composers, painters, architects, and journalists. The admission of medical men, scholars, and scientists is envisaged but not yet a fact. It is thought probable that these may be more efficiently served by the teachers' union. The locals of Union 17 are attached, so far as is possible, to producing units, each theater, newspaper, radio station, etc., being a separate grouping. "One shop one local" is the aim. Exception made for former adherents of the Nazi party, who cannot work anyway, membership is open to all intellectual workers without professional examination. It is also, with minor leniencies, obligatory, after the classical principle of "open unions and closed shops." The right to strike is admitted; but there have been no strikes so far. Frozen wages and frozen prices have not provoked any need for economic adjustment, and the observances by management of contractual engagements is enforced by the Saxon state.

The chief faults of union organization under the Weimar Republic, according to Mr. Pappe, were the multiplicity of unions claiming jurisdiction in a given shop or industry, and a tendency of the arbitration courts to side with management. The present union structure of the Soviet zone, though not in theory monopolistic, is designed to discourage rival jurisdictions; and arbitration courts have been abolished. They have been replaced by a chamber of commerce and industry, of which the membership is one third representatives of management, one third union delegates, and one third state officials, experts on labor and production questions. All contracts have to be passed on by this board; and when they have been accepted, the state police enforces them. The board is thus automatically stacked in favor of whichever group is more powerful in the state government, management or labor. Whether Soviet influence will in the long run exert itself on the side of labor or of capital remains to be seen.

Working regulations for musicians in the Soviet zone demand a forty-eight-hour availability week, with a maximum of around thirty hours' actual work before overtime pay begins. This last figure is thought by most musicians to be excessive, and they are hoping to get it diminished to the twenty-four-hour norm effective in Berlin, a norm comparable to our American week of nine services, where any normal performance or one two-and-a-half-hour rehearsal constitutes a service. Musicians' wages in Saxony are about the same as in Berlin. They vary, according to the skill of the artist and the importance of his post, from a minimum of 300 marks a month ($30 in American money) up to twice that. Opera stars and guest conductors sometimes receive as high as 1,800 marks ($180) a month. The provincial governments in all zones reduce a man's income by nearly half through taxation. Life for all, under these circumstances, is difficult, but not more so in the Russian zone than elsewhere. Artists there receive a higher food ration than they do in the other zones, and political bans are less rigidly enforced than in ours. But interzonal travel is virtually impossible for them. Working in the Russian zone is thus tempting to many, but all know that settling there is an irrevocable act as long as the iron curtain remains closed.

The musical events which this visitor attended in Dresden consisted of two operettas, *Die Czardasfürstin*, by Emmerich Kalman, and a Tyrolean piece called *Monika*, by one Dorstal, standard repertory works both. The performances were musically quite adequate but visually primitive, since an improvised stage in a beer hall and a half-bombed-out suburban summer theater imposed limitations on stage display. The major opera company, directed by Hans Keilbert, who also conducts the Dresden Philharmonic Orchestra, had not yet opened its winter season. It has performed up till now in a Christian Science church. The physical state of Dresden, where the whole center of the city, including its priceless Baroque monuments and noble opera house, was destroyed in one bombardment, is unfavorable to music and drama. Nevertheless music and drama go on, and the conservatory has 180 students. A large theater, the former Schauspielhaus, is being restored.

Space forbids, even if my competency permitted, reporting on the art treasures of the former State Museum, now hung at the eighteenth-century Pillnitz Palace in the suburbs, on the curious absence from this collection of certain famous works, including Raphael's *Sistine Madonna*, and on the fact that the Russians don't seem to be looking very hard for these. Also on the large retrospective show of German modern painting now open at the former military academy. On the 28th of September there is to be held in Dresden a congress of German artists from all the zones.

The United States Information Control Division seemed to this observer both more enlightened and more efficient than the Russian in the fields of journalism and of drama, less so with regard to education, the visual arts (excepting old masters), and trade-union organization. On all the latter subjects our policy is obscure and our action, in consequence, slow. Musically one zone is very much like another, though we have not yet produced with our Berlin Philharmonic as good performances as the Russians do with their Staatsoper or as the British are said to do at the Hamburg Opera House. All field workers everywhere pray for the abolition of interzonal barriers. The Russian field workers in music appeared to me as no less devoted and self-sacrificing than ours and as possibly better supported in detail by their higher officers and by their government at home. The Soviet hierarchy, in any case, has certainly a clearer understanding of what it is up to culturally than ours has. The avowed aim of all the occupying powers is to put an end, and quickly, to Germany's present state of moral, intellectual, and economic anarchy, which risks infecting the whole European continent and sowing destruction broadcast.

October 6, 1946

THOUGHTS IN SEASON

Repertory

IT is a commonplace of contemporary esthetics that music of marked originality is likely to be found shocking by the epoch that gives it birth. The inability is notorious not only of the lay public but of trained musicians to perceive beauty in any work of which the style is unfamiliar. And program makers are aware that this blindness obtains not only with regard to contemporary composition but with regard to the past as well. When one considers the vast amount of music written since 1600 that is perfectly well known, published, and available for performance and that is never given by our operatic or orchestral establishments, in spite of the eagerness of conductors to vary their monotonous routine, one is obliged to conclude, I think, that the tininess of our effective repertory is due to psychological factors that are beyond anyone's power to control.

Epochs, styles, and authors all have a way of becoming invisible, of passing in and out of focus, rather, that is not easy to explain. The facts of this matter constitute the history of taste. Our inability to cope with the unfamiliar is equaled only by our inability to maintain interest in the too familiar, in that which is no longer in any way strange. The vogue of our popular songs is typical. Within a few years, sometimes within one year, it is possible to observe in succession the enthusiasm, the indifference, and the ridicule with which one of these is treated; and we have all experienced the renewed charm of some old song that has been left in limbo long enough to be all but forgotten. There is no way of preventing it; the things we get used to tend to become invisible. They are there all the time, and we know they are there, and we think we love them dearly; but if they were taken away we should half the time not remark any difference.

Schumann's music, for example, is in a decline of favor just now; nobody has a lively feeling for it any more. Interpreters find it more and more difficult to render, audiences more and more difficult to listen to. It is passing out of our focus. Debussy is in an even more curious phase. He is listened to increasingly, understood less and less. Haydn seems to be emerging from his recent obscurity and taking on contours again. Bach, after having been genuinely popular among the *cognoscenti* for thirty years, is losing a bit his appeal for intellectuals. Mozart has, in fact, taken Bach's place of late as the master most admired among connoisseurs. Wagner and Brahms have still a broadly based popularity but a markedly diminishing attraction for musicians. Verdi, though he has lost much of his former power over the masses, has acquired in the last twenty years a prestige in university circles that would have shocked profoundly the scholastic musicians of fifty years ago.

Always, in the case of such revivals, there is imposed a certain falsification upon the original. No matter how much we pretend we are restoring old works to their pristine state, we are obliged at the same time to modernize them somewhat if we expect our contemporaries to take them seriously. Returns to popularity of past styles in architecture and decoration have usually been accompanied, therefore, by complete resurfacing. The nineteenth century unpainted its Gothic monuments and left them a unified gray. It covered up the bare wood of its Louis XVI furniture with a bluish color known as Trianon gray. It built Greco-Roman houses everywhere and painted them white, which is still considered, indeed, to be the appropriate color for classical antiquity. In recent decades flamboyant Victorian interiors, also, have regained their charm through the use of white paint, which was practically never used on them originally but which our age finds cheerful and associates with asepsis.

The Bach revival of the 1830's, which Mendelssohn and Schumann fathered, translated this music into all the idioms of contemporary executant style, using Tourte bows for the orchestral suites and violin pieces, gigantic organs and choruses for the religious works, pianos for the domestic keyboard music, and employing a constant crescendo and diminuendo within all phrases, as was considered necessary at that time for true expression. Bach was modernized all over again in the early years of this century.

His rhythm was made to sound more mechanical, dynamism was everywhere diminished, phraseology streamlined, the harpsichord revived, the old, small, bright-sounding organs restored to use.

A healthy traffic goes on nowadays in the reinstrumentation of eighteenth-century music of all kinds, but we have not yet done over the Romantics very much. Though the nineteenth century is dying slowly, there is vigor in its traditions still. Not for some time will they be forgotten so thoroughly that a resurfacing of the Romantic masters will be possible to envisage. When this does take place, they will lose, of course, the somber patina that a century of daily handling has laid upon them and appear as bright again to us as cleaned and revarnished masterpieces from the past do in a gallery of painting.

Meanwhile, we must put up with our own age, because, whether we like it or not, its habits are for us the facts of life. That age listens to a great deal of new music, likes practically none of it, but would not for the world forgo hearing it. It respects a vast repertory of old music, complains no end at the infrequency with which most of this is heard, discourages firmly the introduction of any of it into the major programs. Exception is made for pre-Romantic works when wholly reinstrumented. It holds to its Romantics with determination, will no more allow them to be restyled than it would consent to having its grandmother's face lifted. Grandma is not kept dressed in the style of her 1880 coming out, however; a seemly adaptation to the mode is encouraged. She is constantly told how young she looks. She is given the place of honor at every ceremony and treated generally with the consideration that we observe toward those whom we know will not be with us forever. Her frequentation is considered to be a privilege for all and of inestimable value to the young.

Whether all this is as it should be I do not know, but certainly that is the way it is. And the concert season just now beginning will, I am sure, hold to its conservative path as relentlessly as all the other seasons have done. These do not vary noticeably from one year to the next or very much from decade to decade. From close up, from a reviewer's seat, their details are clearly always different. But from a little way off, from a summer vacational vantage point, say, they appear as comfortingly alike as successive Harvard graduating classes, Mei Lan-fang, the Chinese actor, confessed to a friend when visiting New York some years ago that he found it hard to tell one Occidental from another.

October 8, 1944

Program Notes

PROGRAM notes used to be a form of belles-lettres. As composed by Donald Tovey in Edinburgh, Philip Hale in Boston, Lawrence Gilman in New York, and Felix Borowski in Chicago, they were charming to read, informative, and often penetrating. At their least so, they were accurate, and their language was genteel. Their purpose was to supplement the listener's spontaneous musical understanding with detailed analyses of the works played and with such appropriate selection of historical data and classic comment as would tend to clarify the music for him, both its style and its content. Of recent years a tendency has been noticeable in program notes toward hastily gathered and often incorrect information, toward the omission of the analysis of form and the quotation of themes, and toward a substitution for the quoting of diversified critical opinion about works of the past of sales talk about how beautiful they are. Even when notes are couched in good English (which is far from always), they are likely to resemble less a scholarly discourse than a publisher's blurb.

The sort of introductions that precede radio broadcasts of high-class music is even more offensive, on the whole, than what the symphony orchestras print in their house programs. The salesmanship note is nearly always dominant. The selection about to be played is praised as something especially picked out for the listener's private delight and brought to him through the benevolence of a loving radio company or some other equally affectionate lessee of that company's time. Since the purpose of all broadcasts is to create good will toward somebody's business, it is almost impossible for the executives of that business to think up a disinterested presentation. Radio disseminates huge quantities of cultural music of the highest quality, but it also disseminates simple entertainment. And, so far, the kind of honorific introduction it has been putting out with its cultural offerings is uncomfortably close to ballyhoo, or the advertising style of the entertainment industries.

It is quite probable that the decline of the concert program note in both scholarship and charm is due to the increased influence of radio's financial prestige on our symphonic organizations. It has not been my observation, however, that this influence is a direct one. Radio companies and the sponsors of cultural broadcasts are likely to show more respect for the radio public's intelligence than managers and conductors do. The conservatism of the Philharmonic's Sunday-afternoon programs is due to no pressure from either the Columbia Broadcasting System or the United States Rubber Company, so far as I can find out. There is every reason to believe, on the other hand, that the Philharmonic management is the timid one. Convinced by long experience in concert organization that the larger any audience is the safer the program must be, that management (and practically every conductor) is equally convinced that a nationwide broadcast is no place to do experimental or unfamiliar music.

The error in this calculation is to suppose that private listeners respond to music in the same way they would if they were gathered together in a hall. Group responses to anything tend to approximate those of the least intelligent persons present. The bed or fireside listener, like the reader of books, responds to art with his full intellectual equipment, no matter how elaborate this may be. He may get bored and turn the music off, or he may wander into another room. But if he listens at all he is not influenced by crowd psychology. The music itself must interest him. The radio people know that a considerable variety in programs is necessary in order to keep up this interest. Their advertisers know, too, that cultural broadcasts and mass entertainment are not the same. When they buy culture for prestige purposes they want the real thing.

It is my suspicion that the writers of concert program notes are reacting, as intellectuals so often do, to the presence of radio in everybody's musical life in an excessive and contradictory fashion. They imagine that because the radio announcing of high-class music is mostly a pretty low-class literary performance the radio public for that music must be ignorant and indiscriminating. This reasoning, which is, no doubt, largely unconscious, carries them to conclude further that the whole music public, since it certainly takes that sort of presentation, probably likes it. In any case, their notes tend to imitate the worst features of radio introductions — inaccuracy, inelegance, and blurb. They are not only debasing in this way a once respectable species of belles-lettres, they are removing from the symphony concert itself that aspect of serious instruction that is no less responsible than their fine musical executions are for the esteem in which our orchestras are held.

To print no program notes at all would be better, if that were practical. Such is the Continental habit. But it is not ours. We have always had them; we like them; we are entitled to proper ones. (We are also entitled to enough light in concert halls to read them by.) Proper ones consist of:

a. Historical information about composers and their intentions that is up to date and verifiable.

b. Analysis, with musical quotations, of the works to be played.

c. Fair statement, with quotations from other commentators and critics, of controversies previously raised by these works.

d. If a work is being performed for the first time, whatever preface the composer wishes to add.

There still are program annotators in the United States who attempt to furnish this information and who do so in graceful language. They are rare, though. What we mostly get is both incorrect and unreadable. This protest is not made out of any wish to delay the ultimate commercialization of our major orchestras. I am inclined, rather, to hasten that consummation if I can, because I believe that radio executives will take care eventually of our conductors' present conservatism about programs. They may even come to the rescue, too, of the program note, though that will be more difficult. I think it would be a good idea for the orchestras to improve their program notes right now, if only for business reasons. Because those notes are a cardinal element in the creation and the maintenance of any American orchestra's intellectual prestige. And its whole intellectual prestige (of which the orchestra's playing ability is only a part) is exactly what any orchestra has to sell to the broadcasters. The chief budget buckler, moreover, of our orchestras in the next ten years is going to be the money that is paid in by broadcasting companies, by lessees of broadcasting time, and by the corporations, mostly subsidiaries of broadcasting, that manufacture gramophone records. This support will be forthcoming exactly as long as the orchestras maintain their nationwide intellectual prestige. And they will maintain that only so long as they are clearly instruments of public instruction.

October 3, 1944

The Piano

THE MODERN pianoforte, though the sound it makes is quite different from anything Mozart or Beethoven knew, is an invention of the late eighteenth century. Its characteristic quality, that which distinguishes it from all the preceding keyboard instruments of domestic usage, is expressed in its name; it can play both loud and soft. Like the modern orchestra, moreover, it can produce the effect that is the specific, the differential characteristic of musical Romanticism; namely, the quick, or expressive, crescendo. Mozart discovered both on his way to Paris in 1777, the modern orchestra at Mannheim and the piano (or fortepiano, as it was then called) at Augsburg.

The first of Mozart's real piano sonatas — the No. 7, in A minor — which was written the following year in Paris, not only makes use (in the slow movement) of expressive crescendo and diminuendo, but (at the end of the first) of an architectural crescendo that is the keyboard transcription of an orchestral effect. The three dynamic levels — soft, medium, and loud — that were never blended in Baroque and Rococo music but merely contrasted are here still used (and Beethoven also so used them throughout his life) for their effects of contrast. But these contrasts are no longer a merely architectural or rhetorical device; they are exploited freely (as in the development section of the first movement) for their value as expression. This is the first of all those romantic and modern piano sonatas, at once intimate and grandiose, that imitate at the keyboard the symphonic style. The scored crescendos of the Mannheim orchestra and the possibility that the fortepiano offered of imitating these on a solo instrument determined in Mozart's lifetime the characteristics of a cycle in musical history that has not yet come to an end.

The evolution of the pianoforte from Mozart's time to ours has been continuous. The instrument Beethoven and Weber knew was already a more powerful one. That of Chopin marked a return to the clear articulation of the earliest ones without any loss of power. Liszt knew at the end of his life something that we should recognize by its loudness as a modern instrument, though he still played it with high fingers and very little arm weight, the keyboard action being lighter than that in use now. Even Debussy knew a lighter piano than we have here, the French Pleyel being a more flexible and less emphatic instrument than our American Steinways, Knabes, and Baldwins.

The twentieth-century piano, nevertheless, as manufactured anywhere, is darker in tone than its eighteenth- and nineteenth-century ancestors. Also, it can play a great deal louder, especially in the bass. The chief motive of its designers has been to provide soloists with an instrument capable of holding its own in concertos against an orchestra of a hundred musicians. Modern piano technique is also designed to make possible, at all degrees of speed, a high degree of loudness. A wide dynamic range is now available to all properly trained pianists. Whether they wish to use it or not, it has been drilled into their hands, as it has been built into the pianos under them. It is less trouble to use it constantly than to refrain from doing so.

As a result, they blow up the piano music of the past to dynamic proportions that are not always an advantage to it. The works of Beethoven, Brahms, Liszt, and, curiously enough, Chopin are not as gravely obscured by the procedure as those of Mozart, Weber, Schubert, and Schumann are. If the solo piano music of the latter composers tends downward nowadays in popularity, that is due, I think, to the fact that overemphasis in the rendering of it has destroyed that mood of ease and of spontaneity through which alone it can be understood.

Wanda Landowska has restored the Mozart piano sonatas to life by removing from their execution all undue exercise of force. And she has not, as is the habit of lesser musicians, allowed them to fall thereupon into dimness and low relief. Her Mozart is as large in thought as it is reasonable in volume. Listening last Sunday night at Town Hall to her vivid evocation on the modern instrument of what these sonatas must have sounded something like (if our knowledge of the past means anything at all) when played by the composer on his own fortepiano made me wish that some pianist with a real understanding of Romanticism (rather than merely an atavistic feeling for it) would give us Schumann's music again, make it clear to us and friendly and direct. We know it is beautiful, but nobody plays it beautifully any more. It needs, I think, a smaller range of loudness and a more precise rhythm, more song, more syncopation, more breath, and a less agonized cantilena than we are accustomed to associate with it.

If much of the great piano music of the past has lost its savor for us, that is not the fault, I think, of pianists, who, as a class, are enlightened musicians, so much as of the modern piano itself. The instrument has evolved so gradually toward its present dynamic range that we are likely to forget we are not dealing with the favorite instrument of the Romantics in the form in which the Romantics knew it. The best pianistic result obtains when a different dynamic gamut and a different kind of touch is employed for each composer. The pianists are certainly at fault who consider loudness a proof of sincerity or a substitute for sound rhythm. But there are many intelligent and consecrated musicians among them who need only to be shown the way of discrimination. Landowska's Mozart is a signpost pointing already to happy hunting grounds. It shows us what delights can be derived from using the piano as a means toward the interpretation of music. That way lies infinite variety. Using all music as a vehicle to demonstrate modern power pianism is not even good showmanship. That way lies monotony and the limitation of repertory.

The violinists have brought their art to something of an impasse by doing a similar thing. With the best intentions in the world, they are mostly unable any longer to conceive music as anything but a vehicle for personal display. If the pianists are to avoid this dead end they must start by limiting their dynamic palette. They must limit it in each piece to what is appropriate to that piece, reserving the full range of it for modern works written with an awareness of their instrument's power gamut. Organists do not turn on the full organ every time they see the sign $f\!f$. Gradations of loudness are the piano's chief source of variety. Using them all up in one piece is both stylistically and psychologically indiscreet. The painter Inna Garsoian recently remarked that a pianist at a grand piano always made her think of Jonah and the whale. Certainly, courage in the face of imminent disaster marks the approach to his instrument of many a pianistic virtuoso. I like, however, to think of that powerful and sensitive mechanism rather as a serpent, deadly if approached with rough gestures, but capable of being charmed by music.

November 26, 1944

The Violin

THE FOLLOWING letter from a pedagogue of the violin expresses the despair that many music lovers have felt about the state to which that noble instrument has come down.

Nov. 1, 1944.

My Dear Mr. Thomson:

I am increasingly concerned with a problem confronting my own profession and have decided to ask you, as a critic of long standing and one who is undoubtedly aware of the situation, what you think of it. I have been playing and teaching the violin for more than thirty years; and I am convinced that the days of great violin playing are numbered, that the time is coming when we shall have to be satisfied with inferior artistry unless something is done about it.

Each season high-lights the situation more, as brilliant new talent and new blood is introduced in all the arts. But for many years we haven't had one outstanding new violinist, and there are no sure indications of any on the way. We have only to count our few remaining artists, who must serve the entire world, to see how very serious it is. Why should this static and lifeless condition exist regarding one of our most important and beloved solo instruments?

If we had no talent there would be an excuse for it. But that is not so. Take, for example, the army of brilliant violin prodigies of ten or twelve years ago. They thrilled audiences throughout the country, amazed artists and critics alike. Whether or not we approve of prodigies, they were at least a substantial indication of talent. We were all sure, and justifiably so, that some of them, at least, would mature into fine artists. Unfortunately, however, they disappointed us. I think, Mr. Thomson, that if we could discover our mistakes with them we might find the key to the whole situation.

That brings us to the point of teachers. In piano we still have great pianists teaching. And we have always a new crop of finished pianists. In dancing, all of the great dancers teach. In violin, then, we need the same thing. More so, perhaps, for the violin is not an easy instrument, and not a profession for self-development at all. Since the birth of the violin all the magic performers have combined their performing gifts with the equally great and necessary profession of teaching; but now not one assumes the responsibility of making artists. It is indeed unfortunate. If we could have more performing artists teaching again, so that there would be a secure means of reaching the top, and if the need for this could be explained, I am sure violin playing would be healthy again.

If you feel for this as I do, your voice, through the press, could help to bring some light and hope to the situation. I am sure it would be very much appreciated. Thank you very much. Sincerely,

Joseph Osborne.

It is not only the wonder children of ten years back that are a disappointment to us. I am afraid the ones of thirty years ago are just as unsatisfactory. They play the violin with high skill, and they have made money. But they have remained wonder children, even into middle age. They still go by their baby names, in fact, of Toscha and Jascha and Mischa and Sacha and the like. Can you imagine what would happen to piano playing if a whole generation of the best started calling itself "Artie" Rubinstein, "Bobbie" Casadesus, "Rudy" Serkin and "Laddie" Horowitz? It is all right to be a wonder child; many of the great have been such. But the status should be scrapped at eighteen if one wishes to take part as an adult in the adult life of one's time.

Technically, the violin is well taught and well played today all over the world. Esthetically, our century has not come to terms with the instrument. The last to be invented among our common types of instruments, it is, nevertheless, the oldest of them, because it has not been altered, to speak of, since the seventeenth century. Scarcely a measurement or a procedure of construction has changed. It is a survival intact of the Baroque age. Only the bow with which it is played has evolved since the days of the Cremona designers, and that attained its present form more than 150 years ago.

The violin has the largest expressive gamut of any instrument in the world. Sweetness, passion, terror, mystery, and grandeur are equally its province. And no other agency of music, even the pipe organ or the lordly harpsichord, can approach its unique fusion of nobility with grace, that particular intensity among opposites that expressed to the century of Louis XIV majesty. Well, our century is not much interested in majesty. Grace in firmness and nuances of nobility are not our preoccupation. We like better displays of power and exhibits of intricate mechanism. The pianoforte is our favorite solo instrument, as it was of the nineteenth century. From there we move to the complex assembly line that is the modern orchestra.

Against these superior efficiencies the solo violinists have taken refuge in sentiment; they have become purveyors of tenderness, of heart throbs, of musical small change. They have presented these minor comforts to us in a packaging of pseudomodernity, silken-surfaced and utterly inconsequential. Their work has been neat in detail but lacking in simplicity, in grandeur of line. They have sacrificed, to be technical about it, steadiness of the bow arm to finicky fingering. Their right arm is so far inferior to the other that many of us have sympathized with the late Leonard Liebling's crack that what the modern world needs is a good violin concerto for the left hand alone.

All this is changing. Mr. Osborne is wrong, I think, in finding the violinists of today lacking in mature musical artistry. The wonder children of ten, twenty, and thirty years ago were. Today violinists like Isaac Stern, Joseph Fuchs, Roman Totenberg (and there are more) can interpret both old music and new with the full breadth of adult thought — straightforwardly, clean, steadily — without shocking their public. Violinists of this water have heretofore been confined to chamber music and to playing in the symphony orchestras as outlet for their musicianship. Technically they are as competent as the preceding generation of virtuosos. Musically they are superior. If their handling of audience psychology is less suave than the streamlined approach of the wonder boys, it is, nevertheless, more attractive to the musically literate. It may be that the solo violin is about to return to its rightful place as an instrument of major music making. I hope so.

November 19, 1944

The Organ

THE MODERN pipe organ and its repertory make a strange dichotomy. The instrument itself is the most elaborate, the most ingenious, the most complex, and the most expensive of all instruments. Also one of the most common. Hamlets that never saw a bassoon or a French horn or an Australian marimba or even a concert grand pianoforte will occasionally house a quite decent one. City people give them away like drinking fountains and stained-glass windows. And yet, in two centuries scarcely twenty pieces have been been written for the organ that could be called first-class music. The learning, the taste, the engineering knowledge, and the skilled handicraft that go into the manufacture of even a reasonably satisfactory instrument are enormous. Nevertheless, not one major composer, since Sebastian Bach died in 1750, has written for the organ with any notable freedom or authority. Very few have written for it at all.

César Franck, perhaps, did the best, though none of his half-dozen best organ pieces is as commanding a work as any of his half-dozen best chamber and orchestral works. Also, Franck's position as a major composer in any medium is doubtful. The organ got much of their best work out of Frescobaldi and Couperin and Handel and Bach, not to mention a hundred other composers of the Baroque age. Since that time it is chiefly the second-rate that have written for it. Mozart, though a skillful organist himself, never wrote a solo piece for the instrument (though Grove's *Dictionary of Music and Musicians* lists seventeen sonatas for organ, "usually with violin and bass, intended to be used as graduales" in the Church service). Mendelssohn wrote six solo sonatas for it that are sound music, if a little stuffy. Brahms wrote eleven chorale-preludes, his last opus number, of which two are genuinely inspired, though neither of these is particularly well conceived for the instrument. And there are twelve organ pieces by Franck that are respectable as music. The rest of the post-Baroque repertory has been written by the Gounods, the Saint-Saënses, the Regers, the Viernes, the Widors, and their like — at its best, second-rate stuff by second-rate composers. Among the modern masters, only Schönberg, and that just once, has produced a work of any grandeur for the organ.

The cause of this neglect lies, I think, in the nature of the instrument itself, which has nowadays little but a glorious moment of history to offer. For the organ, like many another instrument of ancient lineage, did have its hour of glory. This hour, which lasted a good century and a half, say from roughly the year 1600 to quite precisely 1750, covers the whole of that period commonly known to the fine arts as the Baroque. And though in the visual techniques the high Baroque style is associated chiefly with the Counter Reformation of the Catholic Church, the musical Baroque penetrated, both in Germany and in England, to the heart of Protestantism itself.

That was the age that created the fugue, the aria, the free fantasia, the opera, the oratorio. It invented the violin, too, and carried to an apogee of musical refinement the keyed instruments, notably the organ and the harpsichord. It was the age of oratory in music, of the grandiose, the impersonal, the abstract. When it gave way in the middle of the eighteenth century to the beginnings of a more personalized romanticism, certain of its favorite media ceased to have effective power. The oratorio, for instance, has never recovered from that change in taste; nor have the fugue and its running mate, the free fantasia, ever since had quite the authority they enjoyed before. The opera survived by going in for personal sentiment in the arias and by giving up all that was merely grandiose in the set pieces. The violin also, played with the new Tourte bow (an invention of the 1770's), took on an appropriate sensitivity of expression. But the harpsichord fell wholly out of use, a new keyed instrument, the fortepiano, offering possibilities of voluntary accent and of crescendo that were far more attractive to the Romantic mind than the equalized articulation and terraced dynamics of its predecessor.

The organ survived the Romantic revolution, but it lost its primacy among musical instruments. It remained (and remains still) firmly intrenched in its privileges as a handmaiden of religion; but it has never since dared venture far, as the rest of music has done, from the protecting walls of the Church. It plays today the tiniest of roles in the concert hall and in the theater, while attempts to give it a new (and secular) prestige through its exploitation in department stores and cinemas have merely ended by robbing it of what little secular dignity was left to it after a century and a half of cloistered servitude.

Nevertheless, the instrument went on growing. It hypertrophied, to be exact. All through the nineteenth and early twentieth centuries it got bigger and bigger. It grew row after row of additional pipes, which included every possible reminder of other instruments, including the human voice; and the manufacturers imperiled its very existence by weighing it down with every imaginable useless labor-saving device. It went to leaf and flower, grew very little musical fresh fruit. In our time a movement to restore to use the surviving organs of the Baroque age, which are fairly numerous in Europe, and the construction of new instruments modeled after these, have given us a new enlightenment, just as a similar revival in harpsichord-building has, about Baroque keyboard music. This revival, for all its antiquarian nature, has played a role in the drama of modernism. Whether it is capable of reinvigorating the organ as an instrument of contemporary expression I do not know. But certainly the communion it has provided with the Baroque keyboard repertory, which is one of the world's very greatest musical literatures, is a closer one than was previously available. And that has brought fresh ideas into modern writing, just as the studies of medieval chant which the Benedictines of Solesmes carried out in the late nineteenth century had given a new life both to harmony and to the French vocal line, and just as the Greek studies of the late Renaissance in Italy had rendered possible in the year 1600 the invention of the opera.

And so the organ, in terms of its once central position in musical advance, is today, as it has been for nearly two centuries (and in spite of its continuing to be manufactured in ever more and more pretentious format), as dead as the harpsichord. But, as in the case of the harpsichord, an inspired resuscitation has given today's world of music a source of knowledge, of real acquaintance with the auditory past, that has brought the instrument back to a worthy and possibly to a proud position in our creative life. Not that there is anything intrinsically unfortunate about having worked so long for religious establishments. But religious establishments have for so long dallied on the sidelines of musical advance that sacred organ composition, like any other musical enterprise limited to Church patronage, has usually found itself outclassed intellectually in the world of free artistic enterprise. And thus it is that antiquarianism and scholarship, for all their supposed sterility, have, by enabling us to hear Bach fugues as Bach himself heard them, made to music a gift that no other agency could have done, would have done, or, to stick to the simple fact, did do.

August 5, 1945

The Great Tradition

FINDING himself, the other evening, alone and with an open mind, in, of all places, a night club, your reviewer took occasion to reflect upon, of all subjects, the problem of sincerity in musical interpretation. The artists who stimulated these reflections were, in the order of their appearance, Pearl Bailey, Claude Alphand, and Maxine Sullivan, the latter two of whom he has long admired. The other, Miss Bailey, turned out to be no end potent as a personality. But for all the personality, plus high skill in its projection (and, indeed, because of both), her work seemed to lie somewhere without the special interest of his department, in the domain, shall we say, of entertainment rather than of straight musical art.

There are few vocal artists now appearing in either opera or concert whose musical style is so straightforward as that of Miss Sullivan and Mrs. Alphand. Straightforwardness in musical interpretation has become, in fact, so rare a quality that the public does not always quite know what to make of it; and managements tend, in consequence, to discourage it. It is, nevertheless, the gauge of any artist's responsibility toward his art and the hallmark of the Great Tradition.

The Great Tradition in music, either of composition or of rendering, is not the history of techniques, their perfection and transmission. Still less is it the history of styles, of manners, of conventions. It is not the history of anything, in fact. It is a continuity, a thread that runs through all the histories, an attitude of certain artists toward their work that is in concord with a similar tradition in painting, in humane letters, and in scholarship. Its basic concept is that art is an image of reality, a telling of the truth about something. There is no class difference between high-brow and low-brow music, between the "classical" and "popular" styles. Both are exploitable as entertainment, and both are appropriate media for expression. Expression, however, which involves objectivity and hence sincerity, is the grander usage, as we all know.

Straightforwardness in the rendering of music presupposes a respect on the interpreter's part for the authenticity, or truth, of the composition to be rendered. It admits the piece to be intrinsically worth doing. And since the doing well of anything that is in itself interesting gives the nature of that thing precedence over the manner of doing it (that nature being the determinant, after all, of the manner), a straightforward rendition, therefore, is one in which fifty-one per cent, at least, of the emphasis is not centered on either the interpreter's person or his means of operation. It shows us a piece of music that, in turn, shows us a piece of life. It does not offer us anybody on a platter; it merely transports us mentally to a place different from the one we are in.

All musical performance is a kind of acting. And the more completely the performer gets inside the role of each piece he plays or sings the more vividly does each piece impress us with its content. The more completely does he convince us, too, of his artistry. The use of music, or of any other technique, for the enhancement of the personality is an ancient practice and perfectly legitimate. The displaying for their own sakes of personality and of skill is ancient and legitimate, too; and musical performers, even composers, have often enough indulged in it. But it is not the Great Tradition either of music or of acting, which has always been one of keeping the script the center of interest.

In an objective operation like this, skill and charm get used to the full. No one wishes any artist to sacrifice his personal advantages. All we ask is that these chiefly serve the representation of something else. When women as beautiful as Claude Alphand and Maxine Sullivan (and musical executants of high finish they are, too) wear their charms and their accomplishments with so little of ostentation, they operate artistically with an effectiveness that is all the greater for their performance's being about something beyond the mere exhibition of those advantages. I only wish that more musicians worked in that loyal manner.

December 31, 1944

Radio Is Chamber Music

CHAMBER music is a natural for radio, and radio is exactly what chamber music has long needed. Bringing the symphony orchestra or the opera into the home is an adventurous operation involving, at best, so many distortions of both sound and sense that constant advertisements of the wonder of it all have to be added in order to make everybody feel right about it. But chamber music gets broadcast all the time and listened to without any alibis having to be furnished by the Appreciation slaves. Chamber music, in other words, is completely at home in anybody's home. And the radio, which exists in nearly every home, is, along with its elder sister, the gramophone, the universal chamber instrument of our time.

By chamber music let us not mean merely string quartets and the like. Chamber music is any music designed to be executed by a small number of musicians and to be listened to informally. Any instrument or any voice is appropriate to it; and any listener can enjoy it in his own way, so long as he listens in his own person and not as a member of an audience. It includes all the music in the world except that which deals in masses — masses of instruments or of voices in the execution and masses of listeners in the audience, which it is aimed to move as a unit, usually in the direction of applause. It is, in fact, the absence of applause as a mass reaction that distinguishes the opera and the concert from private music, from the music of the home.

Chamber music in public halls, though common enough, is really a recondite exercise. So are symphony concerts in the home. Both require, for full comprehension, a previous acquaintance with the works executed and a large effort of the imagination, to compensate for the acoustic and psychological distortions involved. People do not have to study in advance an opera they are about to hear, unless this is to be given in a foreign language (as is unfortunately the custom here). Neither is it of much value to prepare oneself for direct symphonic listening. Studying concert works *after* the performance, when the sound of them is already familiar, is by far the more rapid method of absorption.

The same is true of chamber music, whether this is string quartets or madrigals or jazz. As long as the circumstances of listening are not too public, anybody who likes music at all can understand without ex-cathedra assistance any piece of any of the kinds of chamber music that he happens to like. At least he can begin to understand it; he can make its acquaintance, which is all that even the most musically expert ever does anyway at a first hearing.

And so, for all the charm of translations and of popular simplifications, it is just as well to remind oneself from time to time that opera is heard at its best in the opera house, symphonic music in the concert hall, and chamber music in some kind of semiprivacy. Now it just so happens that the radio and the gramophone — all the instruments, in fact, of processed music — operate most effectively in the very limitations that are chamber music's characteristic advantages. Individualized instrumentation, complexity of linear design and of rhythm they transmit beautifully. The things they do not transmit well — mass instrumentation, harmonic complexity, and variations of dynamic impact — are exactly the things that, though specific to the large orchestra, are unbecoming, if not downright impossible, to small groups. Not only, therefore, has the radio, by the convenience of its use in the home, become our principal chamber instrument. By the very virtues and limitations themselves of electrical transmission it has enlarged the usage of chamber music as chamber music many thousand times, and with a minimum of falsification.

As a disseminator of chamber music of all kinds, the radio is an organ of unquestionable value to culture. Its services to culture as a disseminator of operatic and symphonic music, though undeniable, are less clear, from the fact that it does not distribute these in anything like so true a reproduction. Listening by radio to music of mass execution is a convenient way of supplementing visits to its public manifestations. But as a substitute for these, though it enriches the lives of many a country dweller and shut-in, it is definitely unsatisfactory, just as reading plays is not a satisfactory substitute for going to the theater. I must say that the music of individualized instrumentation — chamber music — sounds, on the whole, better to me in the chamber, even though electrically transmitted, than it does in a public hall. There is no major change of proportion; and the loss of the living tone is slight compared with the advantages of privacy and of proximity which are gained.

Chamber music needs to be heard close by. Distance lends it no enchantment. The radio gives it to us in close-up. One can hear what goes on. Playing music with friends is a pleasure reserved for few and one that is even less generally available than formerly, since the professional standards of gramophone and radio execution have made everybody a little intolerant of amateur effort. The regular engagement of musicians for making music in the home is a still rarer indulgence nowadays; even the rich don't do it any more. But everybody has a radio and that means that everybody now has chamber music. Some of what the radio emits is massive music reduced to the possibilities of a chamber instrument; and a good deal of what it puts out is, of course, not music at all. There are speeches and soap operas and news. But a quite large part of the music broadcast is chamber music of all categories. It is right that this should be so and highly satisfactory. None of the legitimate reserves, indeed, that everybody has about radio in general applies at all to the broadcasting for private and semiprivate consumption of the music of individualized instrumentation.

January 7, 1945

Symphonic Broadcasts

LAST Sunday this column considered the radio as a chamber instrument, the universal chamber instrument of our time, and commented on the satisfactoriness in general of chamber music heard by that means. Chamber music, we repeat, does not mean merely European music in sonata form; it includes, of course, all the music of individualized instrumentation; and that means madrigals, string quartets, female trios, hillbilly songs, and most of our jazz — all of it, in fact, that is describable as hot. But let us consider today the radio as a purveyor of more massive music, of orchestral and operatic literature. There is no generic term for this, for the music that uses instruments or voices in phalanx. If we contrast its texture with that of individualized instrumentation, it is clearly the music of massive, or massed, instrumentation. If we contrast its acoustical layout and social function with those of chamber music, it becomes simply theater or hall music; and perhaps that is as descriptive a name for it as any.

The transmitting of chamber music from studio to home is a simple matter, a matter of sending it from one room to another. No distortions are involved save those inherent to any transmission; and nowadays these are almost imperceptible, especially if frequency modulation is employed. That is why radio music is naturally and normally chamber music. The transmitting of theater or hall music, however, necessitates two major alterations, an acoustic one and a social or psychological one.

The acoustic distortion involved is the minimization of the specific virtue of massed instruments or voices, namely, the power range. There is very little advantage, excepting that of added volume, in the employment of any body of string players, for instance, or of singers more numerous than the independent lines of the music. I do not mean that sixteen first violins sound like one violin, only louder; I merely mean that sixteen violins have very little expressive advantage over one violin, save that they can play louder. A wide dynamic range is an advantage to expression, however; and the whole flowering of orchestral composition that has made music so glorious in the last 150 years has come about through the invention of the scored crescendo, which makes of this whole range a unified and enormous dynamic palette. The color palette has been enlarged, too; but a large color palette is not basic to orchestral composition. Brahms, for instance, holds one's interest with very little exploiting of it. But nobody ever writes an orchestral work of any length that does not exploit as a major means of expression the full range of orchestral loudnesses.

Orchestral literature is all built to sound clearly both soft and loud, and the maximum spread of clear sonority between these two extremes is attained in halls. In the open air it does not balance properly or carry far, and in small rooms it creates a confused reverberation. Importing this literature into the home, whether by pianoforte transcription, music box, gramophone, or radio, is a matter of reducing it to room size. Neither the instrument nor the room can take it in its original intensity, in its original range of intensities, to be exact. And since this range is almost its whole reason for existence — its specific difference from chamber music, in any case — hearing it in the home, though a pleasure and a privilege, is not at all the same thing as hearing it in a hall. Chamber music is like easel painting. It can be brought into the home intact or in the form of amazingly faithful original-sized reproductions. Orchestral and operatic music is like architecture. It can be studied in the home but not fully experienced there. Its broadcasts and its gramophone records bear about the same relation to their originals that photographs of a cathedral do.

The psychological distortion is somewhat the same, too, because neither cathedrals nor symphonies were ever built for private use. Chamber music and easel painting, yes. But hall music and public edifices are intended for ceremonial usage — mass usage, emotional or intellectual unity, observances in common. Without the presence of a participant public (though the gesture of participation may be limited to applause only) these structures do not have the same quality, the same meaning to offer us. We can study them better in privacy, but we can really know them only in the exercise of their intended functions. Opera music and symphonic music are not different from each other save in the clarity of their literary programs. Both are public statements made to public gatherings. In both cases there is a good deal of musical execution in unison, and the whole thing is heard by rows and rows of citizens sitting elbow to elbow, observing toward one another and toward the performing artists the courtesy of silence, voting their degree of gratitude or approval at the end by the agreed-upon gesture of applause.

Do not think that Beethoven's, or anybody else's, symphonies are not meant to be applauded. They are mass music aimed at mass effect, and this is in no way to their discredit. Applause is not an aim, on the other hand, in string quartets; and this is not to their discredit. It is not an aim in jam sessions, either, or in any of the hotter forms of jazz. It is an aim in musical comedies. It is an aim in all the kinds of music that use massed musicians, excepting only the music of church services, where applause is replaced by the equally communal manifestation of common prayer. Make no mistake about it. Symphonies and operas are formal harangues, not fireside chats.

Chamber music on the radio needs no blurb. But broadcasts

of orchestral music and opera have to be sold to the consumer. Every device of cajolery and of impressiveness is employed in the introductory publicity to make him feel he is part of an audience, to create the illusion of participation in a ceremony. This is a legitimate procedure on the part of the broadcasters and a necessary one. Indeed, what we need is more explanation rather than less. That is why it has occurred to me as possibly of interest to point out to radio music consumers what I think is the true nature of the material they are dealing with.

Radio can amplify the usage of chamber music, has already done so. It can broaden our acquaintance with symphonic music and opera, too. But in the one case the image of reality is resembling. In the other it is distorted. There is misunderstanding of a whole literature if the transmission of an orchestral concert or an opera to a private room is taken to be anything but a rudimentary representation of the real thing. Broadcast chamber music comes very close to the real thing, and sometimes it is an improvement over it. Broadcast mass music gives only a part of the real thing and not its most characteristic enjoyments, which are the expressivity of volume variation and participation in a public event. That is why so much explaining on the part of the broadcasters and so much sales-resistant discrimination on the part of the consumers are necessary for obtaining a cultural result.

January 14, 1945

Surrealism and Music

THE SPRING number of *Modern Music* opens with four articles of homage to Arnold Schönberg on the occasion of his seventieth birthday, of which those by Ernst Křenek and by Lou Harrison are both penetrating and informative. It closes, as usual, with a fireworks display of critical articles that illumines the contemporary music front all across the United States. But the real novelty of the issue is a reflective article on the place of music in modernist esthetics by a man who has admittedly little taste for the art and no precise knowledge about it. The author of this far from undiscerning essay is no less a writer than André Breton, founder, defender of the faith, and for twenty years pope of the surrealist movement in French poetry, at present head of the surrealist government-in-exile in New York City.

Mr. Breton defends his own antagonistic attitude toward music on the grounds that it is identical with that of most of the nineteenth- and twentieth-century French poets. He admits, however, the desirability of some fusion between it and his own art. And he recommends to musicians a "return to principles" comparable to that which has made surrealism for two decades now the chief movement of renovation in European poetry.

The first observation needs no rebuttal. It is, alas, only too true that since the divorce of poetry from music (Thomas Campion was the last in England to practice both with distinction) the poets have manifested consistently a certain bitterness toward the rival auditory art. They have indited odes to it aplenty, I know, and spoken of it on many occasions most feelingly; but their homage has rarely been without guile. Shakespeare very nearly gave the plot away when he referred to music as a "concourse of sweet sounds." (Imagine the explosion that would have occurred had any one dared in Shakespeare's London to call poetry a "running together of pretty words.") The great one eventually carried his campaign for the discrediting of music as a major art to the point of proclaiming it frankly "the food of love." His disinterestedness in this matter has not hitherto been questioned. But music died in England shortly after him.

What Mr. Breton, a poet, fails to consider here is the propaganda for the dignity and the grandeur and, most important of all, the meaning of music that was operated so successfully by the nineteenth-century philosophers. It is not the exceptional suffrages of Baudelaire and Mallarmé that have given to music its prestige in contemporary society but the systematic and relentless praise of its expressive powers by Hegel, by Schopenhauer, and by Nietzsche.

On the fusion, or re-fusion, of the two great auditory arts Mr. Breton adopts without argument the Wagnerian thesis that this is desirable. As a good Marxian he refuses the "reformist" program of closer collaboration between poets and composers, maintaining with some justice that poems "set to music" serve no valid artistic purpose and that opera librettos are and always have been a pretty silly form of literature. He seems to think that the fusion might be operated by some one man working at a high emotional temperature, and he suggests the passion of love as possibly useful to this end. What such a fusion would accomplish beyond a regression to primitive esthetics is not proposed to us. One wonders if Mr. Breton envisages as desirable a similar fusion of the visual arts, the reunion of painting and sculpture, for instance, with or without a framework of architecture, the event to take place by no collaborative procedure. One wouldn't wish that dish on his dearest enemy. The musical theater is only now recovering from Wagner's megalomaniac seizure of all its creative privileges, and convalescence is still far from complete.

That music should take a lesson from contemporary French poetry and go back to principled operations is not a bad idea. That the functioning of the auditory invention be studied in its divergent manifestations of poetry and of music is an even better one. It is probable that persons of strong auditory memory vary in the relation that their auditory function bears to specific bodily regions. Audito-cerebral types are likely to make poets, orators, preachers, and even statesmen. Audito-visceral types, persons whose reactions to sound and to the memory of it are organic (which means emotional) rather than visual or muscular, make musicians. The audito-kinetic make dancers, acrobats, and the like. Persons for whom noise is merely a sexual stimulant, as it is for rats, may reasonably call music "the food of love"; and their type, though common, is a low one in the biological scale.

The fusion of divers artistic techniques through personal collaboration is an ancient procedure. Their simultaneous exercise by one person is an even more ancient procedure, a primitive one, to be exact. The desirability of reestablishing this in custom depends on the feasibility of trying to develop in human beings a generalized bodily reaction to sound in place of the specifically varied ones that seem to be at present a mark of the higher human types. The matter is worth investigating; but so far as anybody knows now, music is better off without its former legal and virtually indissoluble union to the word.

What Mr. Breton does not seem to have grasped about music is that, instead of being behind poetry in its evolution, it is in many ways more advanced. The dissociative process, which has made possible Mr. Breton's whole career and that of the poetic movement he presides over, has long since lost its novelty for composers. The composer who doesn't use it freely is simply not a very interesting composer; his work lacks fancy, surprise, richness, originality, depth. The right of poets to express themselves by means of spontaneous, subconsciously ordered sequences of material has seemed to many in our century a revolutionary proposition. It is, however, the normal and accepted way of writing music. Any imposition of logic upon this, whether in the form of allusions to classical rhetoric or in the observance of the only rigorous syntax known to our time, the twelve-tone system, is considered in some circles as dangerous radicalism.

The Romantic revolution, in short, was successful in music. It won real freedom for the composer. That it was not successful in literature is proved by the fact that Mr. Breton and his friends are still fighting for it. Haydn, Mozart, and Beethoven, sometimes foolishly spoken of as classicists, were the most radical of libertarians; and sonata form, their favorite continuity convention, was, as is well known, no strict formula at all but the slenderest possible framework for the display of musical fancy and for the expansive expression of spontaneous, nonverbalized feeling.

Music's modern movement is another thing from poetry's. The verbal art is still demanding liberty from arbitrary intellectual restraints. The tonal art, that freedom long since gained and the things it was gained for saying long since said, has fallen, through the progressive lowering of its intellectual standards, into demagogic and commercial hands. Its modern movement is based on the demand that music be allowed to make some kind of plain sense again. We seek no loosening of our intellectual clothes; they are so loose now we can barely walk. What we want is readmission to intellectual society, to the world of free thought and clear expression.

It is more than probable that some of the surrealists' psychological devices for provoking and for sustaining inspiration can be used to advantage by composers, since they are largely of musical origin anyway. They cannot fail, certainly, to encourage spontaneity of auditory invention, because they represent a return to the best Romantic practice in this regard. What they do not represent is any kind of novelty for the musical world. They are, in fact, what the post-Baroque musical world is all about. Musicians are only too delighted, I am sure, to lend them for a while to poetry, with all good wishes for their continued success.

April 2, 1944

French Rhythm

WHAT makes French music so French? Basically, I should say, it is the rhythm. German musicians and Italian musicians tend to consider rhythm as a series of pulsations. French musicians consider pulsations as a special effect appropriate only to dance music, and they train their musical young most carefully to avoid them in other connections. In the Italo-German tradition, as practiced nowadays, the written measure is likely to be considered as a rhythmic unit and the first count of that measure as a dynamic impulse that sets the whole thing in motion. In French musical thought the measure has nothing to do with motion; it is a metrical unit purely. The bar line is a visual device of notation for the convenience of executants, but the French consider that it should never be perceptible to the listener.

The French conceive rhythm as a duality of meter and accent. Meter is a pattern of quanties, of note lengths. Its minimum unit in execution is the phrase. Accent is a stress that may occur either regularly or irregularly; but in any case, it is always written in. It may occur on the first note of a measure; but in well-written music it will usually appear more frequently in other positions, since any regular marking off of metrical units tends to produce a hypnotic effect. French music, unless it is written for the dance or unless it aims to evoke the dance, has no dynamic propulsion at all. It proceeds at an even rate, unrolls itself phrase by phrase rather like Gregorian chant.

It is more than probable that the classical Viennese symphonists were accustomed to this kind of rhythmic articulation and took it for granted. That pulsation came into Viennese symphonic execution somewhere around 1830, after the waltz had come to dominate Vienna's musical thought. At any rate, discerning Germans have frequently pointed out the superiority of French renderings of their own classics. Wagner found the Beethoven symphonies far better played by the Paris Conservatory Orchestra than anywhere in Germany, and he based his own later readings on those of the French conductor Habeneck. Alfred Einstein, German Mozart specialist of our own day, has avowed in his book, *Greatness in Music,* his preference for French renditions of that composer. And certainly German organists have not in our century played Bach with any authority comparable to that of Saint-Saëns, Widor, Vierne, Guilmant, and Schweitzer.

This acknowledged superiority of the French approach to classical German music is due, I believe, to the survival in French musical practice of classical observances about rhythm, elsewhere fallen into disuse. Those same observances are responsible, I believe, for the vigorous flowering of music in France that is the most noteworthy event in the musical history of the last seventy-five years. French harmonic innovations have been striking, but so were those of Richard Strauss and of Arnold Schönberg, of Gustav Mahler, even. Everybody has played around at inventing a new harmony. Scriabin in Russia, Ives in Danbury, Connecticut, were no less original harmonically than Claude Debussy. What their music lacks is true rhythmic life. The only music of our time that can compare in this respect with that of the school of Paris is American hot jazz. And this is based on the same duality of meter versus accent that underlies French music.

The French rhythmic tradition is at once more ancient and more modern than any other. It includes the medieval plain song and the Benedictine restoration of this, in which a wholly quantitative syllabic execution without any regular stresses whatsoever turns out to be expressive and interesting. It includes the French medieval and Renaissance music that grew out of plain song, the schools of Champagne and of Burgundy. It remembers its own Baroque and Rococo styles. It is least aware, perhaps, of the domain that is the very center and pivot of German musical understanding, the world of nineteenth-century Romanticism, though Chopin, Liszt, and, curiously, Schumann it considers as its own. All these it thinks of, along with Mussorgsky and Stravinsky and Spanish dance music and the popular music of Java and Bali and Morocco and the United States, as in no way foreign to itself.

The binding element, the thread that runs through all these different kinds of music is an absence of pulsating rhythm. In Greek theory quantities are one element of rhythm; stress is another; cadence (or phraseology) is the third. Pulsation has no place in this analysis. It is a special effect, derived from round dancing, only to be added to musical execution when round dancing is clearly implied as the subject of a musical passage. Its introduction elsewhere brings in a sing-song element that tends to trivialize musical rhetoric. Bach played by Schweitzer or Landowska, Mozart and Haydn played by Beecham (who is no Frenchman but who remembers the eighteenth century as it was) and modern French music conducted by Monteux or played on the piano by Schmitz are anything but trivial.

Other artists in other repertoires have their charms and their especial powers, like Horowitz's Liszt, Toscanini's Wagner, Walter's Brahms. These always seem to me like cases of pure genius, supported (excepting possibly for Walter) by no major tradition. But the others not only are supported by a major tradition; they support it, too. They are constantly tending it, pruning it, watering it, grafting new shoots on it, gathering from it new fruits. The parent stem of that tradition is, I think, a certain approach to rhythm. That approach is as ancient as Hellas, as far-flung as China, Marrakech, and New Orleans, as up-to-date as boogie-woogie or the percussion music of John Cage. I take this occasion to speak about it because there is better access to it right now in New York City than there has been in some years and because I hope some of our young musicians, both composing and executant, may be induced here and now to profit by the occasion. I believe this view of rhythm to be the open sesame of musical advance today exactly as it has been all through history.

November 14, 1943

Expressive Content

EXPRESSIVITY in music is its power of communication. All the music that is any good says something. A great deal of music says things that are clear to all. This is particularly true of music that has words to it — songs, oratorios, and operas. Also of music that has fanciful titles or footnotes — such as *Lullaby, Rustle of Spring, Turkish March, A Faust Overture, Cowboy Rhapsody, Kitten on the Keys,* or *The Sea.* But even music that bears on its title page no such revelation does have meaning all the same. For the passive listener it may be sufficient that a Beethoven or Tchaikovsky symphony seems pregnant with meaning in general, the imprecision of that meaning being part, indeed, of its power. The interpreter can afford no such vagueness. He must make a guess at the music's specific meaning. Otherwise he has no test for determining tempos, rhythmic inflections, and climactic emphases beyond the notes and markings of the score. And these are never enough, musical notation being as inefficient as it is.

Nor can the composer avoid deciding about the character of his work. He may have created it in a fine fury or in a semi-euphoric state of automatism; but if he wants anybody to use his creation he has to provide some clues to its meaning. He must indicate the speed, the loudness, the kind of lilt he wants. If he wishes orchestral performance he must clothe his creation in unalterable colors and accents. No composer can orchestrate a piece without deciding on the expression that he wishes given to every phrase. A theme conceived for flute has quite another character when played in unison by thirty-two violins. Though both versions may appear in the same composition, only the composer can determine which appears first; and that determination involves a decision about the kind of feeling that he wishes his music to communicate, both as a whole and in detail.

Any performance is correctly called an interpretation. The creator creates and then adds, somewhat later, as many aids as he can think of toward a clear interpretation. The final, or public, interpreter thereupon translates the whole into sound, making his own decisions in every measure about the exact inflection that will best transmit what he esteems to be the composer's meaning. If he thinks the composer's specific indication requires violation in order to attain what he believes to be the work's larger sense, he makes that violation and takes responsibility for it before the musical world. He is right to do so, though he should not do so without reflection. The composer's specific indications are themselves not always a part of his original creation but rather one musician's message to another about it, a hint about how to secure in performance a convincing transmission of the work's feeling content without destroying its emotional and intellectual continuity. The latter continuity, of course, is not an end in itself; it is merely the composer's means of achieving, of not interrupting, emotional continuity.

There is no such thing as an abstract, or meaningless, musical work. There are brief musical phrases and formulas so common that they are in themselves neutral, but these are not neutral when placed in a context. They take on meaning, or they underline by a merely apparent neutrality the meaning of something else. The materials of art are all, taken separately, expressively neutral — colors, words, grammar, sounds, and seams no less than metal and stone. The most valuable are those capable of taking on in a variety of contexts a large number of meanings. That is why the oboe is superior as art material to the saxophone. The latter is powerfully affecting but limited in its gamut of expressivity, notably in the direction of self-effacement.

The creation of meaning by the use of musical lines and formulas, familiar and unfamiliar, is the art of composition. Nothing else is involved. Classical and structural observances have no other value, nor has novelty. In themselves they are without significance, and no employment of them in composition has any value beyond the immediate context. Nor are they capable of acquiring any value in a specific context other than that which the meaning of the whole lends to them for that occasion.

A composer's education involves acquiring a vocabulary of useful turns and formulas. The employment of these and the invention of others in musical works with a unique expressive content is the operation that determines a composer's quality as an artist. The techniques of musical composition are many. The purpose of it is single. That purpose is the creation of art. Art is an infinitive multiplicity of unique objects known as works of art. Their materials are limited; consequently they bear to one another a great material resemblance. Where they differ notably is in meaning, or expressivity; and their survival is determined by that meaning, provided their structure is not just too stupid to bear repetition. If that meaning is unique it can be remembered, and reconsulting it is a pleasure. If not, remembering it is scarcely worth while. The original of which it is an imitation is good enough for us.

And so, to recapitulate my theme, expressivity is what a piece of music says. That communication, as is appropriate to music, is chiefly emotional; and its form in memory is auditory, because sound is its medium. The communication can vary somewhat from interpreter to interpreter, from age to age and even from place to place; but such variation is not large. It cannot be, because any piece of written music, to be performable at all, has to have an implied expressive content and some kind of supplementary indication as to the specific character of that content. Otherwise it is sound without sense, and musicians just won't go on with it. Even paid or commanded they won't.

The determination of music's sense is the privilege, in any group, of the leader, though there is always some communal contribution to this. The definition of this expressivity in words is the hardest thing any critic or historian ever has to undertake, though the recognition of its presence, and even the degree of its presence, in any composer's work is not difficult. Most musicians and most habitual concertgoers are able to recognize strength when they encounter it. Sometimes their recognition takes the form of anger, sometimes not. But it is likely to be fairly dependable. Audiences are easily bored by nonentities but not easily angered by them. Active audience resistance to anything is one of the clinical signs by which we recognize quality. Because it is not the direction of an audience reaction that is critical; what is significant is its strength. And that strength, believe me, is not determined by the mere sounds made. It comes from the character, the individuality of the music's expressive content. Audiences have always complained about what they call dissonance in one piece, while accepting the exact same tonal relations in another. Here is proof aplenty, if more is needed, that what they really mind is something in the expression.

April 13, 1947

Intellectual Content

MUSIC, a creation of the human mind, has its appeal for all the faculties of the mind. Its message, its direct communication, is to the feelings, of course. But the methods by which continuity is sustained and interest held are a result of thought taken. And though it is desirable that this thought be not too evident, that it not interfere with the transmission of feeling that is music's both immediate and final aim, it does have a listener interest over and above its functional efficiency, because any construction of the human mind is fascinating to the human mind. This is the workmanship aspect of music, the quality that adds beauty to expression. And so if the power of provoking specific emotional effects can be referred to as music's expressive content, the power of provoking cerebration, of interesting the mind, may legitimately be called, I think, its intellectual content.

The intellectual content of anything — of music, painting, poetry, oratory, or acting — consists of references to tradition, to the history of its own technique as an art, of a wealth of allusions, indeed, to many things under the sun. Expressive content is personal, individual, specific, unique. It cannot be borrowed. If it is not spontaneous it is not sincere, hence not, in the long run, convincing. But intellectual content is all borrowed; it is only the choice and the appropriate usage of allusions and devices that give them validity in any work. Exhibited overostentatiously, they merely prove vanity. Aptly applied they enrich the texture and delight all.

The richness of music's intellectual substance varies from composer to composer. It is greater in Bach, for instance, than in Handel, though the latter, predominantly a man of the theater, has a plainer and more direct emotional appeal. Mozart's frame of reference, likewise, is more ample than that of Haydn. It is characteristic of both Bach and Mozart to use dance meters without the idea of dancing being the only thought communicated. Bach writes between an organ toccata and its fugue a siciliana which is at the same time a religious meditation. And Mozart writes in a piano sonata (O, how often) a slow movement which is both a minuet and a love duet, as well as a piano solo.

The best opera composers have usually avoided, in writing for the lyric stage, any duality of allusion that might weaken the impact of the expressive content. The best concert composers, on the other hand, are those who employ the techniques of multiple meaning, adding thus to simple expressivity contrapuntal interest and the perspective effect of contradictory evocations. It is Beethoven's gift for working opposites in together that gives to his concert music its phenomenal power of suggesting drama, which is struggle. Beethoven has for this reason intellectual content to a high degree. He did not refer much, except in his later works, where he employed constantly the deliberate archaism of fugal style, to the history of composing techniques; but he did manage by careful handling of the contemporary techniques, to make one thing mean many things (as in the variation form) and to make many things mean one (as in the ten-theme symphony form). He holds attention to this day, in consequence. He keeps the listener occupied.

Wagner's operas have the highest intellectual content of any. I don't mean the philosophical tomfoolery of his librettos, either, though this was necessary to him as a pretext for elaborateness of musical texture and for the whole psychological refinement that was his chief legacy to the stage. Puccini's operas have probably the lowest intellectual content of any, though their plots are far from stupid. Their expressive content, which is chiefly self-pity, is powerful by its simplicity. But the emotional composition of this has little depth or perspective, and the musical textures employed are of small interest as workmanship.

Tchaikovsky, Sibelius, and Shostakovitch are demagogic symphonists because the expressive power of their work is greater than its interest as music; it does not fully or long occupy an adult mind. Debussy and Stravinsky are fascinating to the adult mind. They stimulate feelings and provoke thought. Schönberg and Hindemith are overrich of intellectual interest in proportion to their feeling content; they are a little dry, in consequence. Bartók, Milhaud, and Copland strike a sound balance between mental and emotional appeal, even though their intensity in both kinds is less than one could wish it were. Roy Harris oscillates between extreme intellectuality, for which he has little gift, and a banal, a borrowed emotionalism, which he cultivates out of a yearning for quick-and-easy success. At his best, however, he is both moving and interesting. Olivier Messiaen is a similar case, though his musical gift is greater and his mind more ingenious.

The music of the great masters is always good both ways. So is that of the little masters; they merely produce less of it. One could go on for columns describing the music of past and present masters in terms of its vital equilibrium, its balance of heart and head. And one could get into some pretty arguments. Brahms, Bruckner, Mahler, César Franck, Ravel, and Liszt are tough cases to judge. So are the great men of jazz. Schubert, Schumann, Verdi, Mussorgsky, and Fauré are more clear. They were truly great artists, though all suffered from technical deficiencies.

What makes possible the writing of good music, beyond that talent for handling sound that is required for being a musician at all, is emotional sincerity and intellectual honesty. Both can be cultivated, of course; but no man can quite lift himself by his boot straps. Unless he has a good heart (the psychiatrists nowadays call this affectivity) and a strong, vigorous mind, he will not write any music capable at once of touching the human heart and interesting the human mind. Art that does not do both dies quickly. And longevity is the glory, perhaps even the definition, of civilization's major achievements.

April 20, 1947

Ethical Content

JUST as we require of music, in order that it be acceptable as "serious," not only that it move our hearts but also that it be interesting to the mind, there is yet a third qualification about which we are no less exigent. We insist that it be edifying. This demand is as old as time. Every civilization and every primitive communty have recognized a music of common or vulgar usage and another music, grander of expressive content and more traditional in style, a music worthy of association with the highest celebrations of religion, of patriotism, and of culture. This latter kind of music is known to our time as "classical" music (as distinguished from "popular"). Whether its intrinsic content, expressive and intellectual, is all that determines its position of prestige among us I am not sure. The case of jazz, a highly civilized but persecuted music, leads one to think that other factors may be involved. In any case, all the music that our time accepts as noble is endowed by that very acceptance with an ethical content. This means that dealing with it in any way is believed to be good for one.

Saint Clement of Alexandria was convinced that goodness is intrinsic to certain kinds of music and wickedness to others. He encouraged the faithful in the usage of diatonic melodies and regular meters, exhorted them to avoid "chromatics and syncopation," which he believed led to "drunkenness and debauchery." This belief is still widespread. Indeed, the proposition has never been disproved. And though Sebastian Bach employed both devices consistently and convincingly (at least to posterity, though his congregation did complain) in the praise of God, and though Beethoven employed them no less to celebrate the brotherhood of man, the fact remains that when any composer wishes to depict heaven in contrast to hell or the serenities of virtue versus the excitements of sin, he is virtually obliged to use for the one a plainer, stiffer melodic and rhythmical vocabulary than for the other.

Olivier Messiaen has devoted his whole musical career to the purging, so to speak, or conversion to devotional uses, of all the most dangerous musical devices. The augmented fourth (or *diabolus in musica*), the major sixth, the false relation (or use of contradictory chromatics in two voices), the exaggerated employment of chromatics in melodic and harmony, the ornamental dissonance, the integral dissonance, the highest elaborations of syncopated and other broken rhythms, and an almost sinfully colistic orchestration are the very substance of his musical style, though piety is certainly its subject. And yet even he is obliged, for the depiction of evil, to go farther in the same direction and to insert additional violations of custom and of symmetry. I suspect, indeed, that it is not so much the employment in music of all the known picturesque effects that is valuable for suggesting the dark forces as it is a certain absence of symmetry in their employment. There is no reason why the music of the higher spheres should not be represented by the higher complexities and that of man's lower tendencies by all that is banal, bromidic, and puny, though so far no major composer has, to my knowledge, essayed to represent beatitude by interest and fantasy, in contrast to a damnation (as in Sartre's *No Exit*) of boredom by monotony.

The endowing of music with an edifying ethical content is a problem every composer has to face. He may face it by avoiding it. This is the romantic procedure, to assume that art's only connections with morals lie in the sincerity of the artist's personal sentiments and in the honesty of his workmanship. Or he may face it by the more classical method of associating his work with ideas, institutions, ceremonies, and events of an edifying character. Dramas with a moralistic ending, poetry of known cultural value, the court symphony, the patriotic occasion, anything whatever having to do with religion, ancestors, or anthropology — all these are sure-fire associations; and there is no composer, living or dead, of major repute who has not employed one or another of them.

A major problem of our time is the concert symphony. The court guest of Haydn's and Mozart's day was less exigent than we are about moral impressiveness. What he liked was liberty. The nineteenth-century music lover, a bourgeois, loved literary, nationalistic, and travelogue content. In our time many composers have endeavored to satisfy the public's taste for news commentary by using current events and international relations as a subject of musical reflection, but so far the results have not been very satisfactory. No contemporary composer has yet matched Beethoven's mastery of the editorial vein, though they can draw circles around him at literary and exotic evocation. And though a great deal of the supposed editorial content in Beethoven is an invention of later times (that which associated his Fifth Symphony, for instance, with the ultimate victory of our side in the last war), it is perfectly certain that his "Battle of Vittoria" does represent a comment on a news event (over and above its delightful straight reporting) and that his Third (or "Heroic") Symphony is the ancestor of the modern editorial symphony.

But if Beethoven invented the editorial symphony, he also furnished, in my opinion, the earliest precedent for its misuse. That precedent is the final movement of his Fifth Symphony. In this piece, I am convinced after much reflection, the form is determined not by any inner necessity or logic derived from its musical material, nor yet from any expressive necessity that grows out of the preceding movements. I think it is a skillful piece of pure theater, a playing upon audience psychology that has for its final effect, along with the expression of some perfectly real content, the provoking of applause for its own sake. If I am right, here is the first successful precedent and model (the finale of Brahms's First Symphony being the second) for that application to symphonic composition of the demagogic devices that are characteristic of so much symphonic music in our time.

Whether the technique of this demagogy is derived from Beethoven, who fell into it, if at all, only that once, or whether it is an invention of smaller men, there it is, in any case. The similar vulgarization that overcame Italian opera about fifty years ago, a concentration on applause at the expense of communication, is nowhere suggested in the work of the great Verdi, though it is in that of Boïto and of Ponchielli. A tolerance of such procedures gives us that cult of "pure" theater which finds any Broadway melodrama or Hollywood sex trifle a model of dramatic procedure. There is no such model to be found where expressive, intellectual, or ethical content is low. And the modern symphony-about-current-events has somewhere along the line accepted expressive and intellectual standards (chiefly the latter) unworthy of its ethical aspirations.

The symphony, after all, is a romantic form. It is subjective and must therefore be sincere. And though any man can have sincere sentiments about a political matter, I have yet to hear a political symphony, excepting Beethoven's Third, that convinced me that the sentiments expressed were entirely spontaneous. There is a hortatory tone about all such work nowadays that is unbecoming to a form with so grand a history of deeply personal expression. Perhaps the political symphony is eloquent only when inspired by protest or revolt. Perhaps, too, the political passions of our time are less grandiose than we like to think. Certainly they are less impressive than the vast variety of human suffering that has been provoked by their translation into political, economic, and military action.

Somewhere in the modern world or in the history of music there may be available an attitude that would enable composers to view today's political events in a manner at once intelligent, ethical, and compassionate. I sincerely hope such an attitude can be found. Until it is, however, a great deal of contemporary composition, operatic as well as symphonic, is bound to appear to us as animated by either a banal escapism or by an assumption of ethical rightness, of a moral nobility that is not justified by either the intellectual or the expressive context offered in support. On the whole, modern composers have done better work when they have treated history, travel, anthropology, autobiography, sex, and abnormal psychology than they have done with current events. Simple patriotism they handle well, too. Even religion they can be convincing about, though few of them are pious men. Their political ideas, however sound from a voting point of view, have not yet proved adequate for the graver responsibilities involved in concert exposition.

April 27, 1947

Americanisms

FOR all the vaunted virtuosity of the American symphony orchestras, your correspondent has long wondered what, if any, has been, or is likely to be, their contribution to art. American ensemble playing on the popular level has given to the world two, perhaps three, expressive devices of absolute originality. One is a new form of tempo rubato, a way of articulating a melody so loosely that its metrical scansion concords at almost no point with that of its accompaniment, the former enjoying the greatest rhythmic freedom while the latter continues in strictly measured time. Another characteristically American device is playing "blue," using for melodic expression constant departures from conventionally correct pitch in such a way that these do not obscure or contradict the basic harmony, which keeps to normal tuning. Simultaneous observance of these two dichotomies, one metrical and one tonal, constitute a style of playing known as "hot." And although precedents for this are not unknown in folklore and even in European art custom, our systematization of it is a gift to music.

Another device by which our popular ensembles depart from European habits is the execution of a volume crescendo without any acceleration of tempo. It is possible that Sebastian Bach may have played the organ without speeding up the louder passages, but Bach did not know the volume crescendo as we conceive it. He only knew platforms of loudness. The smooth and rapid increase of sound from very soft to very loud and back again is a Romantic invention. It is possible, even today, only with a fairly numerous orchestra or chorus, on a pianoforte, or on the accordion. It is the basic novelty of musical Romanticism; and the nineteenth century invented a fluid rhythmic style, in which pulsations were substituted for strict metrics, to give to the planned crescendo a semblance of spontaneity.

It was the conductor Maurice Abravanel who first called my attention to the rarity of the nonaccelerating crescendo in European musical execution. It has long been used to suggest armies approaching and then going off into the distance, its rhythmic regularity being easily evocative of marching. But aside from this special employment it is foreign to Romantic thought. If you want to get a laugh out of yourself, just try applying it to Wagner or Chopin or Liszt or Brahms or Beethoven or even Debussy. These authors require a fluid rhythmic articulation. And though one may for rhetorical purposes, as when approaching a peroration, get slower instead of faster as the volume mounts, it is obviously inappropriate in Romantic music to execute a subjectively expressive crescendo or decrescendo without speeding up or slowing down.

The modern world, even in Europe, has long recognized the rhythmically steady crescendo as, in theory, a possible addition to the terraced dynamics of the eighteenth-century symphony. In fact, however, European composers have never, to my knowledge, used it without a specifically evocative purpose. Of the three most famous crescendos in modern music not one is both tonally continuous and rhythmically steady. Strauss's *Elektra* is tonally continuous, rising in waves from beginning to end; but it presupposes no exact metrics. Stravinsky's "Dance of the Adolescents" (from *The Rite of Spring*) and Ravel's *Bolero* do presuppose a metrically exact rendering, but they are not tonally steady crescendos. They are as neatly terraced as any Bach organ fugue.

The completely steady crescendo is natural to American musical thought. Our theater orchestras execute it without hesitation or embarrassment. Our popular orchestrators call for it constantly and get it. Our symphonic composers call for it constantly and rarely get it. The conductors of European formation, who lead most of our symphonic ensembles, simply do not understand it. Very few of them understand metrical exactitude in any form. American music, nevertheless, requires a high degree of metrical exactitude, emphasized by merely momentary metrical liberties. Also lots of crescendo, which is our passion. The music of Barber and Schuman and Piston and Hanson and Copland and Harris and Bernstein and Gershwin and Cowell and Sowerby and Randall Thompson and William Grant Still is full of crescendos. It is also full of rhythmic and metrical irregularities. But none of it is romantic music in the European sense, because the crescendos and the rhythmic irregularities are not two aspects of the same device. The separation of these devices is as characteristic of American musical thought as is our simultaneous use of free meter with strict meter and free with strict pitch. These three dichotomies are basic to our musical speech.

Hearing Howard Hanson or Leonard Bernstein conduct American music is a pleasure comparable to hearing Pierre Monteux conduct French music or Bruno Walter interpret Mahler and Bruckner. The reading is at one with the writing. Our foreign-born conductors have given the American composer a chance to hear his own work. Also, they have built up among the public a certain toleration of American music, or encouraged, rather, a toleration that has always existed. But they have built up also a certain resistance to it which did not exist here previous to the post-Civil-War German musical invasion. This resistance comes from a complete lack of adaptation on the part of the European-trained to American musical speech. They understand its international grammar, but they have not acquired its idiom and accent.

In so far as they are aware that there are an idiom and an accent (as several of them are), they are likely to mistake these for localisms of some kind. They are nothing of the sort; they are a contribution to the world's musical language, as many postwar Europeans are beginning to suspect. American popular music has long been admired abroad, but American art music is just beginning to be discovered. It would probably be a good idea for us here to keep one step ahead of the foreign market by building up a record library of American works in authoritative renderings by American-trained artists. Also to accustom our own public to this kind of authoritative collaboration. We shall need both a professional tradition and broad public support for it if we are to accept with any confidence the world-wide distribution of American music that seems to be imminent, in view of the world-wide demand.

Actually we are producing very nearly the best music in the world. Only France, of all the other music-exporting countries, operates by stricter standards both of workmanship and of originality. Not Germany nor Italy nor Russia nor England nor Mexico nor Brazil is producing music in steady quantity that is comparable in quality to that of the American school. And we are a school. Not because I say so, but because we have a vocabulary that anybody can recognize, I think, once it is pointed out, as particular to us.

January 27, 1946

Modernism Today

MUSICAL modernism, as this has been understood for fifty years, is nowadays a pretty dead issue. Its masters are all famous and their works are known to the public. Its libertarian attitude toward dissonance, rhythmic and metrical irregularities, and unconventional sonorities is no longer revolutionary. Children are brought up on these liberties; and even symphony subscribers, a notoriously conservative group, accept them as normal. The only form of modernism that remains to be imposed (or finally refused) is atonality.

In such a situation, with little left to fight for, what future is there for the composing young beyond a prospect of inevitable conformity? How can they avoid being placed in the public's present scheme of things as mere competitors of their elders? How can they be fresh and original and interesting in their own right? Having observed them pretty carefully during the last ten years both here and abroad, I have come to the conclusion that they are doing exactly what anybody could have figured out by pure logic that they would do. They have taken up the only battle left, namely, that of atonality and its allied techniques.

Not all the young, I grant you, are atonalists. There are neo-classicists and neoromantics and even a few retarded impressionists among them. But a generation takes its tone from those who branch out, not from those who follow in footsteps. And today's adventurous young, believe me, are mostly atonal. This position has more to offer them in artistic discovery and less in immediate royalties than any other available, excepting only the tradition of pure percussion. The latter is for the present so limited in scope and so completely occupied by John Cage that there is not much room left in it for anybody else.

The atonal techniques, however, are more ample. One can

move around in them. And the young of England, France, Italy, and the Americas have recognized that fact. Germany and Russia, on account of their lack of expressive freedom in the last ten and more years, are slower in taking up the new manner. There are still too many older ones that have not been accepted there yet. But in the countries where intellectual freedom is the norm, young composers are busy with nontonal counterpoint.

Nontonal music, any music of which the key and mode are consistently obscure, has so far always turned out to be contrapuntal. It cannot be harmonic in the conventional sense, because chords pull everything back into a tonal syntax. And if harmonic in an unconventional way, through dependence on percussive and other pitchless noises, it becomes contrapuntal through the necessity of writing for these in varied simultaneous rhythmic patterns, these being its only source of formal coherence.

Counterpoint within the conventional scales can be of three kinds. That practiced in Europe from the twelfth through the fifteenth century is known as quintal, which means that, read vertically at the metrical accents, the music will be found to contain chiefly intervals of the fourth and fifth. Tertial counterpoint, which was the official style from the sixteenth through the nineteenth century, exhibits principally thirds and sixths when read this way. Secundal counterpoint, which is characteristic of our time, stacks up on the down beats as mostly seconds and sevenths.

Any of these styles can be used with either a diatonic or a chromatic melodic texture. The twelve-tone syntax, the strictest form of chromatic writing, can even be made to come out harmonically as tertial counterpoint. The music of the chief living neoclassicists — Stravinsky, Milhaud, and Hindemith — is diatonic secundal counterpoint. That of Schönberg is mostly chromatic secundal counterpoint. On account of this music's lack of a full acceptance by the general public such as that of the neoclassicists enjoys, it remains, with regard to the latter, though it was conceived, in point of time, earlier, in an "advanced" position. The more vigorous movements among today's young are, in consequence, all more closely related to Schönberg than to the others.

The newer music offers a divergence, however, from Schönberg's practice in its consistent preoccupation with nondifferentiated counterpoint, a style of writing in which all the voices have equal obligations of expressivity and identical rights in rhetoric. The dramatizing of counterpoint into melody, bass, countermelody, and accompaniment is abolished in this style for an equalized texture that recalls the music of the pre-Renaissance period. There are advantages here to intimacy of expression, since the composer can speak in this technique as personally through a vocal or string ensemble as through a solo instrument. The disadvantage of it is that it is not easily applicable to diversified ensembles, where variety of timbre and technique imposes a certain differentiation of melodic style from one voice to another.

The new music, therefore, is mostly homophonic in sound, or instrumentation. It is personal in expression, too, and contrapuntal in texture. Its counterpoint is secundal and generally chromatic. If it were not the latter, it would resemble more closely than it does official, or neoclassic, modernism. It can appear tonal or nontonal when examined closely; and it can follow or not Schönberg's strict twelve-tone syntax, which this composer himself does not always follow. But its chromaticism invariably approaches atonality. This last, let us remember, is not a precise or easily attainable end. It is rather an ultimate state toward which chromaticism has always tended. Its attractiveness to our century comes, I think, from its equalization of harmonic tensions. We like equalized tensions. They are the basis of streamlining and of all those other surface unifications that in art, as in engineering, make a work recognizable as belonging to our time and to no other.

February 2, 1947

"Theory" at Juilliard

REVISING the curriculum is a major American sport. Everybody enjoys it. Students and faculties alike find it invigorating. For presidents of educational institutions it is the *sine qua non* of tenure. It is the perfect mechanism for getting rid of one's predecessor's aides-de-camp and putting in one's own. And it is proof both to students and to the intellectual world that the job is no sinecure but a full-time occupation. It offers to all the comforting conviction of progress. And it is intrinsically good for educational institutions, for without it they do go to seed.

The Juilliard School of Music has just announced such a revision of its "theory" department, "theory" meaning all the branches of musical instruction that have to do with understanding the texture, structure, and composition of music, as distinguished from its performance. The announcement is welcome, not so much because of any notorious inefficiency in the present instruction as because of its fittingness in the general pattern of William Schuman's presidency of the institution, a reign, or regime, that has begun brilliantly and that offers every prospect of continuance with high benefit to American music.

Mr. Schuman is young, vigorous, sincere, passionate, and competent. To follow in his predecessor's footsteps would be neither appropriate nor interesting, though these footsteps have marked out trails of no mean value. Nor is there any question of backtracking and of calling those trails an error. It is simply that Mr. Schuman must go on from there. And the way any first-class American educator goes on from where he took over is to remake the institution into the kind of household where he can live and work with comfort. He must re-form it into his own image.

It is a characteristic of American life that many of our greatest teachers, from Mark Hopkins to Frank Lloyd Wright, have been less the product of schools than of self-education. Now when these men take over the instruction of others, they tend not to destroy the systematic or formal elements of education. They value, rather, the formalities that their own youth was deprived of. But they do tend to alter the content of those formalities. They revise the curriculum with an eye to making it a systematized version of their own nonsystematic education.

William Schuman is a composer and teacher whose preparation has been, in any scholastic sense, of the sketchiest, but whose practical experience in both composition and pedagogy has been marked by continued success. He is a practical man, an autodidact, an eclectic. He has learned his business the easy way (for any American of talent and character), that is to say, by doing it. He now proposes to offer his students a systematized version of his own training; and if all our grandest American precedents hold, he will be successful. He will be successful not because his system is any better than another, but because he is a good teacher and because, like any other good teacher, he must teach his subject the way he learned it.

That way is the way of personal initiative. Schuman proposes to let the students learn methods rather than rules and to derive these from the study of classical and modern music rather than of rule books. The procedure is similar to the famous "case system" of the Harvard Law School, where the principles of law are arrived at through the study of many court cases rather than learned in advance and applied to the interpretation of court cases. It works beautifully if the instructors see to it that the proper principles are arrived at. It works badly unless the student acquires a repertory of principles, in one way or another, along with his repertory of cases.

In musical "theory" instruction the abandonment of textbooks for case books is a normal accompaniment to that revision of the curriculum that takes place in any case about every twenty or twenty-five years. When the old books lose their savor and the older instructors their understanding, the old books have to be thrown out and the instructors changed. The young instructors, when this happens, are likely to teach for a year or so right out of Palestrina's and Bach's and Schönberg's own works. Then gradually they systematize, too, their teaching, settle on certain examples that they have found more useful than others for exposition purposes, and codify the principles of composition, as they understand them, with these tested examples as illustrations. Next, to simplify transmission of their now codified thought, they print, first a syllabus of their course, and then a whole textbook of it. And everything is right back where it was twenty years before. So a new president takes over and throws out the old textbooks and gets some new blood into the teaching staff.

It is the opinion of this writer that one system of instruction is about as good as another, exception made for whichever one has just been in use. Teachers vary in effectiveness, however, and so do students. The ungifted will always blame their failures on the setup. A good teacher and a good student can always come to terms, no matter what system of instruction is in vogue. A good president can rarely come to terms with the system and personnel he has inherited from his predecessor. It is a proof of William Schuman's devotion to his job at the Juilliard School that he has undertaken a thorough revision of its teaching. A busy man and a successful composer, he could so easily have kept the status quo and let his institution quietly run down. But he has accepted the responsibility of keeping a great institution at least as effective as it has been before. He would even like to make it more so. Consequently, he has undertaken a massive curricular revision. This involves lots of work, but there is no other way. There is nothing in the whole intellectual domain so elaborate to install and, once installed, so fragile and so impermanent as any of the pedagogical methods by which civilization is preserved and transmitted.

May 18, 1947

Second-Rate Season

LOOKING back at the music season now approaching its end, this reviewer finds he can remember very little that took place. Discussing it with friends and colleagues, he finds that in the opinion of these very little that was out of the ordinary, in fact, did take place. There were lots of concerts and recitals and the usual number of operatic performances, but unusual departures from routine repertory or from average standards of competence in execution have been almost nonexistent.

The New York Music Critics' Circle will have to make its annual awards on a basis of very few available works, since the new American pieces given here for the first time can almost be counted on five fingers. And our New York situation is not unique. The Pulitzer Prize Committee has been worried all spring lest the number of new American works performed anywhere in America be insufficient to justify the giving of that prize at all. Our City Symphony has been fairly assiduous about novelties; our Philharmonic has been skimpy about them. Philadelphia, not of late a very novelty-minded orchestra, has furnished about its usual quota. Boston, formerly our chief source of fresh musical material, would seem to have gone ultraconventional all of a sudden. In any case, all of the orchestras that play here regularly, excepting the City Symphony, which has kept a lively repertory, have played hardly enough new music, American or other, for anyone but their conductors to shake a stick at.

The local opera companies at the Metropolitan and City Center, as well as the Salmaggi and San Carlo troupes, have long ago disaccustomed us to novel repertory. Of that they offer us literally and exactly nothing, and they do not pretend otherwise. Their policy is identical with that of the New Friends of Music, conservatism for the box office's sake. And the regular run of recitalists follows the same slogan. A few here and there play something new and get applauded for it. But mostly they stick to the conventions. And the conventions would have one believe that the music-consuming public only wants, and will buy, chestnuts.

The falsity of the supposition is proved by the devotion of certain small groups among the public to musical advance and to quality. Nobody pretends that these small groups are capable of supporting large institutions. But they are capable of supporting a great deal more modern music and quality music than they are nowadays being given a chance to do. They flock to hear Maggie Teyte and Landowska and the Cantata Singers. They turn out for Povla Frijsh and for the two-piano playing of Gold and Fizdale. They even mobilize, on occasion, the literary world. They are a devoted public. To throw away their special custom by lumping them with the mass public is to act like a book publisher who would refuse to publish any manuscript not clearly destined to sell a hundred thousand copies.

This latter seems to be the calculation of the recording companies. Their output of anything beyond the Fifty Pieces is pathetically small. They are commercial institutions and may possibly be excused from the cultural obligation, though their virtual monopoly of materials and distribution facilities will one day force a raising of the cultural question. But the orchestras and the Metropolitan are, in theory, intellectual foundations. They are committing intellectual suicide by not appealing to the intellectual public. Let them give standard repertory for the young people and for the musically retarded who are not yet familiar with it. The reciting of sacred texts has no doubt a place in art, as in religion; let it by all means go on. But not to give special concerts for the musically active (concerts that they are perfectly willing to pay admission to) is like making adults take all their meals at the children's table. This is faulty cultural policy and, in the long run, bad business policy, though it is defended at present as a business economy.

Just how much opera companies and symphony orchestras contribute to real musical life is questionable, anyway. They go through a routine about this; and some of their customers certainly get pleasure, even profit. Whether these benefits are worth what the whole thing costs is hard to say. Certainly expensive orchestras are a more important part of music's business setup, which could not do without them, than of our cultural setup, which could. They are the branches of a vast international chain store of music, with interchangeable managements, musicians, conductors, soloists, and repertory. They supply to the public only a very small part of the repertory that is properly their stock in trade.

The performance of this repertory is a public service. Wherever business does not supply it, governments do. Where business does supply it, the circulation is larger; but the number of pieces supplied gets smaller and smaller every year. I have no proposal for remedying the stalemate beyond elaborating the scheme. I do think that supplying all the kinds of music for all the kinds of musical taste in separate concerts and separate series of concerts would serve the public better and that it would, in the long run, be more profitable. Beyond this innocent suggestion, I can only comment, as a regular concertgoer, that giving the same kind of thing to everybody does not seem to me a satisfactory system of cultural operation. I find less and less memorable difference, as any season goes on, between one concert and another; and I do not believe this standardization to be culturally advantageous. Paternalism in cultural matters is always oppressive, even when practiced by enlightened governments. When practiced by business under the guise of philanthropy, it amounts to forcing the consumption of an inferior product. Because art that is not full of variety and surprise is, by definition, second-rate.

May 5, 1946

A War's End

MODERN MUSIC, distinguished quarterly review edited by Minna Lederman and published by the League of Composers, has ceased publication after twenty-three years. Musicians and laymen who are part of the contemporary musical movement will of necessity be deeply moved by this announcement, because *Modern Music* has been for them all a Bible and a news organ, a forum, a source of world information, and the defender of their faith. It is hard to think of it as not existing, and trying to imagine what life will be without it is a most depressing enterprise. Nevertheless, we shall be living without it, whether we like that or not. Some other magazine or group of magazines may substitute their charms for its uses and delights; but none can replace it ever, for none was ever like it.

No other magazine with which I am acquainted has taken for its exclusive subject the act of musical composition in our time or sustained with regard to that subject so comprehensive a coverage. This one reported on France and Germany and Italy and England and Russia and Mexico and the South American republics, as well as on its own United States. It covered musical modernism in concerts, in the theater, in films, radio, records, and publication. Jazz and swing procedures were analyzed and Calypso discovered in its pages. Books dealing with contemporary musical esthetics were reviewed. The only aspects of music excluded from it were those that make up the ordinary layman's idea of music, namely, its composition before 1900, its interpretation, and its exploitation as a business.

Modern Music was a magazine about contemporary composition written chiefly by composers and addressed to them. It even went into their politics on occasion. When our entry into the recent war brought to certain composers' minds the possibility that perhaps our government might be persuaded not to draft all the younger ones, thus husbanding, after the Soviet example, a major cultural resource, Roger Sessions disposed of the proposal firmly by identifying it with the previous war's slogan "business as usual." And when, on the liberation of Europe, consciences were worried about musician collaborators, a whole symposium was published, exposing all possible ways of envisaging the problem. Darius Milhaud, as I remember, said that traitors should be shot, regardless of talent or profession. Ernst Křenek pointed out that Shostakovich, who had accepted from his own government artistic correction and directives regarding the subject matter of his music, was the prince of collaborators. While Arnold Schönberg opined that composers were all children politically and mostly fools and should be forgiven.

In the atmosphere of sharp esthetic controversy that pervaded the magazine and with its constant confrontation of authoritative statement and analysis (for there is practically no living composer of any prestige at all whose works have not been discussed in it and who has not written for it himself), wits became more keen and critical powers came to maturity. It is not the least of many debts that America owes Minna Lederman that she discovered, formed, and trained such distinguished contributors to musical letters as Edwin Denby, Aaron Copland, Roger Sessions, Theodore Chanler, Paul Bowles, Marc Blitzstein, Samuel Barlow, Henry Cowell, Colin McPhee, Arthur Berger, and Lou Harrison. My own debt to her is enormous. Her magazine was a forum of all the most distinguished world figures of creation and of criticism; and the unknown bright young were given their right to speak up among these, trained to do so without stammering and without fear.

The magazine's "cessation of hostilities," as one of its European admirers refers to the demise, is explained by its editor as due to "rising costs of production." Considering previous difficulties surmounted, I should be inclined to derive the fact from a deeper cause. After all, the war about modern music is over. Now comes division of the spoils. Miss Lederman's magazine proved to the whole world that our century's first half is one of the great creative periods in music. No student in a library, no radio program maker, dallying with her priceless back issues, can avoid recognizing the vast fertility, the originality, ingenuity, and invention that music has manifested in our time.

This is all admitted now, and modern music is played everywhere.[1] There is no war about it any more. Our century's second

---

[1] An encyclical of Pope Pius XII, entitled *"Mediator Dei,"* dated November 20, 1947, recommends its use in the services of the Catholic Church. This lifts the ban on contemporary musical styles that the encyclical of Pius X, *"De Motu Proprio,"* had imposed in 1903.

half, like any other century's second half, will certainly witness the fusion of all the major modern devices into a new classical style. That fusion, in fact, has already begun; invention is on the wane, comprehensibility within the modern techniques on the increase. And the public has ceased resisting them as such. The stabilization of modernism's gains is the order of the next few decades. Other organs of musical opinion will no doubt take over *Modern Music's* leadership. But what has been done well and finished off cleanly will remain as history.

No other musical magazine of our century can possibly have the place in history, either as monument or as source material that *Modern Music* already occupies, because no other magazine and no book has told the musical story of its time so completely, so authoritatively, so straight from the creative laboratory and from the field of battle. Its twenty-three volumes are history written by the men who made it. For the history of music in any epoch is the story of its composers and of their compositions. Nobody ever tells that story right but the composers themselves. What Haydn thought of Mozart and Beethoven, however wrong as opinion, is true as musical history. What Heine thought of Beethoven, however right, is literature and belongs to the history of another art. The subsequent recounting of musical history from documents of the period belongs, of course, to still another. Thanks to *Modern Music* the last quarter-century has probably a better chance of being written up convincingly than any other, save possibly those years between 1820 and 1845, when Schumann, Berlioz, Wagner, Liszt, Weber, and Jean-Paul Richter (himself a composer) all wrote voluminously about their contemporaries.

January 12, 1947

Index

Index   iii

A NOTE ON THE TYPE

The text of this book is set in CALEDONIA, *a Linotype face designed by W. A. Dwiggins. Caledonia belongs to the family of printing types called "modern face" by printers — a term used to mark the change in style of type-letters that occurred about 1800. Caledonia borders on the general design of Scotch Modern, but is more freely drawn than that letter.*

The book was composed, printed, and bound by The Plimpton Press, Norwood, Massachusetts. The typography and binding are based on designs by W. A. Dwiggins.